Peace Behind Bars

Also by John Dear:

Disarming the Heart

Our God Is Nonviolent

Jean Donovan and the Call to Discipleship

Oscar Romero and the Nonviolent Struggle for Justice

Seeds of Nonviolence

The God of Peace

The Sacrament of Civil Disobedience

"Come, let us climb the Lord's mountain, to the house of the God of Jacob, that God may instruct us in God's ways, and we may walk in God's paths."

For from Zion shall go forth instruction, and the word of the Lord from Jerusalem. God shall judge between the nations, and impose terms on many peoples.

They shall beat their swords into plowshares,
and their spears into pruning hooks;
One nation shall not raise the sword against another,
nor shall they train for war again.

—Isaiah 2:3–4

If I should pass the tomb of Jonah, I think I would stop there and sit for awhile, because I was swallowed once deep in the dark and came out alive after all.

—Carl Sandburg

Peace Behind Bars

A Peacemaking Priest's Journal from Jail

John Dear

SHEED & WARD
Franklin, Wisconsin

As an apostolate of the Priests of the Sacred Heart, a Catholic religious order, the mission of Sheed & Ward is to publish books of contemporary impact and enduring merit in Catholic Christian thought and action. The books published, however, reflect the opinions of their authors and are not meant to represent the official position of the Priests of the Sacred Heart.

1999

Sheed & Ward
7373 South Lovers Lane Road
Franklin, Wisconsin 53132
1-800-558-0580

Printed in the United States of America

Cover design: James F. Brisson
Author photo: Sally Savage Photography

Library of Congress Cataloging-in-Publication Data
Dear, John, 1959–
    Peace behind bars : a peace making priest's journal from jail / John Dear.
      p. cm.
    ISBN 1-55612-771-5 (alk. paper)
    1. Dear, John, 1959– 2. Catholic Church—United States—Clergy—Biography. 3. Jesuits—United States—Biography. 4. Prisoners—United States—Biography. 5. Government, Resistance to—United States. 6. Nonviolence—Religious aspects—Catholic Church. 7. Peace—Religious aspects—Catholic Church. 8. Nuclear warfare—Religious aspects—Catholic Church. 9. Catholic Church—Doctrines. I. Title.
BX4705.D2849A3   1995
271'.5302—dc20
[B]   95-9248
                               CIP

2 3 4 5 / 02 01 00 99

Contents

For Bill O'Donnell and Martin Sheen

Acknowledgments

I WOULD LIKE TO THANK ALL THOSE WHO HELPED ME DURING MY TIME IN jail for the Pax Christi-Spirit of Life Plowshares action. Most especially I thank my parent; my brother Steve and his wife Janet; Patrick O'Neill and Mary Rider; Jean Chapman; Dave and Debbie Biesack; Sara Arnold; Lynda Ward; Carol Brothers; Elizabeth McAlister; Jim and Shelley Douglass; Walter Sullivan; Tom Gumbleton; Patrick Hart; Mev Puleo; Mark Chmiel; Henri Nouwen; Janice Vanderhaar; Valerie Sklarersky; Anne Curtin Marshall; Mary Anne Muller; Patrick Atkinson; Cindy Pile; Jim Forest; Ken Butigan; Nancy Small; Rena Rae; Elmer Maas; Chris Ponnet; M.J. Park; David and Karen Dear; Ramsey Clark; and Joe Cosgrove.

I would like to thank all those Jesuits who supported me, visited me, and strengthened me, beginning with my provincial, Fr. Ed Glynn, S.J.; Tom Gaunt, S.J.; Richard McSorley, S.J.; Joe Sands, S.J.; Jim Stormes, S.J.; Daniel Berrigan, S.J.; Jim Devereux, S.J.; Gene McCressh, S.J.; Frank O'Connor, S.J.; George Anderson, S.J.; Frank Moan, S.Jl; Steve Kelly S.Jl; Simon Harak, S.J.; Brendan Hurley, S.J.; and Frank McAloon, S.J.

I would also like to thank Colman McCarthy for his support, Robert Heyer for originally bringing this journal to publication, and Jeremy Langford and the staff at Sheed & Ward for keeping this book in print.

I want to extend my deep gratitude to my "partners in crime," Phil Berrigan, Lynn Fredriksson and Bruce Friedrich, for sharing these remarkable days with me. Thanks expecially to Bruce for his careful editing of the manuscript.

I dedicate this book to two dear friends who have encouraged me to take the stand for peace. Thank you, Bill and Martin.

Foreword

by Philip Berrigan

I want to make a special appeal to soldiers, national guardsmen and policemen: "Brothers, each one of you is one of us. We are the same people. The campesinos you kill are your own brothers and sisters. When you hear the words of a man telling you to kill, remember instead the word of God, 'Thou Shalt Not Kill!' God's laws must prevail. No soldier is obliged to obey an order contrary to the law of God. It is time for you to come to your senses and obey your consciences rather than follow a sinful command."

—Archbishop Oscar Romero
March 23, 1980, the day before he was assassinated

A government that is evil has no room for good women and men except in its prisons.

—Henry David Thoreau

A government swollen with bloodshed and killing will regard those who reject killing with uneasiness and suspicion. It will regard those who resist its killing with umbrage, rage, and reprisal. Their civic destiny is a jail cell.

Whenever I come across commands or obedience in the Bible, I think of John Dear. Because if one honors a command, one must honor obedience. John honors both.

The Bible is full of commands. Christ repeatedly uses commands in his teachings: "Follow me!" "Love one another!" "Love your enemies!" "Bless those who curse you!" "Do to others as you would have them do to you!"

God has the perfect right to command us, having made us and having died to ransom us. Moreover, doesn't everyone need a teacher, guide, and loving example?

American Christians are flagrantly ambiguous about commands. On the one hand, we virtually ignore God's command to follow Her Son, to love our enemies, and to do justice to the poor. On the other, we put on a deaf and dumb show of obedience when the empire imposes nuclearism as its religion, when it commands taxes, silence and conscription of young people for the military. Indeed, the domination system—government, transnationals, military, and patriarchy—keeps the individual under a tight rein of slavish obedience, a parody of the true obedience we owe God.

If one disobeys the domination system, consequences follow—public disgrace, imprisonment, and loss of property.

Peace Behind Bars is John Dear's expose of both America's love affair with the bomb and military killing and secondly, Christian equivocation about violence and mass murder. It is a stunning chronicle of Christian nonviolence, hope, and resistance. Step by step, it rigorously records a Plowshares witness against a nuclear-capable fight bomber, the Air Force's "work horse" (the most potent killer during the Persian Gulf war), the F-15e Strike Eagle. With intense dramatic impact, John Dear relates our arrest, jailing, indictment, and the legal railroad the government calls a "trial of your peers," marked by an *in limine* motion suppressing any reference to the Bible, international law, United States foreign policy, nuclear weaponry, or the Gulf war. Finally, it details the grim consequence of confinement in a little North Carolina dustbin.

Dear spares nothing of himself in this altogether extraordinary account—anguish, uncertainty, humiliation, loneliness, misunderstanding from family and friends, public indifference, and imprisonment in a cell smaller than that of a zoo animal.

What drew John Dear to this modern enactment of Calvary? Certainly, sensitivity to God's commands and obedient response. But also, awareness of criminality in high places, injustices so towering as to be unprecedented—the bombings of Hiroshima and Nagasaki, revenge for Pearl Harbor, and threat to the Russians; rejection of international controls of nuclear weapons; repeated nuclear confrontations with the Soviets; creation of a permanent war economy; a $19 trillion war chest from 1940; scores of "broken arrows" (American/Soviet accidents with nuclear weapons systems); interventionism (one per year since 1946); and superpowerism since the Soviet Union's collapse. And much more of nuclear terror, political psychosis, and their progeny.

How do believing and loving people co-exist with such stupendous lunacy? The fact is, they don't. If they do, they cease to believe in God and show compassion to the poor.

John Dear refused to co-exist. He was subject to authority, to God's command. And he learned obedience, recalling that marvelous teaching from the letter to the Hebrews: "Son though he was, he learned obedience from what he suffered" (Hebrews 5:8).

—Philip Berrigan
Baltimore, Maryland
1999

1

The Action

ONCE I STEP ACROSS THE LINE, MY LIFE WILL BE CHANGED FOREVER. There is no going back. I start walking. There. I've done it. I am now officially, illegally, on government property. The Seymour Johnson Air Force Base in Goldsboro, North Carolina. It's Tuesday morning, 2 a.m., December 7th, 1993. I am breaking the law. I have just walked across a downed fence onto a military base. I keep on walking.

It is dark. The middle of the night. There are four of us: 70-year-old peace activist Philip Berrigan; 30-year-old homeless advocate Lynn Fredriksson; and 24-year-old Catholic Worker Bruce Friedrich. The plan is to keep on walking through the woods, through the fields, over the runways, onto the tarmac, to one of the enormous F15E nuclear fighter bomber aircraft where we will hammer on it to fulfill Isaiah's mandate to "beat swords into plowshares" and Jesus' command, "Love your enemies."

We are sure we can get in without trouble. In keeping with the spirit of nonviolence, we will wait for the authorities to arrest us, so that we can stand up publicly and explain what we have done and why we have done it.

Wait a minute! Here comes a car with bright headlights, along the fence, straight for us. Quick! Duck into the bushes. There are not supposed to be any security cars! That was a close call.

Here comes another security car! Should we turn around and call off the action? No. We will press on and trust in God's grace to get us through. We start walking again.

We reach the woods and another caravan of security cars, military trucks and construction equipment passes. We dive into the bushes as they ride within ten feet of us. They drive by slowly and we turn to one another: "They must have discovered our presence. I'll bet they were alerted to our coming." We look into each other's faces. We crouch in silence. Then Phil says, "Let's go on."

We are now walking through the woods in the pitch black. Stumbling, tripping, trying to make our way, following Lynn who seems to know the correct direction. We walk along a creek's edge hoping to find a narrow place where we can jump across, but no luck. We take the plunge. The cold water is up to our waists. We walk ten yards through it and come to a hillside along the other side of the creek. Bruce looks over the top and a security car sits not too far away with its lights on. We decide to sit, collect our wits, pray in silence and then determine what to do next.

I am wearing my dark blue winter coat. In my pocket is a hammer on which I have engraved: "Swords into Plowshares," "Disarm Now," "Seek the unarmed Christ," and "Love your enemies." I look up at the sky and watch the stars. The fear that has been with me all evening does not let up. What if I am caught? What if they shoot one of us? What if they shoot me? What if I get killed? What if they put me in jail? What am I doing here?

We had listened to a song earlier in the evening, and now I find myself humming its words. "Fearless. We must be fearless. Trusting the power of love, counting on help from above, we must be fearless, fearless, fearless!"

I say a little prayer. I think of all the suffering peoples I have known around the world. I remember the wars I have experienced in El Salvador, Guatemala, the Middle East, Nicaragua, the Philippines. I contemplate Hiroshima and Nagasaki. I see before me the crucified Christ, who taught and preached active nonviolence. All around me, I sense the Cloud of Witnesses of which the scriptures speak. I invoke the recent saints who took risks for the sake of Gospel peacemaking—Gandhi, Martin King, Dorothy Day, Ita Ford, Jean Donovan, Oscar Romero, Ignacio Ellacuria, and Franz Jaegerstaetter. I feel the presence of the God of peace. God is opening a way for us to enact the biblical command to disarm.

We look at one another. We listen. We all agree: keep on walking.

Lynn goes first, then Bruce, then Phil, and finally myself. Over the hill, along the edge of the forest, we walk. In the distance, we barely make out the tarmac. We ease our way along the edge of the woods. At one point, another caravan of military vehicles passes by and we lie motionless on the ground. In the distance, at the top of a slight hill, we see a clump of five pine trees with some bushes, and we make our way to that point to regroup.

We approach the cluster of pine trees and we are stunned. There before us, like a movie set, is the entire Seymour Johnson Air Force Base, all lit up. It looks like three airports spread out in front of us. Within each area stand 20 to 30 of the F15E nuclear fighter bomber airplanes, at least 75 altogether. Air force personnel are working on each plane and each plane seems to be lit up with engines running. Security cars, trucks, tanks, construction equipment, fire trucks, and other military vehicles circle the airport area. They are in the midst of full-scale war games. We know they are on alert to bomb Bosnia-Herzegovnia. Perhaps the bombing will begin any day now, maybe even tonight. We are speechless. Lying on the pine needles under the pine trees close to Lynn, Bruce and Phil, I am astounded. And I think: So this is where all the money that should be helping the poor and homeless is spent. While the nation sleeps, the war machine speeds on in full gear.

We lie there contemplating the scene before us. We collect our strength, and then we proceed. Bruce and Lynn first. Then, Phil and I. We walk, bent low, for what seems like a long time. Then, when it is clear that no one is going to stop us—no one even notices us—we walk plainly ahead. Finally, across fields of grass and an asphalt tarmac we approach our goal—a single F15E fighter bomber that is not lit up and has no personnel around it. The plane is waiting for us. The God of peace has set this one aside for us.

Bruce and Lynn start hammering the pylons which hold the bombs. Then, they hammer on a guidance light and the Lantern all-weather flight pod and pour out of baby bottles their own blood onto the fuselage and into the air intake valves. I arrive next. The plane is much bigger than I thought it would be. Underneath the fuselage of the cockpit, a small, narrow fin hangs down in the air—the bomb tracking radar device. I look at it intently. This is it. I swing my hammer and hit it directly. Thud! Not even a dent; not even a paint chip. My whole body shakes from the reverberations. By this time, Phil is standing under a wing, about to strike the bomber as well. I can see dozens of soldiers running towards us now, machine guns ready. Time enough for one more swing! I look directly at the grey fuselage beneath the cockpit, and swing my hammer. Thud! Again, not even a chip in the paint. But at long last, by the grace of God, I am striking a blow for nuclear disarmament. I thus join the historic movement of nonviolence. I think of the book of Isaiah and the Gospel of Jesus and I am exhilarated.

"Put down your hammers and come to the other side!" the soldiers are yelling at Phil and me. Bruce, Lynn, Phil and I stand together on one side of the plane surrounded instantly by 20 soldiers with machine guns. "Put down your hammers," one of them yells. "We are unarmed, peaceful, nonviolent people," I reply loudly. "We mean you no harm. We are here simply to disarm this weapon of mass destruction." I repeat our intention several times. Meanwhile, Phil and Bruce lay out our banners: "Disarm and Live!" and "Pax Christi-Spirit of Life Plowshares." One of the soldiers screams into his walkie-talkie: "This is the real world! These people were hammering on our plane. Def-Con Charlie. This is the real world! Exercises Cancelled. This is the real world! I repeat, War Games Cancelled." At the same time, Bruce reads from our statement:

> The Pax Christi-Spirit of Life Plowshares act in the spirit of Isaiah 2: "They shall beat their swords into plowshares and their spears into pruning hooks; nation shall not lift sword against nation, neither shall they learn war anymore." We seek the peace of Christ who requires that we put down the nuclear sword and love our enemies. We humble ourselves before the Spirit of Life to disarm F15Es at the Seymour Johnson Air Force Base, expose these nuclear-capable weapons, and begin the process of disassembly and conversion. We use the symbol of blood to illustrate the murderous purposes of these weapons, the blood already spilled in wars in Iraq and other areas of F15E deployment. We beat the F15E with household hammers—symbols of transformation dictated by Isaiah.

> The Pax Christi-Spirit of Life Plowshares occurs on "Pearl Harbor Day," in the season of Advent. The unconsidered patriotism

of the day stands as antithesis to its spiritual significance—Advent as arrival, for some the coming of Jesus the Christ, for others the renewal of hope through revolutionary nonviolence. . . . Pearl Harbor and World War II combined to initiate: worldwide economic restructuring which further divides the rich from the poor and leave the U.S. a world-class empire; the nuclear massacres at Hiroshima and Nagasaki; and the beginning of American militarism. While 50 million died in World War II, for the past few decades over 40 million people have starved to death each year. They starve because we remain complicit in the building of F15Es rather than demand that these resources feed hundreds of thousands of children. Our silence contributes to violence, cruelty and greed.

In the spirit of nonviolent disarmament, we say No to nuclear weapons, No to militarism, No to the Seymour Johnson Air Force Base, No to the F15E, No to the U.S. government that finances and develops this genocidal weaponry and No to an economic system which has been elevated to the status of a deity.

Nonviolence invites us to say Yes to environmentally sustainable cultivation and socially just distribution of food; Yes to adequate housing, decent education, universal healthcare; Yes to self-determination throughout the world; Yes to healing the earth; Yes to peace; Yes to children; Yes to community; Yes to love and understanding. We visit Seymour Johnson Air Force Base, then, to say No to death and war, and Yes to peace and life. We invite all to join us in this nonviolent transformation.

Before we know it, we are lying on the ground and the soldiers are searching us. One of them grabs my chest pocket, where he discovers a small Salvadoran cross which I had engraved with the names of people I love (from my family to Jesuit friends to Gandhi and King). He rips it out of my pocket and throws it behind him. It hits the F15E bomber and falls to the ground. I lie next to Lynn who lies next to Bruce and Phil. We join hands together and start to pray. "Thank you. Thank you. Thank you," we pray. "May our action bear fruit. May it help our nation to disarm. May it help proclaim your reign of nonviolence," I pray. Lynn is crying, overwhelmed by the power of the action itself. We are ordered to stand and walk 20 yards onto a grass lawn and lie face down.

Through the corner of my eyes, I see we are surrounded by soldiers with loaded machine guns aimed at us. Behind them, a row of police cars centers their headlights on us. I am transported in time to the early morning of November 16th, 1989, to the green lawn in front of the Jesuit house at the University in San Salvador. Six Jesuits are forced to lie face down in the grass. Government soldiers surround them and one by one, blow out their brains. The image frightens me.

For 30 minutes, we lie face down on the ground. Every now and again, a soldier approaches and questions one of us. "What did you do to that airplane?" "We simply tried to disarm it by hammering on it," one of us replies. One of them yells at Phil, "Did you put a bomb in our airplane?" "What do you think we are—crazy?" Phil asks back.

Eventually, several of the soldiers grab me by the arms, handcuff me and escort me to a waiting police car. I turn and see the F15E bomber, with hammers lying beneath—an image engraved in my memory, an icon of peace. After a few minutes, Bruce is put in the back seat of the car with me. We talk about the action. "It was so beautiful," Bruce keeps saying. The police come by and tell us to be quiet. We continue to talk. Then, Bruce is taken to another car. We are all separated.

I sit in the back of the police car. An officer gets in, turns around and says as he turns on the radio, "Let's have some Christmas carols." With that, I hear the sound of angelic choirs in my ears, a heavenly chorus like a Cistercian chant: "Christ was born for you, Alleluia." Over and over again, it's "Alleluia!" I bow my head and weep for joy and gratitude. The singing touches my very soul as if God herself were thanking me for this disarmament action. "Thank you," I whisper. "Thank you."

As we drive away, I look out the window and see row upon row of young air force personnel in their military fatigues, gawking at me in the car. Some are angry; some smile, even laugh at us and our protest. All of them are affected. Then, the choir bursts into song. "O come, all ye faithful, joyful and triumphant. . . . O come ye to Bethelehem. . . . O come let us adore him, Christ the Lord."

The four of us are escorted from our police cars, up a staircase into a military office building and put in separate rooms. I am put in a tiny, empty room and the door is shut behind me. I sit on the floor and, for the first time, begin to rest.

An hour passes. I wonder what will become of me. How long will I be held? What will jail be like? Will I be locked up for years? Might they release us? I try to be still. To pray. To be at peace. I do feel a deep peace, more than relief—a blessing.

We are escorted again to the police cars and transferred to another building. This time, I am in a larger room, and I lie down on the floor in the sunshine. After several hours, a tall, dark haired man wearing a green suitcoat enters the room. "Al Koehler, FBI," he says. "I understand you are a Jesuit priest. I want you to know that I am a Catholic, that I attend a church in Raleigh, and also that I was one of the FBI agents who arrested Father Daniel Berrigan on Block Island 21 years ago, after he had become a fugitive. I can't believe that here I am in North Carolina, questioning another Berrigan and his friends." With that introduction, he orders me to remove all my clothes so that he can search me. After he examines me, he proceeds to ask me questions about my life, my family and my work. I respectfully decline to answer. He leaves. I am alone in the sunshine.

Eventually, after we are photographed and fingerprinted, at around 2:00 p.m., the four of us are taken together in a police van to Raleigh where we appear briefly in court before a magistrate. We will have a hearing on Friday and probably be indicted on felony charges for destruction of government property. The government is claiming we did $100,000 worth of damage, but we recall that this government, according to the Pentagon budget, pays $600 for a household screwdriver.

We say goodbye to Phil, who is taken to the Smithfield County Jail. Lynn, Bruce and I are led together in chains to a police van and taken away. I am exhausted; my heart is full, my soul content, but my future has never been so unclear. As the van speeds along the Carolina highways, I look out at the passing pine forests, hoping to find consolation. In the peace of creation, I find it.

Up ahead, near Henderson, a place is being prepared for us.

2

The Vance County Jail

December 9th, 1993

Through the long, horizontal window in our tiny cell, I look out at two rows of barbed wire atop two tall fences which ostensibly protect the outside world. Out there I see Carolina pine trees, needles on the ground, green bushes, and blue sky. I'm sitting here with Bruce in the Vance County Jail in Henderson, North Carolina, some 60 hours after our disarmament action at the Seymour Johnson Air Force Base.

Bruce and I live in a large cellblock with 60 other men. The two of us share a cell with two others. Yesterday, Wednesday, Bruce and I began a bible study on the Gospel of Mark, and also sat in silent meditation and prayed the rosary together. Then, we had Mass together in our cell. A local priest came to see us and we got out for 15 minutes to an enclosed basketball court. The other inmates call me "preacher" and "priest" and shake our hands. When we appeared on the late evening news, the entire cellblock erupted in applause. But I had already gone to sleep by then.

Today, we prayed and slept and talked about the action all day and about God and how our lives had brought us to this moment. This morning, one prisoner, a young guy from Mexico, asked me to hear his confession and grant him absolution. So we sat in the corner of the cellblock and he proceeded to tell me his life story—and all the trouble he had caused. He is broken, remorseful and filled with the grace of God. Later, Bruce and I had a large group of visitors, including my father and my brother, Steve, who lives in Chapel Hill and works with the rural poor. My parents are terribly upset with me, deeply shaken by my arrest. Tom Gaunt, a Jesuit priest in Chapel Hill, on the other hand, reports that my Jesuit provincial, Fr. Ed Glynn, S.J., offers his complete support.

After visiting with everyone and talking with Bruce and the other inmates, I am amazed at these blessed, intense, grace-filled days. Advent is definitely here. God is present to me and yet I wait for God to come anew into my new life here in jail. In my prayer I have a sense of Jesus' love for me and his joy over this nonviolent act of disarmament. As I sit here aware of his presence, I feel a deep peace. God has not abandoned us. Sitting here in jail, in legal jeopardy, God has never been so present.

It is very good to be here with Bruce. He is a 24-year-old member of the Dorothy Day Catholic Worker house in Washington, D.C. I see in him true devotion to the poor, a brilliant mind, a searching spirit, and a generous heart. While Bruce was at Grinnell College in Iowa, Mitch Snyder, the housing advocate, came to speak and challenged him to leave school and join the struggle for justice for the poor. After spending a year at the London School of Economics, Bruce quit college, moved to Washington, D.C., became a Catholic, started housing the homeless and demonstrating for justice and peace. Each summer, he has fasted for several weeks to mark the anniversaries of the atomic bombings of Hiroshima and Nagasaki. In three active years, he has broken the law regularly. He received a felony conviction for pouring blood on the statue of Columbus at Union Station during the ceremony marking the 500th anniversary of Columbus' arrival. Since we arrived here, Bruce has been regaling me with stories of his experiences in the D.C. jail, the Morgantown Federal Prison and, worst of all, the Norfolk City jail. His encouragement and confidence will help get me through whatever lies ahead.

Lynn Fredriksson sits somewhere in this jail in the women's section. She is a 30-year-old peace activist who ran a shelter for homeless men in Baltimore, Maryland. A graduate from Williams College, she left law school to serve the poor and work for justice and peace. She has traveled in the former Soviet Union organizing against nuclear weapons, lived across the street from the White House in the permanent peace vigil, and co-directed the National Office of "Women Strike for Peace," as it opposed the U.S. massacre in Iraq. Lynn is not a

Christian but she has been willing to go through this action with three Catholic men. As the only woman in our foursome, she will suffer from being alone and separated, but she will be a source of strength and inspiration to the three of us because of her passion for justice, disarmament and peace.

Phil Berrigan, at 70, continues to be a guiding presence in our lives. What can I say about him? I look at his life and I marvel at his steadfast resistance to evil, his faith in God, his willingness to sacrifice. As a priest, he became a leader in the civil rights movement and the anti-Vietnam war movement. In 1967, he formed the "Baltimore Four" and poured blood on draft files. In 1968, with his brother Daniel, he joined the "Catonsville Nine" and burned draft files to protest the war. In 1980, with Daniel again, he and his friends entered the General Electric Plant in King of Prussia, Pennsylvania and hammered on nuclear nosecones. The "Plowshares Eight" was the first of over 50 Plowshares actions here in the United States and around the world, including Australia, England, Denmark, and Germany. Altogether, Phil has spent over seven years of his life in jails and prisons. He has been arrested perhaps 200 times in demonstrations against war and nuclear weapons around the country. Phil, his wife Elizabeth McAlister, and their Jonah House community have focused their energies in Washington, D.C. since 1973. Phil is like a biblical prophet. He speaks God's commandment to disarm and live—whether we want to hear it or not; whether it will cost him imprisonment; or whether he is ignored. Perhaps his greatest gift is his fidelity to his prophetic vocation. As I have known him over this past decade, I have been challenged by his determination to oppose the government's commitment to the big business of war. I would not be in jail today, pursuing the biblical command to disarm, if it were not for Phil and his brother, Dan.

The four of us met together regularly during these past months to plan this action and discuss the consequences. We looked at the militarism of our society; the biblical teachings on justice and peace; the specific realities of the Seymour Johnson Air Force Base and the F15E; and the prospects of jail, trial and years in prison. We prayed together, ate together, laughed occasionally, and strengthened one another with the resolve to proceed. At the heart of such a life-changing act is community. I could not have done this alone. I need these friends to walk with and to endure jail.

These friends and many others have brought me to this place. I lie here on my bunk in this ugly cell and confess a certain peace at being here. Ever since I began reading Gandhi, King and Dorothy Day, I have longed to share in the struggle for justice and peace that risked jail and imprisonment. I have been arrested many times protesting war at the Pentagon and the White House, Trident submarine launchings, the Nevada Test Site, Livermore Laboratories, and the S.A.C. Base in Omaha. I have seen so much suffering in the war zones of the world, particularly in Central America and the streets of our cities. In Washington, D.C., where I've been working since my ordination this past June (1993) at St. Aloysius' church and our homeless shelter and drop-in center, the Horace McKenna Center, I have been confronted with the injustice of poverty afflicted on people living in the shadow of the U.S. Capitol. All these experiences, these people, the pressing need for justice and peace, propelled me to this jail cell. Tonight, I hold all these people in prayer. We pray for our families, our fellow prisoners, for all those who struggle for justice and peace, and for our world. As we break bread, we offer our hearts and lives to our God.

Today while reading the psalms, I remembered that God has special compassion for prisoners. Since I am now in jail, I believe God has a special compassion and love for me, as I share the sufferings of the poor. I look around me and realize that I have finally entered into a living solidarity with the North American poor. I have entered their prison life. Even though I am white, upper-class, and well-educated, I cannot leave this jail cell. I cannot go out to the movies. I cannot go out for a walk in the park or a swim in the ocean or a meal at a restaurant or a visit with friends. I'm not going anywhere. I am tasting something of the powerlessness of the poor. This powerlessness is the daily lot for the one and a half million people currently packing our country's jails and prisons.

I am learning here about my vow of poverty. I have hardly anything, and yet, God takes care of me. So as the scriptures say, though I am poor, I am rich indeed, rich with the blessings of God.

3

The Robeson County Jail

December 10th, 1993

Bruce, Lynn and I were taken in chains to the Raleigh Federal Court-house. For several hours, we waited in holding cells on the fifth floor of the courthouse, with a beautiful view of rural North Carolina. Fi-nally, Phil was brought in and we had a reunion with much laughter and discussion. Phil, Bruce and I were chained at the feet and hands and brought in to the court. The four of us declined the help of lawyers and decided to stand *pro se,* as our own lawyers. We refused to accept any conditions of release, such as promising not to demonstrate against war again. The judge declared that we were "a danger to society" and that there would be no bond. We were hustled back to the cell and then to a waiting van. Then, the four of us were driven to the Robeson County Detention Center in Lumberton, near the South Carolina bor-der. We have no shoes and no books. Our few belongings remain at the Henderson jail (and the Seymour Johnson Air Force Base).

And so, on this the 25th anniversary of the death of Thomas Merton, the great Trappist monk and prophet, the U.S. government de-nounces me and takes me to jail to begin my own monastic life.

When we arrived at Lumberton, Lynn, Phil, Bruce and I were separated and placed in different cellblocks. I write these lines sitting on my bunk in a room with four bunk beds and a toilet. The room opens into another room with two tables and a TV set that blares at full volume. Six other inmates live in this unit. Before coming in here, I was forced to strip, hand over my clothes and put on fluorescent orange sandals and an orange jump suit with a tag at the neck that says, "Made in El Salvador." My only possessions are a bible, this note pad and pen.

Suddenly, a deep loneliness and depression descend upon me. The key source of my pain is the grief that my family feels over my arrest and imprisonment. My parents and brothers, except for my brother Steve, are terribly upset with me and although I understand, I find this very disheartening. I slept for an hour and ate an orange and two pieces of bread for dinner. I struggle through several psalms. I sit back upon my bunk and try to pray. I feel a slight lifting of that heaviness. I think I know how Dan Berrigan felt during those dark, heavy first months at Danbury prison (described in *Lights On In the House of the Dead*). I pray for strength to remain strong in the faith, hope and love that led us to the air force base in the first place.

Tonight, I am four days in jail and it feels like a lifetime. My life has changed irrevocably with this action and imprisonment. We face ten years in prison. If we are indicted on conspiracy felony charges, we could get up to 20 years. Phil speculates that we may indeed get five years. The challenge before me is not only to survive, but to use this incarceration as an opportunity of grace and spiritual growth. These days offer a living solidarity with the poor, the possibility of serious bible study, and most importantly, a deepening of contemplative prayer. I shall pray for disarmament, justice, peace, the conversion of hearts, and the nonviolent transformation of the world.

*

Everybody here spends his day playing cards and watching tv. The exception is Rafael who is from Mexico. In Spanish, he tells me that he shot someone in the arm during a fight and has been here for many months. He is sad and lonely. He never talks to anyone since no one else speaks Spanish. He paces the perimeter of the two rooms over and over again. He looks up at me and smiles but I see a terrible loneliness in his eyes. What must he be going through? What does it mean to be a refugee in jail? I shall try to take time to listen and be present to him.

I open the book of Isaiah for a word of consolation: "Fear not for I am with you. Because you are precious in my eyes and glorious and I love you." I may just sit here in my upper bunk, like Buddha or Gandhi, and meditate on that affirmation for the rest of the night.

December 11, 1993

Broken lives surround me this morning, from the guards to my fellow inmates. Cereal and bananas were dropped through a slot in the door at 6:00 a.m. after the lights came on at 5:00 a.m. I sat in prayer for an hour, and meditated on Jesus saying to me, "My love will never leave you; my covenant of peace will never be shaken."As I ponder the risen Jesus and contemplate his life and suffering, I begin to see anew the depth of the ordeal he went through. Yes, I may be imprisoned for years, but no one will take me down the corridor to a torture chamber, as in the third world or the life of Jesus. No one will whip me, abuse me, put thorns into my head, and nail me to a cross. Jesus' suffering puts mine in perspective.

Slowly, I get to know my cellmates and learn of their suffering. A young man with three kids was arrested for drug dealing and brought here last night. He told me his story and is hoping a friend will come and pay his bail. As I watched, he called home and his young wife told him she's leaving him and hung up. He's devastated.

For me, these early hours will be the most important hours of the day. It is quiet, except for heavy snoring. I sit alone at this steel table and write in silence. The television does not come back on until 11 a.m., praise God. I would like to keep a schedule but I have no watch and no sense of time. I enter the Advent spirit of waiting and hope for the coming of grace and peace.

*

The only way to understand our action and this imprisonment is through the eyes of faith. God led us through our action and God accompanies us here in prison. I will always remember being loaded into the police car just after we were arrested and Bruce getting in with me and saying, "God was with us." God will use this action and the love behind it to help proclaim God's reign of nonviolence. And so, in this faith, I trust in God. The task before me is to rely on the Spirit of God, to dwell in peace, and to share that peace with the other inmates.

*

The past 24 hours have been awful—the noise, the television, the yelling, this uncomfortable, orange jumpsuit, and the boredom. Frankly, the combination of these factors in these close quarters seems to me a modern-day torture. I can no longer think straight. I can't hear myself think. I find it hard to pray. Instead, I lay on my top bunk with the Bible open and read page after page from Isaiah, the Psalms, the Gospel of Mark and Paul's letter to the Romans. A few basic themes encourage me: "Do not be afraid; It is I." "Have faith." "If God is for us, who can be against?" Yet, I wonder about my faith—or more accurately, my lack of it. I hope that I can continue to believe and trust in God and dwell in peace throughout the difficult days that lie ahead. If today sets the standard, I'm in for a very trying ordeal.

Whenever I am down, I summon the spirits of those great saints, martyrs, and peacemakers who inspire me. I call out their names now and beg their intercession for me and my friends: Mohandas Gandhi, Dorothy Day, Martin Luther King, Jr., Thomas Merton, Franz Jaegerstaetter, Therese of Lisieux, Elizabeth Ann Seton, Francis and Clare of Assisi, Ignatius Loyola, Oscar Romero, Ita Ford, Maura Clarke, Dorothy Kazel, Jean Donovan, Ignacio Ellacuria, Nacho Martin Baro, Segundo Montes, Joaquim Lopez y Lopez, Juan Ramon Moreno, Amando Lopez, Elba Ramos, Celina Ramos, St. Peter, St. Paul and Mary of Nazareth. "Be present with me here and give me strength in the days ahead."

*

Thinking of these noble souls causes me to reflect on the profound influence of Daniel and Philip Berrigan on my life. Their life witness of nonviolent resistance to evil demonstrates what it means to put the Gospel into action in these *kairos* times. Yesterday, in court, the FBI gave us each a report with our arrest and conviction record. Phil's was so long. He said nonchalantly that it only listed "the basic incidents." "Actually," he continued, "there are many more." Dan and Phil remain committed to breaking the laws which make war and nuclear weapons legal. They are prophets for our time and I consider myself blessed to share in their public struggle for peace. From the

Catonsville Nine to the Plowshares Eight to here in the Lumberton jail
with Phil (he's in a unit down the hall), Dan and Phil have kept the
light of peace burning in a dark time. They have paid an enormous
personal price for this witness. They have been burned many times.
Many people like myself find strength from their steadfast conviction.
This afternoon, I thought of the retreat Dan and I led just four week-
ends ago in the Blue Ridge mountains near Roanoke, Virginia. With a
group of college students, we reflected and read from the Gospel of
Mark. During our time, we walked in the glorious countryside. It was a
beautiful autumn day with my great Jesuit brother. That day remains a
precious memory now.

Tonight, some relief: a substantial and delicious vegetarian dinner consisting of a large salad with cheese, lettuce and tomatoes, an
orange, an apple, crackers and a peanut butter sandwich. I feel better
already.

December 12, 1993

Today is the feast of Our Lady of Guadalupe and I dedicate this
day in prison to her and ask for her intercession for me, my friends
and for all those struggling nonviolently for justice. "Lady, bless our
witness that it may bear fruit in peace for your Son and bring greater
glory to God."

Last night before going to bed, I reread Paul's letter to the
Philippians. The central theme of Paul's great letter from prison is a
message I need to hear in this prison: "Rejoice in the Lord always!
Again I say rejoice!" Let these words be mine:

> The majority of the brothers and sisters, having taken encourage-
> ment in the Lord from my imprisonment, dare more than ever to
> proclaim the Word fearlessly. . . . I shall continue to rejoice for I
> know that this will result in deliverance for me through your pra-
> yers and support from the Spirit of Jesus Christ. My eager expec-
> tation and hope is that I shall not be put to shame in any way, but
> that with all boldness, now as always, Christ will be magnified in
> my body, whether by life or by death. For to me, life is Christ
> and death is gain. . . . The Lord is near. Have no anxiety at all,
> but in everything, by prayer and petition, with thanksgiving, make
> your requests known to God. Then the peace of God that sur-

passes all understanding will guard your hearts and minds in Christ Jesus." (Phil 1:14,18-21;4:5-7)

A relatively peaceful night. I try to fall asleep by 8:30 p.m. or so, just as the tv is the loudest and the shouting the strongest. The lights stay on 24 hours a day here. Remembering my visit with the Trappists of Gethsemani in Kentucky, I rise early for an hour of meditation. My prayer focuses on the risen Jesus and I ask for the grace of joy and the consolation of sharing in his resurrection. I try to be present to him and to listen to him. I sense his vulnerability and all he has been through. I listen to his affirming words. They sustain me through the day.

I showered and brushed my teeth and I feel refreshed. The man brought in on Friday, whose wife is now going to leave him, was just bailed out. He left thanking us. God bless him on his journey. We have a new cellmate, brought in on a "driving while intoxicated" charge. Instead of doing 120 hours of community service, he chose to do seven days in jail. Six of us fill this cell: two young African-Americans brought in for selling drugs; Rafael the Mexican; and a 19-year-old youth with very short hair, the loudest and most violent of the bunch, charged with "breaking and entering." He has been threatening everyone, yelling at the guards and the other guys, and screaming at the television.

*

Sunday afternoon. Time stands still. I do not want to complain but I am shocked at how hard I am taking this jailtime. I suppose I am crushed by the pain my parents feel because of my imprisonment. I find the confinement, the lack of exercise, and the inability to go outdoors stifling. Still, I thought two years in the Jesuit novitiate; two hard years of philosophy studies at Fordham; two unhappy years teaching high school students in Scranton, Pennsylvania; four peace-filled years of theological reflection at the Jesuit School of Theology in Berkeley; travels to war zones in El Salvador, Guatemala, Nicaragua, the Philippines, and Haiti; and intensive work among the homeless in Washington, D.C. would have prepared me for jail. This marks a new reality in my life and my heart breaks under the weight. The action was beautiful and deeply blessed, but I already feel the pain of rejection. I wish people would simply support me as I undergo this brutal confinement.

The government, the military, the FBI, and the media all conspire against me. I am deemed "a danger to society." I have spent my life opposing war, promoting disarmament, teaching nonviolence, resisting injustice, trying to practice compassion—yet I am "a danger to society." In the eyes of some of my family and friends, I am a disgrace and a scandal. Suddenly, I am poor, powerless, humbled. I have publicly challenged the culture and its presupposition that violence is acceptable. And I am thus rejected.

I cannot claim any nobility for myself. Though I wish to follow Jesus, to be his suffering servant, an apostle of Gospel nonviolence, I have far to go. I know that God wants to break through the obstacles to love, to shatter the instruments of war that have their roots within me.

I pray that God will work many miracles through my suffering. Martin Luther King, Jr. used to say that "unearned suffering is redemptive." God, may this suffering which we are undergoing for our disarmament action be redemptive for many people and be a channel of your peace for our world. Do not abandon me God. Rather, come quickly and let me feel your consoling presence. I need you.

*

Who indeed is the danger to society? My friends and I labor for peace, struggle for justice and spend our lives promoting nonviolence. We are called "a danger to society" by a government that maintains over 20,000 nuclear weapons. Last Tuesday morning, we came upon some 75 F15Es ready to wage war, perhaps even nuclear war. We saw hundreds of men with weapons ready to kill on order. We watched tanks, trucks and bulldozers play war games so that they would be ready to kill at a moment's notice. Who indeed is the "danger to society"?

Our world has never encountered a more dangerous institution than the U.S. military force. It can kill hundreds of thousands of people in minutes. With its nuclear arsenal, it can destroy entire countries, whole continents and even the world. Its nuclear program and radioactive waste already pollute the air, destroy our waters, and threaten the stratosphere. Though the Cold War is ostensibly over, this killing force is still accepted as part of life. We enter into secret war games and call a halt to the practice for death, only to be thrown in prison and publicly labeled as dangerous to society. What a sick culture. It will take a widespread conversion of heart to the way of nonviolence before we turn the corner from our path toward self-destruction. I only hope that more people will speak out against the madness of militarism.

My friends and I tried modestly to help spark disarmament. We wish to prevent a great catastrophe from happening. If the judge truly recognized this, he would have put the military on trial and ordered all nuclear weapons and F15Es dismantled. Alas, he becomes instead a tool of the war machine. His court extends the war department.

If we lived in a sane world, we would recognize these weapons of mass destruction as the real danger. We would all be horrified by their very existence. We would be shocked by our own willingness to use them, at the fact that these F15Es killed hundreds of thousands of people during the Gulf War. We would insist that these funds be spent on food for the starving masses, houses for the world's homeless, jobs, healthcare, education and care for creation. But we do not live in a sane world. Society accepts war, violence and nuclear weapons as normal. In a world of violence, Gospel peacemaking manifests a real threat to the powers of violence. Serious nonviolence threatens to overturn the tables of the unjust, warmaking status quo. If everyone took up hammers, entered nuclear facilities around the country and began beating bombs into plowshares, the Pentagon would lose control over society.

In our world, nonviolent peacemakers pose a huge danger to society. We have seen this before: Gandhi, King, Dorothy Day, Romero, Ita Ford, Maura Clarke, Dorothy Kazel, and Jean Donovan were all considered dangerous because of their peacemaking. Indeed, the most dangerous person who ever lived is Jesus—totally unarmed, nonviolence personified.

Everything Jesus did was illegal. He broke all the imperial laws of violence which control the world. He turned over the tables of systemic injustice. For this great work, he was arrested and jailed. He was charged with inciting revolt, opposing payment of taxes, and maintaining that he was the Messiah, greater than the Emperor (Lk 23:2). He was executed alongside violent revolutionaries. Yet God affirmed the dangerous, peacemaking life of Jesus and raised him from the dead.

In that same spirit, I believe God summons us to beat swords into plowshares, to renounce war, to love our enemies, and to embrace the way of nonviolence. Trying to proclaim this message and struggling to be faithful to the God of nonviolence are worth whatever chains, jails, trials, persecutions, sufferings and years of prison the government might demand.

*

I sit in prison and my thoughts turn to God. I place myself at the mercy of God and beg that God might have mercy on us all and save us from our own madness. Though I suffer, I am not alone. God hears my prayer. Jesus Christ is with me. The Spirit of the Lord is upon me. I shall not fear. Instead, I trust in God. I have faith in God. I continue to love everyone and rejoice that the reign of God is at hand.

O God, have mercy on me. Grant me a deep peace and a deep faith. Give me confidence, that I may trust in you, for I am poor and in prison, rejected by many and ostracized. I feel alone. I am isolated. My heart breaks and I fight to restrain tears. Do not be far from me. Come close, right now, and console me. Give me joy. Let me taste the resurrection. Let me not be weighed down by death, but dwell in life. Let me live in the light, in hope, not in darkness or despair.

O God, I love you so much. I am so faithless and weak. I am so small and vulnerable. I am afraid. Please come to my assistance. Do not let me suffer much longer. Return me to my friends. Let us at least be together in prison, so that we can pray together and study your Word together and build community together. God, nothing is impossible for you. I ask you to do this for me, for us, in your mercy. I thank you for hearing my prayer.

*

I've been reading the Bible on and off all day—Genesis and Exodus; the Psalms and Micah; Luke and Romans. There is nothing for me to do but read the scriptures, pray, talk to the guys and write in this journal. I cannot think straight through the noise and commotion.

I ponder the Gospel passage where Jesus sleeps in a boat during a storm while the disciples fear the boat will capsize. After he awakes and calms the wind and sea, he asks the petrified disciples, "Why are you terrified? Do you not yet have faith?" (Mk 4:35-41). This captures my feelings: afraid, terrified, alone, abandoned by God, in the middle of a violent storm, at the brink of death. What do I fear? I am afraid of complete abandonment; of being hurt or injured by a prisoner or guard; of having a nervous breakdown; of causing pain and sorrow to family and friends; of being killed in prison. "Do you not yet have faith, John?" I hear. "Lord, I believe; help my unbelief. Increase my faith. Fill me with faith so that I may know that all will be well, that the days ahead will be grace-filled, that our action will bear good fruit."

"The Lord looked down from heaven and beheld the earth, to hear the groaning of the prisoners, to release those doomed to die." (Ps 102:21)

December 13, 1993

I struggle to maintain my spirit. I struggle with lack of support by some of my relatives and the place itself. This morning, one inmate left and another arrived. At 9:30 a.m., we were let outside to the basketball courtyard for 30 minutes. Wearing only this orange jump-suit and sandals, I was very cold. The blue sky was stunning. I bought some paper, envelopes and stamps in the canteen and stood around freezing. I asked the police officer in charge if I could be moved into the same cell with Phil and Bruce.

I'm really closing in on myself. The situation is quite oppressive. I've been trying to focus on two things to gain some perspective: First, I think of all the poor of the world who suffer much worse than I do, from the starving masses of Africa to those on death row. I remember, for instance, an elderly woman I met on a bus in El Salvador. She had no legs and dragged herself around the countryside, the city, the bus. Second, I think of beautiful places, good friends, and the wonderful days of my life. I remember days with my brother novices in the Jesuit novitiate and my friends during my theology studies in California. I recall walking through Yosemite National Park with a Jesuit friend; watching the seals at Santa Cruz with Dan Berrigan; retreating along the Oregon coast with Jesuits; the glorious party at my parents' house in Maryland after my first Mass; retreats at the Abbey of Gethsemani in Kentucky and Holy Cross Abbey in Berryville, Virginia; my Casa San Jose community in Oakland; my summers in El Salvador and Guatemala. These memories sustain me. I see how blessed my life has been, blessed most of all with peace. I know I will not be here forever, but at the moment, it is hard to believe that I will ever leave.

*

With this action, I wished to offer a modest service to humanity, a symbol and a clue about how we might all live in peace. I tried to do something serious with my life, to put my life at the service of peace. Life is so short, the sufferings and injustices around the world so grievous, that it seemed only right that I hammer on that weapon of mass destruction. This action represents most the contribution I can make with my life at this time. I risked my life for the sake of disarmament and nonviolence. Now I am imprisoned, soon to be condemned by the courts, dismissed by the media and ostracized by many relatives, friends and churchfolk. Yet I place all my trust in God and have faith that God will take care of me.

*

The soap operas are on. My Mexican friend is pacing back and forth, and the young man who has been so contentious has decided to make some kind of Christmas decoration for himself. He asked me how to spell the name "Jesus."

Christmas comes next week. Perhaps Christmas in jail gets closer to the original event—Jesus' life of poverty, powerlessness, and suffering.

I have been expecting a visit from my brother, Steve. Instead, my name was called and someone asked for my arm through the slot in the lower part of the door and I was given a shot to test for tuberculosis. The nurse argued with me about why I should allow her to give me this test, but the episode seemed so surreal and inhuman that I hesitated. In the end, I decided I might as well take the test and know if I'm coming down with tuberculosis, which is very common in jails and prisons. Steve must not have been able to clear the red tape and get in to see me. My expectations are dashed once again. Instead, I'm trying ever so slowly to write a few letters. And I have taken up an appropriate book of the Bible—Job.

I sit on my bunk in prison blankets and sheets (my own sack cloth and ashes), pondering my predicament, appealing to God. Yes, I asked for this. Yes, I knew what I was getting myself into. Nonetheless—God, give me strength to endure it all.

*

6 p.m. Relief! A visit. I was able to walk the long hallway to the visiting room with Bruce, who looks as ragged as I do, but who is smiling and in great spirits. He's been reading the Bible, writing letters and watching tv. His enthusiasm is contagious. He has a touch of Gandhi's satyagraha—all good cheer, laughter, joy, zeal. We discovered Phil in the visiting room. Through glass windows, we spoke with our friends Patrick O'Neill and his wife Mary Ryder, our primary support people, and my brother Steve. Phil is thriving. Steve reports that he has been inundated with calls from people around the country, including various Jesuits and peace movement friends. A nun in Raleigh fasted on Friday for us. Many people send their prayers. And I think: We are not alone. I am not alone. God has not abandoned us.

*

Dear God, I come before you this evening to ask for the gifts of faith, hope and love. Increase my faith that these fears and doubts might cease once and for all, so that I may finally become a faithful companion of Jesus. Give me hope that I may no longer wallow in despair, but that, instead, my heart might be centered on you. Help me not to fall prey to the despair so prevalent in this society.

Give me love that I may love everyone. Help me not to be afraid or to be filled with hatred or to be indifferent in the face of injustice. I want to love you with all my heart, all my mind, all my soul, and all my strength and my neighbor as myself. I want to love even my enemies. To have such faith, hope and love is to be blessed. In your mercy, give me these graces. Then, I shall be a faithful follower of Jesus. Amen.

December 14, 1993

At 6 a.m., I was awoken and reunited with Phil, Bruce and Lynn. We were taken to the Fayetteville courthouse for a hearing. The Grand Jury is deciding whether or not to indict us on two counts—destruction of government property and conspiracy. The FBI asked for ten samples of our signatures to match the signed statements we left. (I prefer to think they were asking for our autographs.) We were held in a holding cell all day and tonight driven back to Robeson County.

What a joy to see my friends. In the van, Lynn turned to us and said, "It lifts my spirit so much to see you all." We all agreed. Lynn is such a rare and noble human being, a committed peacemaker, dedicated to the poor, humble and nonviolent, a real inspiration to me. What a scandal that the government shackles the hands and feet and waists of my noble friends. Instead, they should thank us, release us, heed our advice, and dismantle every weapon.

Bruce, Phil and I sat in the holding cell all day. While Phil slept, Bruce and I told jokes. Later, Phil and I talked about the life of Thomas Merton. Phil commented on Merton's isolation in the monastery during the turbulent 60s. He was brilliant and deeply concerned, Phil pointed out, yet he was far removed from events. At the end of the day, we were told that we would be arraigned next week, just before Christmas, and go to trial in about two months. We'll be in this hellish Robeson County jail for months to come.

When I returned to my cell tonight, I felt like I walked into *One Flew Over the Cuckoo's Nest*. The poor young man who shaved his head last night with "magic cream" kicked the walls, cussed out the guards, yelled, screamed and dangled (upside down) from the bars of the skylight. A few minutes later, while sitting on my bunk writing letters, three police officers with white gloves burst in to search the room. One went through all my papers. Perhaps this is what daily life was like under South African apartheid or the Third Reich.

December 15, 1993

This morning, out of the blue, the young man who has been acting up and causing trouble was suddenly and inexplicably removed, along with another cellmate. The cellblock instantly became peaceful. I have moved to a top bunk in the corner, around the corner from the next room and its tv. Maybe it will be quieter here. We now have two new cellmates who are reading books.

This morning, we were taken to the canteen where I bought stamps, envelopes and paper. Along the way I spoke with Bruce for 15 seconds. I passed his cellblock, knocked on his window and there he appeared, giving me the peace sign. "I'm reading Matthew, all about the woes," he said with a smile. "I prefer the blesseds," I replied. Outside, it was freezing cold and pouring rain and we stood in line for 20 minutes to buy things from the canteen window. The inmate in line in front of me started singing and praising God. "Thank you, Jesus, for this cold rain," he said. "I'm so happy. You gotta be happy if you believe in the Lord," he says to me. "Hey everyone," he shouts. "I see a tree. And look, there goes a bird!" A delightful character.

The other prisoners all express interest in our plight. One of the new cellmates pressed me for all the details. Like many others, he said, "I support you, but I hope you will be careful. I don't think I could do what you've done, but I agree with you."

After lunch, a guard came looking for me and I thought, this is it, I'm being moved. Instead, I was brought to the doctor's office for a physical examination. I was put in a holding cell with Bruce and several other inmates. We let everyone else go before us and sat talking together for several hours before our turn came. We discussed our cells, our cellmates, our letter writing, bible reading and phone calls to our families. After this glorious visit, the physical exam lasted 30 seconds. This place does not care one iota about our physical, mental or spiritual health. Prison is a form of low-grade torture which crushes the human spirit.

I am back on my cellblock now and it is full. Four new people have arrived. One is working hard cleaning up the place. Another has chastised Jerome, a short, heavy inmate whom I like, for cussing. "You're going to have to stop using those big words," he said, "if you're going to be my friend and you're going to have to start reading the Testament as well." With that, a third prisoner came over and presented Jerome with a book on how to read the Bible. These Christians manifest great dignity, even though they've been subjected to poverty, oppression and injustice.

Tonight, I spoke with my housemates at the K Street Jesuit community in Washington, D.C. Fr. Ed Glynn, S.J., the provincial superior of the Maryland Province, was visiting. The former president of St. Peter's College in Jersey City, he had given me his permission and blessing to proceed with our action last fall. Tonight, I thanked him for his support. When I met with him last fall, he told me that, as a teacher, he had always tried to get his students to ask themselves, "What is it I want to say and do with my life before God?" As I explained my Plowshares witness to him, he saw it as what I want to say with my life to God and to humanity: that we are called to disarm the world and become people of nonviolence. In that light, he encouraged me to go forward and promised to speak out in support of me, come what may. In the past week, he has consoled my parents. "He's our brother," he told my mother who is surprised at the support from the Society of Jesus for my "crime."

Thursday morning, December 16th, 1993

After a deep sleep, I got up around four this morning and prayed through some psalms. A cup of lukewarm coffee at 5 a.m. perked me up a bit. As I sit before God these days, I imagine Jesus and sense a new awareness of his spirit. I feel his presence, his personality, his character. He manifests the gentle spirit I find in Gandhi and King, and in the countless oppressed peoples I have befriended in Haiti, El Salvador, the Philippines, Nicaragua and elsewhere. This morning, I understood that Jesus is ground zero, that totally empty being who radiates God. He is completely selfless. Jesus is pure nonviolence, pure peace, pure simplicity, pure compassion, pure love, pure light. This morning, as I write and the seven other inmates sleep, I sense the pure presence of Jesus here, present to me in this awful dungeon. As I feel his humble presence, I suddenly feel both unworthy and deeply blessed. How does one begin to explain this spirituality to others? I just know that though I am a sinner, a selfish, self-righteous, arrogant, egotistical, violent person, I am blessed by the God of peace who comes to me in Jesus. And so, this morning, I praise God.

> "I will give thanks to you, O Lord my God, with all my heart, and I will glorify your name forever. Great has been your kindness toward me. . . . You, O Lord, are a God merciful and gracious, slow to anger, abounding in kindness and fidelity. . . . Give your strength to your servant." (Ps 86)

*

Everything I've read about Christians in prison for their nonviolent witness to Christ rings true. Whether it's St. Paul, St. Edmund Campion, Dorothy Day or Dr. King, the experience remains the same: God comes close to those in prison. God's spirit is unleashed on the person who suffers imprisonment in a spirit of obedient love. God is a God of prisoners, a God of the poor, a God of the oppressed—but most of all, as the life of Jesus testifies, a God of nonviolent resisters. God is a God of nonviolence and peace.

Perhaps what is needed most in our sad church and sad world is a new image of God. We continue to imagine that God is a god of war. We create God in the image of ourselves. Since we are warmaking people—violent, unjust, cruel, self-destructive, hellbent on blowing up the planet—we imagine that God must be that way, too. We know no other image. But God is not at all like that. God is not a god of violence; God is the God of nonviolence: God is boundless mercy, endless compassion, unconditional love, true justice and deep peace. Perhaps when we as a people finally realize this spiritual insight, when we worship the God of peace and begin to reflect the nonviolence of God, then finally we will repent of our violence, renounce war, beat our swords into plowshares, and become—like God—nonviolent.

*

I am feeling good today. I see what a great grace this whole experience is. Knowing myself, I begin to realize how unworthy I am of this grace. I spoke on the phone with a friend who asked, "How can you be feeling good if you are in jail and facing ten, possibly 20 years in prison?" I said it was because our action was so holy and beautiful and because God is pouring out so many blessings of love and grace on me here.

A statement has arrived in the mail signed by "Alexander B. Denson, United States Magistrate Judge." It is entitled: "The United States of America vs. John Dear." It explains from the government's perspective what happened in court last week and how I am charged "in a criminal complaint with destruction of government property. . . . The defendant reportedly commits such acts as a protest against United

States policy," he writes. "The defendant poses a danger to the community such that cannot be met by any conditions of release the court could impose. Accordingly, he is ordered detained pending trial. In his zeal to protest this government's policy, the defendant has embarked on a plan to damage or destroy government property. . . . The court has no alternative but to detain the defendant pending trial."

The envelope has been stamped, "Season's Greetings."

4

Christmas in Jail

Friday, December 17th, 1993.

God of prisoners, be with us. They handcuff us. They shackle our legs together. They lock us behind bars. They take away our clothes and belongings. They strip us and search us. They order us about. They force us to wear orange jumpsuits and fluorescent orange sandals. They put out greasy, unhealthy food. They keep the TV blaring all day long to make us numb. They permit us only two 15-minute visits a week. In short, they treat us like animals.

God of prisoners, liberate us. Free us from all that enslaves us. Break the chains that bind us all. Liberate us from the violence, racism, sexism and militarism that creates these dungeons. Help us to be human to one another, to care for one another, to heal one another, and to be nonviolent towards each oher. Create the world anew into your own nonviolent reign. We prisoners cry out to you, God of liberation. Hear our cry.

*

"Disarmament is not only a command out of the scripture," Phil told a reporter who interviewed the four of us this morning. "It's also an imperative for survival." "I'm inspired by Gandhi's idea that truth is not to be sought through legislation, but truth is to be sought in jails, and if necessary, on the gallows," Bruce said. "What we were doing was not attempting to destroy something, but to create something," Lynn added.

On the way back from the interview, I asked the guard on duty if it would be at all possible to reassign me to a cell with Phil and Bruce. He told me to write a letter to the sergeant on duty. So I wrote and explained how we were Christians, that we wanted to spend our days together praying and studying the scriptures, and since it was Christmas, why not give us a break. The next thing I know, I'm told to pack up and move into a new cell and here comes Bruce and then Phil. A great reunion. Immediately, Bruce has us exercising. Phil and I were laughing as we did our pushups. We talked all evening long. At one point, we called Dan Berrigan, filled him in on our situation and heard from him about our friends who have gone to Bosnia-Herzegovnia on the "Seeds of Peace" mission. Finally, at 10:30 p.m. a pile of mail arrived for us, which we shared and enjoyed. It is great to be together again.

*

We were up early, drinking coffee and sitting in silence. We wrote some letters together and did some exercises. Finally, we began our bible study.

We opened to the Gospel of Mark. "The beginning of the Gospel of Jesus Christ, the Son of God." A bold, exciting, politically radical opening line. In those days, after the latest war or military intervention, the Roman troops would parade throughout the empire, announcing the latest victory which they called the gospel of Caesar. Now instead: "Behold! The Gospel of Jesus"—a victory of another sort.

John the Baptist enters, fulfilling Isaiah, preparing a way in the wilderness, calling the people to repent of the social sins of war and injustice. What does it mean to prepare for Jesus today? How do we offer God's message to the world today? At Seymour Johnson Air Force Base, we tried to continue that cry in the wilderness which is a cry for peace. We tried to offer a message from God. Why do the crowds flock to hear John? Because he offers serious political (and spiritual, nonviolent) critique of his culture and of the empire. The crowds long to hear this message; they hear enough about personal sin from the synagogue pulpit (so to speak). The poor want to hear truth.

Then Jesus arrives. God affirms Jesus, and immediately the Spirit drives Jesus into the wilderness. He is tempted by Satan as he dwells among the wild beasts. Angels minister to him.

The wilderness produces social-political transformation. Nonviolent social change begins in the wilderness. As Gandhi said, "Social change never comes from parliaments or pulpits but only from the courts, the jails and sometimes the gallows." Jail is a modern-day wilderness: locked up, on the margins of society, we are deprived of everything and removed from society.

People fear the wilderness. The culture tells us that safety and power reside in the city. God dwells in the wilderness. From the margins, the winds of change stir until eventually a new center is created. But we fear the loss of reputation, the loss of social standing and the loss of freedom which occurs in the wilderness—in jail. We fear being among prisoners, among rapists, murderers, drug dealers, and thieves. Yet it is here in this wilderness where we confront our true selves. In the wilderness, Jesus faces all the temptations to power—economic, political and religious. He refuses the temptations to "power, prestige and possessions." And because he does not give in, the angels minister to him. In jail, we are likewise challenged at the deepest human level. Each moment we are invited to confess our faith. The wilderness pushes us to the deepest level of faith.

One actual wilderness in our country—the Nevada desert—has become a place where all the temptations are played out. In Nevada, we find Las Vegas, an empty city of greed, power, prestige, money, and false pleasures. A few miles away at the Nevada Test Site, the U.S. government has desecrated the earth with nuclear explosions over 1,000 times since the 1940s. The military deliberately releases radiation into the atmosphere. Into all this evil, into this jail even, comes the nonviolent Jesus with "the good news" of victory. He rejects the powers of violence and domination and embraces God's way of nonviolence. From Seymour Johnson Air Force Base to the confines of our wilderness jail cells, we struggle to do the same.

*

Christmas is one week away and I cannot think of a better place to be. I am glad to be reunited with my friends. We are by and large

ignored by the media and the country, which we expected. We find
ourselves on the margins of society, with the poor, with God. Our
families, friends and some faith-based peace groups know of our incarceration. But most importantly, God knows we are here. We speak and
act simply because it's right. That's enough to go on. We do not not
care about results, efficiency, or success; our primary focus is on the
truth of nonviolence. Results are in God's hands. The unknown nonviolent resisters who opposed Hitler's Germany and were killed were
right to resist, despite their anonymity. Before God, such resisters are
welcomed and blessed. Similarly, we are called to stand up for peace
and justice, even to risk our freedom and our lives in the process, as
Jesus did. If we are loving, faithful and nonviolent, God will use us to
transform our world's injustice into God's justice. The main goal: to
trust God completely.

December 18th

This morning we opened to Mark 1:14-20, the beginning of Jesus' Galilean ministry and the call of the first disciples. Jesus begins
his public work after John is arrested, as if he is so moved by John's
arrest that he decides to take up the work and risk the same fate. The
message of Jesus: "This is the time of fulfillment. The reign of God is
at hand. Repent and believe in the Gospel." This reign of God is indeed now, Bruce comments. Perhaps, I add, it is as close as the hammer in our hands.

In 1985, when I lived and worked for a few months in a refugee
camp in El Salvador, I talked with Ignacio Ellacuria, the president of
the Jesuit university in San Salvador, who was later assassinated in
1989. "The purpose of our work here at the Jesuit university is to proclaim the reign of God," he told us. "In El Salvador, that means denouncing the anti-reign and its wars, the bombings, the death squads,
the U.S. military aid, the starvation and the poverty." Along with the
other Salvadoran martyrs, he gave his life proclaiming that reign of
God's peace and justice.

"Everything connected with the reign of God begins with the
commandment, 'Thou shalt not kill,'" Phil said. "Everything in Christian life is based on this foundation against killing. Nothing is going to
happen until we stop killing one another. That's the first step towards
loving our enemies, which is the summit of the Gospel. The bottom

line is to stop killing one another and prevent others from killing one another. People need to withdraw their complicity in this system of nuclear weapons and institutionalized killing in order for the reign of God to be at hand today."

As we read about the call of the first disciples, we began to discuss community. "The first public act of our Lord," Phil pointed out, "was to call disciples and form a community, the most political act possible." "All are called to share this community," Phil said. "The call of Jesus is an imperative: Come, follow me." North American Christians are called to enter community and to resist the forces of death. Community and resistance—these are what it means to respond to Jesus' proclamation of God's reign and to live in that reign as modern-day disciples.

*

The Pentagon scales back and the economy booms, the evening news reports. All is well in the empire. Meanwhile back in the cell, it's been a slow day with the usual routine of reading, exercising, long naps, and talking with our cellmates.

By and large, the other inmates are friendly. We have a Cuban here on drug charges, three pleasant young African-Americans also here on drug charges and one African-American here for stealing a car. He has been having a hard time in lockup. Occasionally, he shouts or hits the wall. He lectured us at length on Islam and Christianity the other day, mouthing some awful fundamentalist prejudices in the process. The guys watch tv all day long and play cards late into the night. When the lights go out at 11:30 p.m., they begin intense conversation about drugs and women. This discussion, laced with foul language, does not end until at least 2 a.m. So far, I've been able to fall asleep quickly. Bruce, on the other hand, has tried a different routine. He sleeps from 1 to 4 in the afternoon, and from 7 to 10 in the evening, until the mail comes. Then, he stays up until 3 a.m. so that he can read, write and pray in silence. Then, he sleeps for an hour or two and we all meet by 5 a.m. for coffee, cleaning up the cell, breakfast, bible study and Eucharist.

Today, we sat at the barren stainless-steel prison table and shared a beautiful liturgy. After our bible study, we took a piece of Wonder

Bread and offered our prayers and intercessions in memory Jesus. The risen Christ is so present to us in these barebones liturgies. We recalled Dan Berrigan's poem about liturgy with the warden in the Baltimore County Jail, shortly after the 1968 Catonsville Nine anti-war action. Dan calls such Eucharists, "prisoners' pot luck."

Later, Phil told long stories about the Catonsville Nine action and the many draft board actions between 1968 and 1970. Then, we spoke again of Thomas Merton and how Merton became a prophetic voice to the nation, calling us to renounce racism, violence and nuclear war. Phil also spoke of Dr. King and how King eventually spoke out eloquently against the Vietnam War. Phil also told about vigiling outside the home of Dean Rusk in 1965, and speaking with him about the Vietnam war. Phil has continued to struggle for peace all these many years, whether people notice or not. Bruce and I continue to be amazed and fortified by his commitment.

December 19th, 1993

This afternoon, I had a good visit with my mother. Later, Bruce and I spent several hours pacing in the cell in an effort to get some exercise.

The cornerstone of our day remains our bible study sessions followed by Eucharist. Today, we examined Mark 1:21-28, Jesus' first healing, where he cures a demoniac of an unclean spirit. We focused on the setting of his first public act: the synagogue. Mark begins his gospel with Jesus disrupting the sabbath and driving out a demon in the local synagogue. The Gospel concludes with Jesus turning over the tables in the temple. What is Mark trying to tell us? Phil suggests that perhaps Jesus believes that the religious community needs to be whole and just before the rest of society can be whole and just. Perhaps the real problem, he ponders, lies within the religious community. Though the synagogue is based on cleanliness and holiness laws, perhaps the people have unclean spirits. The religious community does not realize its problem, but Jesus does and addresses it. He calls out the evil spirit of violence which possesses the synagogue and temple. He challenges their complicity with imperial Rome and its systemic injustice. And when they are confronted with the nonviolence of Jesus, they can respond only with violence. "Have you come to destroy us?" the dark spirit asks. They project onto Jesus their own predilection to destruction.

Given the modern church's complicity with systemic violence, perhaps this Gospel commands us to undertake acts of nonviolent resistance and healing within and for the religious community. Can we confront the government and military without seriously challenging the church's complicity? We let these questions linger as we shared more stories. Bruce told how he disrupted a huge "Knights of Columbus" Mass at the Shrine of the Immaculate Conception in Washington, D.C. during the Persian Gulf war. Phil shared a decision he made long ago to ignore the institutional church and to concentrate all his efforts on the nuclear warmakers. After they were jailed for the Plowshares Eight action in 1980, Phil and two friends wrote from jail to all 350 Catholic bishops, asking them to condemn nuclear weapons. Only five wrote back. I spoke of keeping vigil outside the U.S. bishops meeting at the Omni-Shoreham Hotel in Washington, D.C. I walked inside to the meetings and discovered that the only outside group allowed to lobby and display literature to the bishops was—the Pentagon. Outside the bishops' meeting room stood a huge display table with material aimed at recruiting chaplains to the military. Is the institutional church possessed by the spirit of militarism like the synagogues and the Temple of old? We looked at one another.

*

Tonight, Bruce and I paced the cell for 45 minutes while Phil read a cheap novel about a football team. Football has been blaring from the tv all day long. We pace and talk about food.

Bruce: Perhaps they'll serve eggplant parmigiana with a Caesar salad.

Me: With a glass of white wine, garlic bread and broccoli.

Dinner arrives: two slices of Wonder Bread, two spoons of peanut butter, a very greasy vegetable soup and two saltine crackers.

*

Dear God, you know me through and through. You understand my thoughts. You see the workings of my heart. You know my failings. Even though I would be holy, humble and compassionate, inside, I am arrogant, egotistical and selfish. Though I profess to walk your way of nonviolence, I still feel and act violently towards others. Gentle God, I join this nonviolent, disarmament action for the purpose of promoting your reign, yet, even here in prison, I remain self-righteous. You know my sin. Have mercy.

I can only turn to you and beg your pardon. Help me to be merciful and compassionate towards every human being. In your kindness, be merciful and compassionate to me. In your mercy, grant me a humble spirit that I might radiate Jesus and become a true instrument of your peace. Thank you.

December 20, 1993

At 6 a.m., we read from Mark 1:29-39 how Jesus' fame spread throughout Galilee; how he cured Peter's mother-in-law; how he healed people of many diseases; how he got up early and prayed alone in the wilderness; how he went forward to the other villages to proclaim the reign of God. A day in the life of Jesus! Among the poor and marginalized, he is famous and beloved for his healing. But as he heads towards Jerusalem to commit nonviolent civil disobedience in the Temple, the crowds turn on him.

At Peter's house, we see Jesus at his base of operations. And the Jesus we meet is kind and compassionate—so human, healing the sick woman who proceeds to minister to the community. This little story contradicts the institutional church's law of mandatory celibacy. The first Pope is married.

The next morning, we read, Jesus departs before dawn for a deserted place, to pray to God in solitude. Mark makes only two other references to the prayer of Jesus: after he heals a possessed boy (9:29) and in Gethsemani (14:32). "Prayer is about faith," Phil suggests. "Prayer is about trying to be faithful." We share our prayer lives. Phil likes to begin his day praying on his knees. He remembers A.J. Muste saying once, "I only feel human on my knees." When he and Liz McAlister are painting houses (to earn a living), Phil takes hours to contemplate the Lord's prayer and the Magnificat. Liz does the same: no formal prayer time, no long wordy prayers—just a life of contemplative prayer.

I speak of a conversation this fall with a Jesuit who holds that St. Ignatius was against long meditation periods. Ignatius wants Jesuits to take five or ten minutes a day to sit with all the violence, hostility and hatred in our hearts and place that before God. In this process, we deal with ourselves as we are, and God comes to us and helps us. Such prayer (or consciousness examination, as it is called) leads to self-knowledge before God, which is essential for faith and true Christian living.

Our action, I continue, is a profound offering of faith. We believed God would bring us safely to the plane. And so, we placed our fear and anxiety to the side, though we faced the possibility of being killed. Continuing that faith in prison, Phil suggests, means building community. In our action, we concentrated on the cross. Here in prison, we concentrate on community-building.

This afternoon, we share a good long visit with Lynn, Patrick O'Neill (the head of our support committee) and a lawyer. We discuss the impending trial and support work, but spent most of the time laughing about our new digs. Meanwhile, Phil, Bruce and I fast today to center ourselves in our prayer for peace.

December 21, 1993

Bruce continues to do 300 pushups a day and several thousand other exercises while Phil jogs around for ten minutes or so. We've all taken up walking, pacing back and forth for 45 minutes. A pile of mail arrived last night, including poems from Dan Berrigan and Christmas cards from Marietta Jaeger, Nancy Small of Pax Christi, and Altheia Diggs of St. Al's. This morning, I spoke with my mother and friends at St. Al's.

It's 11 a.m. All our fellow inmates are asleep. During our bible study this morning, we took up the scene of Jesus praying in the desert, how his prayer leads to public preaching about God's reign and to serious nonviolent action (exorcising demons and healing outcasts—Mark 1:35-39). Next we discussed Jesus' healing of the leper and how he commands the healed leper to confront the religious establishment with this healing. This act constitutes serious nonviolent resistance to the authorities, who might have killed him to keep the status quo in tact. For sure, we conclude, healing has political and spiritual consequences. Jesus' healings were intensely political, subversive acts which threatened to revolutionize and tear down the entire unjust social order. The healed are sent, like the disciples, to become nonviolent resisters. Who of us obeys? Complete healing requires taking up Jesus' cross of nonviolent resistance to evil. In the end, Jesus is the only one completely committed to nonviolent resistance. Nonetheless, he calls us to follow.

December 22, 1993

This morning we discussed Jesus' healing of the paralytic (Mk 2:1-12). First, Jesus operates out of his home base in Capernaum, where he organizes service to the poor and nonviolent revolutionary activity against the oligarchy. Then four amazing men carry in their friend on a mat. Jesus does not say, "Don't mess with my roof" or "Get to the back of the line." He immediately recognizes their faith and declares the paralyzed man forgiven. Their extreme measures are praised as a sign of faith.

All these factors work together: faith, community, forgiveness, following Jesus, healing. Perhaps we could say healing comes from following Jesus which comes from forgiveness which comes in community which comes from faith. Phil spoke of John 20:23 where the risen Jesus tells the disciples that "whose sins you forgive are forgiven them; those retained are retained." In the original Greek, I noted, we find a better translation which makes more sense: "Whose sins you forgive are forgiven them; those people you retain (or bind) in community, are retained (or held bound) in community." In other words, as this story explains, forgiveness involves community and vice-versa.

After Bruce went off to canteen to buy some stamps and envelopes for us, Phil and I talked about Bruce and Lynn, and what sterling people they are. Perhaps the greatest challenge before them, however, will be to stay with peacemaking for the long haul. Community, we concluded, will be essential if they are to live a lifelong commitment to resistance against imperial violence.

*

I wrote to my parents about the emotional paradox of deep peace and joy in jail. How can I feel peace and joy in jail, at Christmas, with the prospect of years of prison ahead of me? I feel I am doing something (however small and feeble) for world peace, for salvation history, for justice for the poor, for nuclear disarmament. Do not all good and noble deeds come with a price? Isn't suffering a requirement of any real nonviolent social change? Isn't imprisonment and even death the lot of peacemakers, from Christ and the early Christians to contemporary figures like Mohandas Gandhi, Martin Luther King, Jr., Dorothy Day or Franz Jaegerstaetter, all of whom were imprisoned? God blesses us. Nonviolent resistance to violence inevitably leads to prison. But if we go in a spirit of love, faith, hope and forgiveness, we receive abundant blessings, deep peace, even joy. This Christmas, I feel my life approaching the story of the original Christmas, a story of poverty, powerlessness, and nonviolent resistance leading to arrest, jail and execution. I hear anew the message of the angels to the poor shepherds of Bethlehem: "Glory to God in the highest and on earth peace to all people" (Lk 2:14).

*

Dan writes: "There's such a sublime power in the action! More, it is so desperately needed by decimated desolate church and state, citizenry and bishops. Cuts through, cuts across, cuts deep. Defines, underscores. Tells the truth, that rarest 'no' to the awful omnivorous machine. You know the one. It eats the Clintons with ease, the all but nonchalance it showed in chewing up the wicked and willing predecessors (predators) on the rickety throne."

*

In the cell next door where I used to be, a fight has broken out. One guy flipped out over a card game. He had been yelling all night. All of a sudden before lunch, we heard him screaming, "I'm going to kill you. I'm going to kill you all." He took the broom and began flailing before anyone knew what was happening. The police came in and hauled him away. Others were taken to the doctor, noses and mouths bleeding. Blood stains the floor around our cell door.

One of the dangers of jail is that the smallest incidents can flare into violence. We feel this ourselves. Yesterday, Bruce chastised me for writing what he thought were too many letters, thus using too many stamps, instead of mailing letters out to one of our communities so that they could, in turn, mail out our enclosed letters (and conserve our meager stamps in the face of piles of mail). Though it was a small matter, Bruce exploded. I took it hard and then reflected on my own reaction. Such ups and downs are typical of community life, but in the context of jail, they fester and mushroom. Here we are in the same room 24 hours a day, seven days a week, with one toilet and one shower. We need to be prayerful and centered on God. It is no wonder that the poor guy went crazy next door and lashed out in violence. Indeed, the wonder is that every cell does not explode in bloody violence. It's a wonder all people in prison do not kill their guards and one another.

*

Nuclear disarmament is not just a political matter—it is a spiritual matter; a matter of life or death; a matter of survival; a question of soul. We can no longer afford to go about our day to day lives and ignore our government's plans for mass murder. We need to stand publicly and take action for disarmament and peace. It's a sin to build a nuclear weapon, as Richard McSorley writes. It's a sin to build an F15 bomber. It's a sin to work at the Seymour Johnson Air Force base; it's a sin to work at the Pentagon, or for a Salvadoran death squad or for the South African apartheid police force. It's a sin to be silent in the face of the F15E and nuclear weapons. The time has come to sin no more, to repent of the sin of war, to renounce our violence, and to become people of nonviolence.

*

Dear God, these poor prisoners around me are going stir crazy. All the cards have been stacked against them since birth. They never received decent education, healthcare, or other opportunities. Now in jail for drug dealing and robbery, they climb the walls. They suffer under the racism, violence, brutality, cruelty, and inhumanity of the police guards and courts. Indeed they are treated as less than human.

God of the poor, I would offer a kind word to these fellow prisoners. More, I would like to offer them justice, liberation, blessings and a new future of peace. But I do not know how. I am weak and sometimes afraid. I am as helpless as they are. Come yourself and set us all free. Give us each the grace we need. Lead us all into new life.

December 23, 1993

Last night one of our cellmates, Andrew, cracked up. For hours, he barked like a dog to the top of his lungs. Then, he would growl like a German shepherd. Quite terrifying. I didn't know what he would do next. I thought for sure (and quietly hoped) that the police would come in and take him away. Bruce eventually told him he was being obnoxious. Andrew mocked Bruce but eventually stopped.

This morning, five police officers burst in wearing white plastic gloves and searched every inch of our cellblock. They went through all my papers. I sat at the table reading the Psalms, trying to pray for them and repress my anger and hostility. They showed total contempt for us—no compassion. God bless and heal them.

*

We resumed the Gospel, this time studying Jesus' call of Levi the tax collector, Jesus' dinner with tax collectors and sinners, and the punchline, "Those who are well do not need a physician, only the sick. I have come to call not the righteous, but sinners" (Mk 2:13-17). Levi was called by Jesus at the custom's house where Levi had collaborated with the empire, doing the work of the Romans and taking money from the poor for himself. He left his livelihood and even faced capital punishment for disobeying Roman authority. He responds not merely to an invitation, but to a command.

Jesus deliberately associates with the marginalized. His involvement with outcasts makes him an outcast as well. This scene of Jesus' intimate association with outcasts encourages us in our attempts at solidarity with the poor, America's outcasts. Being in prison for peacemaking is the closest solidarity we can achieve with the poor. As Dorothy Day once observed, the best way to fulfill Matthew 25's command to visit Christ in prison is to be in prison with him.

The Scribes and the Pharisees found Jesus' healings of the poor tolerable, but to sit down at table with such people was downright scandalous. We experience the same phenemenon by being here at table with prisoners. People say to me, "It's so good that you help the poor at the drop-in center and church shelter." But demanding justice, resisting the forces which kill the poor, sitting at table with criminals? "Outrageous!"

The conclusion of the story: we all need Jesus. We are all sinners. We all participate in injustice and we legalize our systemic injustice. Everything is allowed by the law: war, nuclear weapons, racism, sexism, homelessness, poverty, the starvation of millions of people each year, and the destruction of the environment. Slavery was legal. The holocaust was legal. The bombings of Hiroshima and Nagasaki were legal. Jesus calls us to repent. We have our work cut out for us.

*

Jesus, I know you are here in our midst. I recall that you said, "Whatever you do to the least of these, you do to me." I remember that you specifically said, "When you visited those in prison, you visited me." Show your face to me.

Here we are, trying to walk in solidarity with the marginalized and the oppressed, with you. We visit the imprisoned by becoming imprisoned for the Gospel. We are here as they are. None of us can leave. We will bear the stigma (honor?) of being felons for the rest of our lives. Do not hide your presence from us. Let your spirit dwell in our midst. Send your peace among us. Come and feel at home among us here behind bars and we shall be free.

Christmas Eve, December 24th, 1993

Jail is a very appropriate place to be as we mark the birth of the Prince of Peace. We were up early. From 7 to 11:30 a.m., Phil, Bruce and I took up again the topics of faith, community life and forgiveness, in the light of Jesus' healing of the paralytic. We each confessed our long failings at community life, our resentment towards the drudgery, our lack of forgiveness, and our lack of faith. But Jesus insists that we build community. We pledged to build community among ourselves here in jail.

Our sharing became very personal as we discussed our life experiences, Phil at Jonah House in Baltimore, Bruce at the Dorothy Day Catholic Worker House, and myself in the Jesuit community. Staying with it, being faithful, forgiving each other, correcting each other, loving each other, taking time away together, we agreed, are all crucial for the life of faith.

I do not know how prisoners survive. In truth, many do not. I've heard too many stories of prisoners killing one another. Here, our cell-mates watch tv. Larry, the Cuban, is writing a letter. Andrew paces back and forth in silent rage. The others, Charles, Andre, and Mike, play cards as they watch TV. Phil, Bruce and I sit on our bunks reading. Bruce and I have become serious about our ritual walks, up to an hour now after lunch and then again for another hour after dinner. Meanwhile, Bruce insists on his vegetarian diet: no meat, no dairy products, no fish. He exercises fiercely. I'm just getting by, still amazed that I'm here at all. It's hard for me to imagine that I may be in prison for years to come. I prefer not to think about it.

Tonight, I read of Shadrach, Meshach and Abednego—how they refused to worship the king's golden statue; how they were thrown into the fiery pit; how they sing and praise God and live (Dn 3). This is our story. We refuse to worship the nation's idol of death at Seymour Johnson Air War Base and so we have been thrown into this fiery furnace, the Robeson County Jail. The flames of violence kill the spirits of those in prison. Nevertheless, we sing and praise God and God protects us. We expect further miracles to come.

I ask Bruce what was the best Christmas of his life. He replies, "This one, being here in jail with you and Phil." In a world of violence, poverty and death, being in jail for nonviolent resistance is the place to be on Christmas day.

*

Someone sent in a quote from Daniel Berrigan: "I would like to say as simply as I know how, to other Christians, that I'm convinced that in our lifetime we have no contribution to make to one another or to the world at large except a modest and consistent No to death. Our churches can go tomorrow; our schools could have been closed yesterday; our institutions ground under by the next wave of tanks or the next phalanx of violence. And what will remain of Christianity except that we have said audibly and consistently and patiently over our lifetime: 'We are not allowed to kill. We are not allowed to be complicit in killing. We are not allowed to commit the crime of silence before these things.'"

Christmas Day, 1993

It is a great grace to be here in jail for active nonviolence and Christian discipleship. After mail came in last night, we stayed up talking and the authorities left the tv on. We heard live coverage of the Christmas Mass from St. Peter's. The jail cell was filled with hymns and prayers!

This morning, after coffee, we read Luke's tale of the birth of Jesus—how his poor, homeless parents journeyed to Bethlehem because of the oppressive emperor's census; how the angel appeared to the poor and how the poor rejoiced at Jesus' birth. "Do not be afraid," the angel announces. "Behold, I proclaim to you good news of great joy that will be for all people. A savior has been born for you. . . . Glory to God in the highest and on earth peace to people of goodwill." Peace comes to people of goodwill. We spoke of the angels who have come into our lives, and how we tried to proclaim this good news at the war base.

Being in jail on Christmas day is not just counter-cultural, but anti-cultural. The culture has no sense of Christ's spirit. People spend billions of dollars in an orgy of consumerism, exchanging presents while ignoring the plight of the poor and the demands of discipleship. As George Anderson of St. Al's says, "We cannot mark Christmas without remembering—and taking up—the cross." This morning, I feel that we are living the cross of nonviolent resistance. Instead of marking this day with the cultural spirit of materialism, we sit here in poverty. The only gifts we have to give each other are a piece of broken bread and an embrace of peace in Jesus' name. That is more than enough.

This feast marks the incarnation of the God of nonviolence. God has become human, and it follows that all human life is sanctified: we can never justify harming another, much less killing another or waging war or silently supporting systemic violence. Christ's birth among the poor in the rural outskirts of an empire calls us to enter the world of the poor and to take up Christ's nonviolent resistance to imperial violence, even at the risk of our own arrest, imprisonment and death.

Be not afraid. Give glory to God! Rejoice! Peace on earth has come! We spoke about our fear versus our faith. Faith, we conclude, is the antithesis of submission to fear. Faith implies nonviolent action and love. Fear is another name for death. Having fear does not mean we are not faithful, but giving in to fear denies our faith. The life of faith is a series of confrontations with fear, with death. In the light of grace, faith pushes us to declare: "I will not be controlled by fear or death." So, here we are, confronting the power of death, which rules in this awful jail. Into our midst comes the Christ—bearing gifts of peace, joy, hope and grace. Good news indeed!

*

Dear Jesus, on this Christmas night, I thank you for coming into our war-torn world. Thank you for entering the world of the poor, for becoming a vulnerable child, for teaching nonviolence, for taking up the cross of resistance, for undergoing death without retaliating, for forgiving us and showing us that death does not have the last word. From the crib to the cross, you, Jesus, are the way of peace. Send again your angel with the glad tidings of peace. Come tonight into this cold jail and grant us your gift of peace. Our hearts long for your presence.

5

A New Year Begins

December 26th, 1993

To celebrate Christmas, we enjoy some snacks which we had saved all week. Phil regales us with stories about his father, growing up during the depression, struggling to survive with five older brothers. I tell about my own family, my grandfather's newspaper business which my father inherited, and growing up in the aura of the family publishing company. A delightful evening. Such evenings will be essential in the days and months ahead.

December 27th

Today is the feast of John the Beloved disciple. We read in the Gospel of Mark how Jesus was asked why he did not fast (2:18-20). "The wedding guests do not fast when the bridegroom is in their midst; later, when he is taken away, on that day they will fast." We fast today to center ourselves in prayer for nuclear and personal disarmament. We discuss our experience of fasting—Phil's 30-day fast in Danbury prison in 1972; Bruce's two 26-day fasts for nuclear disarmament; and my 21-day fast for an end to U.S. military aid to El Salvador. We fast quietly, privately, as prayer, as an act of resistance and hope.

Fr. Gene McCreesh, a Jesuit priest from Charlotte, N.C., visits this morning and encourages me to pray through Ephesians 3:14-19 for the strength to be centered in God's love: "For this reason I kneel before God from whom every family in heaven and on earth is named that God may grant you in accord with the riches of God's glory to be strengthened with power through God's spirit in the inner self and that Christ may dwell in your hearts through faith, that you rooted and grounded in love may have strength to comprehend with all the holy ones what is the breadth and length and height and depth and to know the love of Christ that surpasses knowledge so that you may be filled with all the fullness of God."

This afternoon, my brother David visits. He strongly disagrees with our action and with my willingness to risk imprisonment. "What good does this do?" he asks. "Plowshares actions make no difference. People think you are crazy."

I explain to him the need to disarm. We are just beginning the process of disarmament. I believe that this is what God wants us to do, that this is what Jesus would do, that it fulfills his command to love our enemies, and that we follow Gandhi, King and other peacemakers. I tell him that we acted in the same spirit as the abolitionists who broke laws and risked their lives nonviolently to abolish slavery; we are trying to abolish war. We may not live to see the abolition of all nuclear weapons, but it is a struggle worth our freedom—and our lives. We did not even dent the war machine, but we offered a symbol to the country. Future generations will view our Plowshares actions as the beginning of the end of such weapons.

*

I have moments here in jail when I think to myself, "So this is what St. Paul, Gandhi and Dorothy Day meant!" I have a deep sense that grace is at work in our day to day lives, in our suffering and confinement, that these days may be redemptive. "The only thing to do in a time of war is to fill the jails," Dorothy Day once said. "Widen the prison gates," Gandhi wrote to the British imperialists. "The nonviolent resister should approach the jail cell as a bridegroom approaches the bridal chamber."

December 28th

This morning, at Eucharist, we remember all our friends who have gathered in Washington, D.C. for a "Faith and Resistance" retreat to mark the feast of the Holy Innocents. Some friends will block the entrance to the Pentagon this morning to protest the ongoing slaughter of the innocents, the world's children.

We discuss at length what community might mean in jail. What are our expectations? What has our experience been? What happens if they try to separate us again? Do we resist the police? How do we form a community with everyone in our cellblock? How do we continue the resistance begun in our action? How do we live together in jail, at peace with one another, even though we share these small confines and are with each other 24 hours a day? How do we remain committed to peacemaking for the long haul? Where do we find the Spirit of God in our day to day prison life?

Phil suffers from an abscessed tooth. Bruce and I walk as much as two hours each day now. Today, I write 14 letters and tonight, enjoy the best meal yet—salad, fruit, a peanut butter sandwich and a little tuna fish.

Outside, a cold spell has hit. I have not been outdoors in over two weeks. Everyone is frustrated, stir crazy. I would be too without Bruce and Phil and our community prayer. For me, today has been a fulfilling day. We had coffee at 6 a.m. and then I swept the floor of the cell while Bruce mopped. We talked and prayed from 7-11 a.m. After lunch, we walked for an hour and fifteen minutes. I wrote letters all afternoon, took a shower, had dinner, walked for another 45 minutes and then watched the evening news—hearing about U.S. threats against North Korea. We have hundreds of nuclear weapons aimed at North Korea but we are telling them they are not allowed to have one. During the 1950s, the U.S. government (in conjunction with Quaker Oats) fed cereal laced with radiation to disabled children during secret experiments, according to a report from Hazel O'Leary, head of the Department of Energy.

Phil is reading in his bunk below me and Bruce is sleeping on the top bunk a few feet from me. I sit here tonight oddly content and at peace. I remain convinced that we are profoundly blessed by the God of peace for willingly entering this dungeon. Jesus is present here in the other prisoners, in Phil and Bruce and in the Spirit I feel within me. Like Shadrach, Meshach and Abednego, we praise the God of peace. Blessed be God forever.

December 29th

The men stayed up late last night and I overheard their conversation. They were talking about their experience of racism, prejudice and "the boys"—i.e., the Ku Klux Klan. One of the guys told of driving through Florida at 4 a.m. on a deserted road and seeing, up ahead, eight men dressed in KKK robes, stopping a car. He told how he quickly turned around and headed the other way. The others told stories of not being waited on in gas stations or restaurants within the last few months. They compared the experience of racism in the North and South. Most agreed that New Jersey was the most racist state they knew. I lay on my bunk, under my sheet, with chills going down my spine as I heard these awful tales, and felt ashamed of being white and appalled by the inhumanity of racism.

Then, the guards came in at 4:30 a.m. and took away Larry, our Cuban friend here on drug charges. He was gone before I had a chance to say goodbye.

During our coffee time this morning, we held our first "check-in," to report to each other how we are doing—what's on our minds and in our hearts. We agreed to follow through with yesterday's discussion, to intentionally build community, support one another, become good Christian brothers—and to include Lynn as best we can. She is at the other end of the building in solitary confinement, so that she can be free of the cigarette smoke and the constant noise. She writes that she is holding up fine. Phil declared this morning that out of the dozens of jails and prisons he has been in, this is the worst.

Jerome, from next door, announced to me with a chuckle this morning that my church back home will never allow me back as long as I continue with this scraggly beard. Secondly, he and the other cellmates want to know just how we got onto that air force base anyway. I tried to explain that military security is a myth, that we could do it again if we wanted to, but even more significantly, that we had prayed beforehand and that we believe that God led us onto the base.

*

The Gospel of Mark (2:21-22) calls for "new wine in new wineskins." This "newness" led us to discuss the need for an entirely new society, a new way of living as the human family. "The Gospel is about nonviolent revolution," Dr. King used to say. What are the ingredients of this nonviolent revolution, this new human society? The Gospel makes it plain: nonviolence, voluntary poverty, resistance to evil, community, prayer, hospitality, solidarity, and care for the earth. This new nonviolent revolution rules out reform. Jesus doesn't stand for reform; he is about personal and social nonviolent revolution. The three of us do not vote or seek public office. People often explode with anger when I tell them that like Dorothy Day and Thomas Merton, I'm a Christian anarchist. They are not too upset that I go to jail or risk my life living in a violent inner-city neighborhood or travel into the war zones of El Salvador or Haiti, but when I mention that I don't vote, people get apoplectic. Bruce explains it this way: 1) he votes with his life; everyday, especially in jail, he tells the government what he thinks; 2) voting is "the opiate of the masses." People think that all they have to do in a democracy is vote; actually voting every four years and not doing anything else is the antithesis of democracy. 3) Voting is about real choices, but we are never offered any real choices. We might be able to vote whether we want 22,000 nuclear weapons or 21,000 nuclear weapons, but we will never be allowed to vote for total nuclear disarmament. A few years ago, we could vote to spend $40 million or $90 million to the death squad government of El Salvador. That is not a choice. As Clarence Jordan said, "We don't want to shuffle the deck; we want a whole new deck." New wine and new wineskins!

Perhaps the first true nonviolent revolution was the resistance, crucifixion, and resurrection of Jesus. To follow Jesus in his social revolution of nonviolence, we must undergo the cross. "Because we tried to embrace the cross of nonviolent resistance to the state at Seymour Johnson Air Force Base," Phil wondered, "perhaps we are experiencing a minor resurrection here in jail." Someday, the angel will roll away the stone of this tomb and we'll walk out reborn.

Tonight, we had a good long visit with Lynn and a local lawyer, a feisty Southern woman who kept us laughing. Lynn seems well, though she has not been outside and only leaves her solitary cell every three days or so to make a phone call. We tried to do some business in preparation for our trial, but we were so giddy with jokes and stories that we just decided to enjoy each other, especially Lynn's company.

*

Dear God, tonight, here in jail, I am tired. I am tired of the long day, the tensions among the other cellmates, the bars, the awful food, the bright lights, the blaring TV, the mean guards, and the basic inhumanity. I'm tired of having to explain to family and friends why I'm here. I am tired of rejection and misunderstanding.

But tonight, I think of Jesus and recall his life. He was completely rejected by every single family member and friend and even betrayed by a close friend. He suffered not only arrest and jail but execution. So many people around the world tonight suffer. They are starving, homeless, sick, dying, lonely, abandoned. So my complaint seems paltry. I ask you to take me and place me close to Jesus and use this experience for your work of salvation. Do with me here whatever you want for the coming of your reign of peace and justice. Thank you, God, for being with me.

December 30th

Jesus deliberately breaks the law protecting the sanctity of the Sabbath (Mk 2:23-28). He invokes scripture and declares that the Sabbath is for human beings and that "the Human One" is Lord even of the Sabbath. He is provocative, troublesome, scandalous, and correct. The Sabbath, in effect, kept the people pacified, under control, silent. The Pharisees promise to keep the people under control in exchange for their own prestige and the power granted them by the imperial authorities. The consequences for breaking the Sabbath were serious, including ostracism from the synagogue. Jesus is free of the false law. He obeys the living God and calls us simply to be human with one another.

We need to do the same today, to break the laws which oppress us by keeping us under the control of mad nuclear warriors and Wall Street conglomerates. Like Jesus, we shatter the reins of death, in our case by hammering on a nuclear bomber at a war base. We cite Jesus as the basis for our religious witness. Jesus was free of imperial control; we are as well.

The whole day was spent writing letters. Liz McAlister writes that during the retreat in Washington, D.C., nine people blocked the doors to the National Rifle Association; six people at the Pentagon; and nine at a local gun shop. None were arrested. Billy Neal Moore, my friend who had been on death row for 16 years before he was granted clemency in 1990, sends his prayers. I used to write to him in prison. Now, he is married and writing to me in prison. We are both amazed at these changes.

A flier came in the mail: "The 20th century has been the most violent in human history. War has accounted for an estimated 110 million deaths—more than 1 million per year. Structural violence—hunger, poverty, preventable disease, racism—has caused another 19 million deaths per year. In all, at least one billion deaths have been caused by violence in this bloodiest of all centuries. In the U.S. alone, a Vietnam-equivalent of 52,000 Americans are killed or kill themselves each year, and hundreds of thousands more are injured by guns. The epitome of this propensity for violence was the advent of nuclear weapons in 1945. Some 200,000 human beings were immediately killed by just two bombs, while tens of thousands more died in the decades following from radiation-induced maladies. After nearly 50 years of nuclear arms build-up, despite recent treaties, some 48,000 nuclear warheads representing more than one million Hiroshimas exist in today's arsenals."

*

God, the lights have gone out in our cell tonight, except for one or two dimmed fluorescent bulbs. They remind me of the spiritual darkness of this place, but even more urgently, the darkness of our world, plunged into an abyss of violence. Tonight, I come to you again and ask with all humanity for the grace of light—the light of nonviolence.

No, we are not worthy. We are helpless. We are blind. We walk about in the dark. We wage war, hurt each other and treat each other miserably. We do not know what we are doing.

Turn on the light. Let your light go on in every human heart. Rescue us. Save us from this dark hellhole. You are God. You are the light of the world. You are our only hope.

Come. Delay no longer.

December 31st

The cell is full again. A young man who talks at the top of his voice from early morning and through the night has joined us. He is loud and we will have to endure him and respond with kindness and compassion as we can. Indeed, some of the late night conversations have hit all time lows, revealing deeply ingrained misogyny, homophobia, fascism, and anti-semitism. We are all disturbed at this, and Bruce has spoken up and challenged it.

This morning, this last day of the year, before our little makeshift Eucharist, we take up one of the most challenging stories of the Gospel: the healing of the man with the withered hand (Mk 3:1-16). It is the Sabbath. In the synagogue, Jesus calls the man to stand before everyone. Then, he puts the truth to them clearly and boldly: "Is it lawful to do good on the Sabbath or to do evil, to save life or destroy it?"

The question lingers: It is *the* question of our times. Are we about doing good and saving life or doing evil and destroying life? With our Plowshares action, we tried to pose this question to the nation; we also tried to do good, save life, and stop the mad, insane destruction of life. This challenging question is never well received. The crowd responds to Jesus with silence. He grows angry and grieves at their "hardness of heart," "their closed minds." He heals the man and immediately they plot ways to kill him.

The symbolism of the withered hand. Earlier, we met a possessed man in the synagogue; now we meet the crippled man. Here we see what the synagogue does to people: it leaves them possessed and crippled. To the extent that they pacify people today, our churches are equally guilty. Instead of inspiring people to act justly and save life, the churches possess and cripple people. The churches are often silent in the face of death and the destruction of the planet. They work in complicity with the forces of evil and destruction. Like the Pharisees, many church people actually plot murder in their hearts by supporting the possibility of war. Jesus gives us an image of the faithful human being: standing up in public, healing people, challenging our complicity, urging people to do good and save life, and upsetting the decorum of our liturgies with the life and death questions of reality.

Jesus is not lukewarm. He deals with matters of life and death. He gets angry and mourns over our silence, complicity, hardness of

heart. Imagine what he thinks today over our wars and nuclear preparations! If he gets angry in the synagogue, what must he feel about Seymour Johnson Air Force Base or the Pentagon? He still grieves. If we
are not about doing good, saving life, resisting evil and publicly protesting the forces of destruction, then we can not claim to be followers
of Jesus. It is a lifelong struggle.

Phil told us a story about our friend Thomas Gumbleton of De-
troit, Michigan. Bishop Gumbleton was asked to speak to a thousand
students at a Jesuit high school. As he outlined U.S. military intervention in Central America, the U.S. plans for nuclear war and the ongoing systemic war against the poor, he noticed that the students had no
reaction. It occurred to him then and there that the church teaches sin.
These students had been taught silence, complicity, violence, injustice,
consumerism, greed, blind patriotism, and idolatry. We stand in a
worse position than that synagogue in Capernaum. We are not only
silent: as devout church people, many of us prefer to do evil. We willingly work for the Pentagon or military industries or multinational corporations so that we can live comfortable lives. We need conversion.

It is now close to midnight and we're all up, reading and writing
letters. We celebrate the new year with peanuts, pretzels, oranges,
crackers, and a peanut butter sandwich. We've been saving up all
week. It turns out to be a quiet evening.

The National Jesuit News has reported our action with a headline
and quoted my provincial, Fr. Ed Glynn, who fully supports me. "John
follows a long line of Christians who have made a choice to act and
are willing to live with the consequences. I'm proud of John. He's a
good Jesuit. Every decision is weighed by the greater good being
served and he sees this as an educational moment, in a much larger
context."

*

Dear God, one year closes and another begins. Time moves on.
History moves ever forward. I feel so small here in this jail cell. I
contemplate the world, the human race, and all human history. To you,
a thousand years are as a moment. Yet, you are here in this small
space with us. Thank you.

A new year! God of peace, we need some newness in this world, some new peace, new justice, new disarmament. The world longs for renewed good news, the eternal good news of nonviolence.

May this new year see a change of heart among us all. Have mercy on us, O God. Come among us still. Provoke us, do not give up on us. Give us a spirit of repentance.

Do not leave us to fend for ourselves. Help us turn back to you, so that the earth may flourish forever in peace.

January 1st, 1994

The new year begins with Bruce waking me and offering me a cup of coffee at 5:30 a.m. The coffee was unusually strong, the best cup since we've been in here. Since none of the others take it, we split eight cups between us. The celebration continues! We broke into long stories about our families and friends. After cereal and a banana, we turn to the Word and Eucharist.

Kirkegaard writes that Christianity is "a do it! religion." Today's simple text, Mark 3:7-12, describes Jesus in action, attracting crowds from the entire region, healing them, and exorcising demons. Jesus does not let possessed people name him because naming indicates control. It occurs to us that the possessed people who were calling out to him, "You are the Son of God," either mock him or praise him so they will not have to follow him. In either case, Jesus rebukes them. We notice that Jesus avoids praise intended to inflate his ego. He is humble and keeps the focus on God and God's reign of justice and peace.

The crowds of people press in on Jesus! So many had unclean spirits. This means that they did not believe, were idolatrous, that they practiced violence. "What are the consequences of not believing in God?" Phil asks. We see them everywhere: militarism, injustice, street killings, despair, hate, fear, apathy. If we believe, we are healed. We will renounce violence, practice nonviolence, trust in God, care for one another, feed and house everyone, and disarm.

*

As I sit reflecting on my bunk and Phil sits reading in the lower bunk, I look back over this past year and am amazed. The year has been filled with so many blessings beginning with my Casa San Jose community life in Oakland; my theology studies; the republication of my book, *Disarming the Heart*; helping to organize the Good Friday witness at Livermore Labs; and finishing my Master's degree in theology from the Jesuit School of Theology in Berkeley. In June, I moved from Oakland to Washington, D.C. was ordained a priest; celebrated a first Mass at St. Aloysius' church and had the party of a lifetime afterwards at my parents' house with all my friends gathered from the four winds. Other vivid memories: demonstrating against the launching of a Trident Submarine in Groton, Connecticut on July 17th; taking a retreat on Block Island; vacationing with Jesuit friends at the Outer Banks; working with the homeless at the McKenna Center in D.C.; speaking on Gospel peacemaking in many places around the country; and presiding at my brother David's wedding and my niece's baptism. Finally, the year climaxed with our Plowshares action and my imprisonment. A year of grace upon grace, blessing upon blessing, peace upon peace!

The prayer of St. Ignatius, at the heart of my ordination prayer these past six months, has been answered: "Take, Lord, receive, all my liberty. . . . "

Now, I look ahead to this new year. I hope that this new year is also marked with grace upon grace and peace upon peace, not only for me, but for our world. May our God grant us renewed peace, justice and disarmament in this new year.

6

The Long Days of Winter

January 2nd, 1994

We begin the day by reading Mark 3:13-19, the story of Jesus climbing the mountain and calling 12 friends to be apostles. He offers three duties: 1) to be with him; 2) to go forth and preach; 3) to drive out demons. We too are called to be with him on his campaign of revolutionary nonviolence. We need to form communities of peace where his spirit is present, where we can dwell with him. We too must go forth and proclaim the reign of God as Jesus did. We too are commanded to drive out demonic power. An apostle brings light into the darkness of killing, and drives out the demons of violence. We see our action at Seymour Johnson war base as such an action—an exorcism. We tried to expose the evil deeds of the air force and to drive out that demonic violence by beginning the process of disarmament.

*

Theologian Jim Douglass writes that the jails are the new monasteries for our age. We resist the forces of death and end up in jails and prisons where we find the God of peace blessing us. In jail, we encounter the God of nonviolence. In the nuclear age, many people who seek peace resist nuclear weapons and experience God's peace in jail.

*

From CURE (Citizens United for Rehabilitation of Errants): "The number of inmates in state and federal prisons doubled from 1973 to

1980 to 329,821. In 1990, there were 755,425 and this year, there are
one million. At the same time, the country's jails hold close to half a
million inmates while ten million are processed every year. Thus, the
U.S. now has the highest incarceration rate of any industrialized nation
in the world. The U.S. spends almost $25 billion a year on construc-
tion of prisons and management of inmates. The average cost of con-
structing a prison bed is over $50,000. However, when states 'buy'
prisons on credit, typically by issuing long term bonds, the cost will
double or even triple. The average operating cost to keep a person
incarcerated can range from $15,000 to $30,000 a year. New York City
pays over $50,000 a year ($150 a day)." Instead of building schools,
we build jails. Instead of building homes for the homeless, we build
jails. Instead of rebuilding our cities, we build jails. Jails are the future
of our nation. Unless we as a people convert and have a change of
heart, we have nothing in store for us except further violence.

January 3rd

I fell asleep last night as the other inmates yelled and screamed a
few yards from me. This morning, bible study was interrupted by a
canteen break. Despite the cold weather, everyone, including Bruce,
went outside to purchase food and other items. Phil and I stayed behind and enjoyed the peace and quiet.

Mark's Gospel tells that Jesus' relatives "set out to seize him, for
they said, 'He is out of his mind'" (Mk 3:21). They were upset with
him because he was drawing attention to himself, disrupting the synagogue, disturbing the peace, and by extension casting aspersions on
them. He must have been hurt by their rejection. We shared our experiences with our own relatives, how each of us has had relatives who
think we are "out of our minds." These accusations hurt, but Jesus'
family problems console us. Through it all, Jesus remains focused on
God and God's will. We struggle to be with him.

*

Here I am, 10 a.m., sitting at a steel table. Bruce writes across
from me. Phil sits on his bunk, writing too. We're not going anywhere.
We have shared a simple Eucharist to remember Jesus, offered our
prayers for peace and drawn strength for the days ahead.

8 p.m. We reunited this afternoon with Lynn, Patrick O'Neill and a lawyer. Lynn is well and Patrick entertained us with stories from his own 1984 prison experiences, a result of his involvement with the Pershing Plowshares. His letters at that time challenged me profoundly and helped me in my path to our action at Seymour Johnson Air Force Base.

*

Every two minutes somebody somewhere in the U.S. is shot. Every 14 minutes somebody dies from a gun wound. Each gun injury involving hospitalization costs over $30,000. A license to sell a gun costs 83 cents a month. A gun rolls off the assembly line in America every ten seconds. America imports another gun every 11 seconds. There are 246,984 gun dealers. In 1990, guns killed 37,184 people in the U.S.. In 1993, more than 485 people were murdered in D.C. alone, the murder capital of the nation.

The little guns will not stop killing until the big guns are disarmed and dismantled. There is a direct connection. Thus, we address the big guns at Seymour Johnson Air Force Base and elsewhere, even though it is unpopular to do so.

January 4th

A full day. A good visit this morning with my former Jesuit provincial—Fr. Jim Devereux, S.J., from Charlotte, N.C. This afternoon, I wrote over 20 letters to friends all over the country.

One of the central missions of Jesus is expelling demons from people. This morning, we studied Jesus' answer to the charge that he is possessed. "How can Satan drive out Satan? If a kingdom is divided against itself, it cannot stand" (Mk 3:23-30). All kingdoms and empires are rooted in violence and lies. The reign of God is the only pure reign of nonviolence and truth.

"No one can enter a strong man's house to plunder his property unless he first ties up the strong man. Then he can plunder his house." Thus, Mark sums up Jesus' life—tying up Satan and plundering Satan's empire through active nonviolence. Initially, the imagery evokes breaking, entering and violent struggle. But within the context of Jesus' nonviolence and the empire of violence, the parable relates something else entirely—the power of nonviolent resistance to evil in a world where violence and war are legally structured into the framework of society. This parable explains the work of Jesus and the disciples as they confront the forces of death. Jesus does not resort to violence and domination to disrupt the empire. Jesus plunders the house of imperial violence in a steadfast spirit of love and truth. It culminates in the nonviolent direct action which Jesus takes in the Temple: He turns over the tables of systemic injustice in acts of nonviolent resistance that subvert the empire and knock down its underpinnings, so that it eventually crumbles down.

As Ched Myers writes in his book, *Binding the Strong Man*, this parable is best understood from the perspective of Jesus' revolutionary nonviolence. Mark does not depict Jesus as a strong man or a stronger man. One does not tie up the strong man by being a strong man; you cannot beat the strong man with violence. That is his venue exclusively. Jesus binds the strong man by being a weak man. We bind the imperial strong man through nonviolence. We overcome the strong man by disavowing everything for which the strong man stands. Jesus uses suffering love and peaceful resistance (even to the point of dying on the cross and forgiving his enemies) to defeat the strong man. We are called to the same nonviolent plundering.

We see such dramatic nonviolence when Gandhi walks to the shore, picks up the illegal salt, ties up the British empire's "business as usual," plunders the unjust economic order and helps bring down "the strong man's" control over India. We see such active nonviolence when Rosa Parks refuses to give up her seat on a Montgomery bus and so disrupts the house of segregation. We see such confrontative nonviolence when Dorothy Day refuses to go indoors during a New York City air raid drill and so disrupts the unanimity of the empire's preparations for nuclear war. We see such public transforming nonviolence when the Catonsville Nine burn draft files with homemade napalm and so rock the warmaking ship of state.

Never before have I tried to plunder the strong man's house as we did on December 7th when we hammered on the nuclear fighter bomber at the air force base. The Gospel calls us to keep breaking through the demonic control over the world with the power of nonviolence. Though the parable challenges, understood within the context of active nonviolence and my own concrete situation of action and imprisonment, it consoles.

January 5th

We as a people suffer hardness of heart. Our willingness to use nuclear weapons and destroy creation signifies this massive hardness of heart. The way to change our hearts is to convert. As we disarm the weapons, God disarms our hearts. Our relationship with God intimately connects with our relationship to all humanity, especially to our enemies. As we love our enemies, our hearts melt and God's own loving Spirit takes over. Jesus is the only soft heart, the only unarmed heart, the only clean spirit, the only one not possessed by empires and death. He invites us to disarm our world so that he can disarm our hearts and fashion them after his own heart.

January 6th

11 p.m. This morning, my brother Steve visited for 30 uplifting minutes. His work as director of a non-profit organization which brings plumbing and heating to the rural poor throughout North Carolina inspires me. He and his wife Janet have two adorable children, Patrick and Katie, and I heard all about their latest adventures. Steve talked about my parents and the local support committee which continues to speak out about us. I have not met many of them, but their concern and efforts to publicize our action and imprisonment hearten me. This afternoon, Patrick O'Neill visited with a lawyer, and we had a marvelous reunion with Lynn. Patrick smuggled in a pile of books, candy, soda, stamps, money, a newspaper and more mail. Kindness at its subversive best!

*

After Jesus' mother and brothers come to see him, he turns to his circle of friends and asks, "Who are my mother and my brothers? Whoever does the will of God is mother and brother and sister to me" (Mk 3:31-35). The passage speaks to me of my own family and their mixed reaction to my action and imprisonment. We discuss Jesus' summons to do the will of God. What is the will of God? Everyone in our society could give a different answer to the question. And yet, we insist that some specific ingredients are necessary: disarmament, peace-making, nonviolence, resistance to evil, seeking justice, and loving our enemies. As Phil says, we are commanded to do these things. The will of God is that we do good and save life. That requires that we resist the forces that do evil and destroy life. As Christians, the will of God is to follow Jesus on his campaign of nonviolent transformation. These days, God's will for some of us is that we resist the ways of war, go to jail, stand with the oppressed, and suffer with the victims of violence. Compassion means "to suffer with." God wants us to be compassion-ate, just as God is. God wants us to "suffer with" the suffering people of the earth. In this way, we are mother and sister and brother to Jesus.

Friday, January 7th, one month since the action.

After yesterday's visits and conversations, I was exhausted to the point of sickness. Phil has a chest cold. Today, we had an abbreviated bible study and went back to bed. I rested again throughout the after-noon, and wrote some letters. In the middle of the afternoon, the guards called me out into the hall and chastised me for receiving and sending out so much mail. "There are going to be problems with all this mail!" they said. "What problems?" I asked. "The Federal Mar-shalls will never let you carry all this mail around with you." "Don't worry," I replied (like Obe Won Kenobee). "There won't be any prob-lems." They are turning back much of our mail. All books and newspa-pers have been shipped back. They read and censor all my outgoing mail.

We continue to discuss family relationships in light of disci-pleship and how Christ commands that our primary focus be God's will. "The bloodline takes second place to Christ," Phil suggests. I feel this during these holidays as my family tells me how they wish I were with them instead of in jail for nonviolent resistance. I think of Christ and how he wants us to do God's will first, to know the whole of humanity as God's family, and to focus on discipleship.

*

Dan Berrigan sent me a quote from a letter from Thomas Merton to the Polish poet Czeslaw Milosz:

We should all feel near to despair in some sense, because this semi-despair is the normal form taken by hope in a time like ours. Hope without any sensible or tangible evidence on which to rest. Hope in spite of the sickness that fills us. Hope married to a firm refusal to accept any palliatives or anything that cheats hope by pretending to relieve apparent despair. And I should add that for you especially hope must mean acceptance of limitations and imperfections and the deceitfulness of a nature that has been wounded and cheated of love and of security; this too we all feel and suffer. Thus we cannot enjoy the luxury of a hope based on our own integrity, our own honesty, our own purity of heart.

January 8th

Over coffee, Phil quotes Charles Peguy. If you act for justice, you get half the world supporting you. If you act again, the number of people supporting you decreases. If you keep acting for justice, eventually, like Christ, you will be alone.

This morning, we take up the parable of the Sower, Mark 4:1-9, which begins with the striking scene of Jesus sitting alone in a boat on the Sea of Galilee, preaching to a crowd of people on the shore. This parable offers the greatest explanation of why people do not accept the Word of God in their lives. It urges us not only to hear the Word, but to accept it, to live it, to do it. If we live God's word, our lives will bear fruit. Jesus calls us to be detached from results, to let go of control, and to live out God's Word with total confidence that God will tend to it.

All of this is very difficult for me. My all-American nature pines for results, success and effectiveness. Yet, detachment is required. For years, I prayed that my life would bear fruit—more than a hundredfold. Now, I pray that I may be faithful. I try to leave the outcome in God's hands. Being in jail helps me let go of the desire for results. I am powerless. Everything is in God's hands. Perhaps for the first time I am experiencing just how out of control my life really is—and how dependent I truly am on God.

Sunday, January 9th

Yesterday afternoon, I wrote articles for the New York Pax Christi newsletter and the Bay Area Pax Christi newsletter. Bruce and

I walked for almost two and a half hours, telling jokes and stories. Another huge pile of mail came in. Dan's letter to Phil closes, "I send this off with a Cole Porter tune, 'You're the top; you're Mahatma Gandhi. . .'" Friends from around the country write. I am spending about six or seven hours each day trying to answer them. Meanwhile, Bruce has made a commitment to forgo reading in the evening to be a fourth in the card games of the other inmates.

"The mystery of the reign of God has been granted to you," Jesus tells his community (Mk 4:1-20). And then, almost in the next breath, "Do you not understand?" In so many ways, I hear these words addressed to me. The reign of God has been revealed to me in my life; in the Society of Jesus; in the work of nonviolent resistance to evil; in my experiences in El Salvador, Israel, Haiti, Guatemala, Nicaragua, and elsewhere; among the homeless; and here, now, with this action and imprisonment. Yet I still have doubts. I still do not understand.

Why do people not accept and live out the Word of God? the Gospel asks. Because the persecutions which inevitably come turn them away and because they get caught up in worldly anxiety and the lure of riches, Jesus answers. One requires roots in order to withstand persecutions. One needs faith, prayer and community.

How do we understand the Word? How do we proclaim it? Both require great effort, study, and discussion with those more experienced. "Faith and understanding do not come overnight," Phil pointed out. We have to concentrate all our hearts and lives on the Word of God to make it real in our lives.

January 10th

Our cellmate, Andrew, flipped out again last night. He yells, barks, screams out rap lyrics and pretends he's a marine marching back and forth in the cell. Beyond the noise is the potential for physical violence. He scares me. Bruce and Phil sit quietly on their bunks. I try to stay centered in Christ who is so present to me. I can feel Christ's confidence and strength. Together, we endure this poor, broken man's violence. Andrew continued his insanity into the morning, but once the three of us sat down with our bibles and began praying, he settled down.

Meanwhile, during the middle of the night, an angry guard broke in and demanded that Bruce take down the Nativity picture and Plowshares artwork that he had glued to his bunk with toothpaste. Our "peace" sign near the TV also came down. Bruce wanted to argue and resist the guard, but held back because he feared the guard might transfer him and split us up.

This morning, we revisit the parable of the Sower. The point of the parable, Bruce explains, is steadfastness. The parable explains three factors which keep us from the Word of God: 1) power; 2) prestige; 3) possessions. As Richard Rohr writes in *Simplicity*, the Word requires total renunciation of power, prestige and possessions. In jail, it is easier to approximate such renunciation. The challenge is to live out this renunciation for the rest of our lives.

Phil observes that steadfastness requires both doing good and resisting evil. Many people do good, but few go on to resist evil. If you do good and do not resist evil, eventually you will be praised and honored. As Dom Helder Camara wryly points out, "When I feed the hungry, they call me a saint; when I ask why people are hungry, they call me a communist." The key factor according to Jesus is resisting evil, which eventually leads to persecution, rejection, imprisonment and even death. As the parable makes clear, if we continue to resist evil (doing good is presumed), our lives will bear fruit in astronomical proportions, though we may know nothing about it. A good yield in those days was sixfold. Jesus gives the dramatic conclusion that such faithful lives will yield thirty, sixty, or the (unimaginable) hundredfold.

January 11th

Phil visits with a local minister while Bruce plays cards with the other inmates. I write to a friend that our action was, as Gandhi might say, an experiment in the truth of nonviolence. How different is our experience from Gandhi. He never knew a society like ours with its Trident submarines, F15E nuclear bombers, and Pentagon. We live in a much worse situation and need to "experiment" in nonviolence with a renewed commitment. Gandhi enjoyed the luxury of space, outdoor work, and silence in his prison "retreat." The noise here would challenge even Gandhi.

*

The peace movement needs to connect with the justice movement if we are to have either peace or justice. White people need to join people of color in their struggle for racial and social justice, and people of color need to join with white people in the pursuit of disarmament. White people like ourselves must accompany and learn from African-Americans and other people of color if the beloved community is to be realized. We are among a handful of whites in this jail of nearly 400 people. In this cell, I'm beginning to see a real connection between nuclear weapons and racism, as well as peacemaking and solidarity with the disenfranchized. The action has opened up the possibility of sharing in the life of the marginalized. We join the African-American community here in prison, and share our commitment to peace, nonviolence and disarmament. They teach us about justice, liberation and equality.

January 12th

This morning, Andre, our 18-year-old friend who talks incessantly at the top of his voice, left. We will miss him. He was full of life, always laughing, singing constantly, truly alive.

We read Mark 4:21-23 and talked about the command to let the light in your lamp shine from the lampstand, and how everything that is hidden is made visible and everything secret brought into the light. In other words, we must drag dark things out into the openness of light. We must unmask evil, name it and try to limit its destructiveness. To expose evil deeds may bring ridicule on us, but eventually exposure mitigates and then vanquishes the evil. On December 7th, we exposed the war games and the preparations for war that continue on under the cover of darkness. We shined the light of truth on militarism. Though the darkness strikes back and punishes us, the light will overcome. We stand publicly and continue to insist on the light of truth.

*

It's midnight now. Phil sleeps while Bruce talks to the other guys. I sit here at the steel table, around the corner, under the tv, which is mercifully off. Down the hall, I hear the sound of various card games. Today was a full day, from the intense sharing and bible study this morning to non-stop letter-writing and efforts to write an article. Patrick O'Neill came by this afternoon and we had a long, lively meeting with Lynn. Patrick smuggled in peanuts, candy, figs, banana bread, oranges, mail, articles, books and even dental floss! Perhaps most importantly, he brought a secret stash of instant coffee to add to the blackish water that is served each morning. Lynn flourishes now that she is in a cellblock with other women.

I am tired. I want to pray but I don't know how. My thoughts are jumbled and though I have a certain peace, the loud conversations around the corner do not inspire quiet meditation.

There is nothing romantic about jail. It is inhuman, oppressive, and violent. The cold steel table on which I lean my head as I write reminds me of reality. All of jail screams out reality—the world is cruel and unjust. I will die not understanding how human beings can be cruel to one another. I will never understand how they harm and kill and massacre others. How can we imprison other human beings? How do the guards sleep at night knowing how poorly they treat us during the day? How do we survive this inhumanity?

Tonight, I think of you, Christ. I think how I fail you, how I betray and deny you, how I turn from you. In your presence, I am reminded that you are faithful, you are strong, you are confident. You are my security. I ask that I may always be at your side as your faithful friend and companion. Take away my faithlessness. Grant me faith. Make me into a saint, into your faithful friend and disciple. You, Christ, are our peace. Be with us. Be with me.

January 13th

The arrival of the broom and mop wakes me at 5 a.m. and I fall out of my perch and start sweeping. When coffee arrives, we add our secret ingredient and voila! a semi-decent cup of coffee. We hope that it will not get captured during a search and so we hide it carefully.

"To the one who has, more will be given," Jesus declares in our Gospel text. "From the one who has not, even what he has will be taken away" (Mk 4:25). This proverb speaks to us of reality. As we choose faith, our faith grows. As we choose money, career and ego, our little faith diminishes further. We go from faith to faith, from grace to grace. Here in jail, we experience this spiritual truth. Though our faith is small and weak, the risk of action as an act of faith blesses

us with an increase of faith. As Bill Frankel-Streit says, "We act ourselves into faith, not visa-versa."

These winter days offer tremendous grace. We receive faith, insight into the scriptures, Eucharist, community, letters from friends far
and wide—the hundredfold! As we offer up our physical freedom, God
lends us new spiritual freedom. We experience what Liz McAlister
calls "the mystical experience of freedom in prison for making peace."

Tom Lewis writes, "I need to be free enough to go to jail." We
reflect on Archbishop Romero, his humility and faith, how he could
tell a reporter two weeks before his assassination, "I am not worthy of
the gift of martyrdom, but if my life is accepted, I pray that it will be
the seed of liberty for my people." We ponder the countless Central
American martyrs who offered their lives in the struggle of justice and
peace. They were blessed with deep faith. We contemplate the life of
Franz Jaegerstaetter, the Austrian farmer who refused to fight for the
Nazi military; who did not heed the pleas of his three girls, his wife,
priest and friends; and who went alone to his death. The evening before his execution by the German military (on August 9, 1943), his
face radiated the peace and faith he knew in his heart. Today, he is
recognized by many as a true saint. We too will be granted deep faith
if we can keep to the narrow way of the Gospel.

The only response to such grace is gratitude. Thank you God for
bringing us here to jail. Thank you for all the blessings and graces you
pour out on us. We are not worthy. Thank you.

January 14th

Phil and I awake at 5 a.m. to sweep and mop the floor. Coffee
arrives at 6 a.m., we study the Gospel, share Eucharist, hold our
"check-in" and write letters together until lunch at 12:15. After lunch
and an hour's pacing with Bruce, I sit and meditate for an hour. Then,
I write an essay on jail for George Anderson's booklet, "Jesuits in
Jail." Tonight, another 25 letters arrive plus books by Dostoyevsky and
Tolstoy. I start *The Brothers Karamazov.*

"This is how it is with the reign of God," Jesus explains (Mk
4:26-29). A sower sows a seed and carries on with life; the seed
grows; eventually at the harvest, she wields the sickle. The parable
points to God—who sows the word, tends God's reign, and reaps the
harvest. I read it as a reminder to let go of results and leave the out-

come of everything in God's hands. This letting go of control does not mean passivity, but rather active nonviolence to the point of imprisonment, and even death. We do not build God's reign: we proclaim its coming, and we drive out the demonic violence that impedes it. The letter of James encourages us: "Be patient sisters and brothers until the coming of God. See how the farmer waits for the precious fruit of the earth, being patient with it until it receives the early and the late rains. You too must be patient. Make your hearts firm because the coming of God is at hand"(Js 5:7-8).

*

During the height of the Vietnam War, Dorothy Day declared that the only way to end it was to "fill the jails." "Imagine the changes that would come if we filled the jails of the United States in resistance to the nuclear arsenal," Phil marvels. At the height of India's independence movement in 1937, 300,000 protesters were in jail, including the first, second and third ranks of the Indian Congress Party. "All the leaders were locked up," Gandhi wrote later, "and the movement for independence was never stronger." Filling the jails crippled the British. Perhaps similar resistance today would cripple the nuclear weapons manufacturers. At this moment in U.S. history, perhaps ten people are in jail (including the four of us) for resisting nuclear imperialism. Why so few? How do we invite more to risk jail? Why are we afraid of going to jail? Will the day ever come when North Americans fill the jails in protest of militarism? We offer these days for the coming of that future day.

*

I have the sense today that I am being pruned—of selfishness, possessions, desires, ambitions, lust, greed, ego, honor, power, pride, gluttony, sloth and despair. A certain dying to self takes place. I only hope that I can let go completely and be reborn in Christ. I want the works: to be completely possessed by Christ in body, soul, mind, spirit and heart. Why not? If others can become saints, why not me too? I bring these days and my full heart to Christ and ask him to transform them. Each moment provides grace upon grace upon grace.

January 15th, Martin Luther King, Jr.'s Birthday

"The reign of God is like a mustard seed, the smallest of all, which grows to become a large shrub" (Mk 4:30-34). What a shocking image this parable must have been to the disciples, who want Christ to take over the world militarily and establish the global power of Israel. The mustard shrub image of God's reign contrasts with Daniel's image of the imperial reign as a tree that covers the world and touches even the heavens. God's nonviolent reign begins modestly, almost micro-scopically. God's reign comes to us hidden, small, the tiniest of seeds. It spreads slowly, but eventually subverts and transforms us all. The lesson this morning invites us to be small, to let go of results, to accept the slow coming of God's reign, and to recognize that God's way is not the way of the Pentagon, the White House or the world.

In John's Gospel, Jesus calls us to become like seeds that die as they fall into the soil—only to be reborn. We feel like small, unnoticed seeds for peace, hidden away, buried alive in the bowels of the empire, in this awful North Carolina county jail. We trust God's reign. God is in charge. I struggle to remember this truth.

*

Dr. King's life stirs within me a great hope. "Truth crushed to earth will rise again," he proclaimed. "Unearned suffering is redemp-tive." I am convinced that the truth of nonviolence and resistance to war will bear fruit one day, in part because we suffer and are impris-oned now. In our action and in many others like it, we sow seeds for the downfall of militarism. We are filled with hope. The nuclear arse-nal will be dismantled. The outcome is certain.

January 16th

This morning's bible study challenges us to a greater faith and fearlessness. Jesus heads off in a boat with the disciples to the Gerasene district, the enemy territory where he will confront imperial forces (Mk 4:35-41). Jesus falls asleep. A violent storms breaks out. Terrified, the disciples awaken Jesus. "Do you not care that we are perishing?" they ask. He quiets the storm and turns to them. "Why are you so terrified? Do you not yet have faith?"

The parable aims at the early community's fear of persecution from the empire; it speaks to us, too, having just walked through war-games and nuclear fighter bombers. The fears I felt throughout this past fall come to mind. Mainly, I fear death. I thought I had overcome my fear of death while living in El Salvador's war zones. Last year, however, a plane I was traveling in was tossed about by a terrible storm and I was terrified at the prospect of crashing and dying. The antidote to fear is faith in God, trust in God. This means love for others. The night before our action, I confessed to Lynn while we were out for a walk that I was afraid. "What are you afraid of?" she asked. "I'm afraid of being killed." "I thought you were a person of faith?" she asked. Her question stopped me in my tracks.

This afternoon, my parents visited. I know it is very hard for them to see me in jail, in a prison uniform and scraggly beard. They do not understand why I voluntarily risk and accept imprisonment. Nor do they grasp my interest in the scriptures. Nonetheless, they are kind and generous. I am grateful for their support and their fidelity to me. I know it tries them.

Lynn writes from her cell down the hall: "I think the three weeks I spent in solitary were important, even necessary, for me. Intense and deep days. However, I am very glad for this community of women with whom I am now. I actually feel spoiled that I have two windows when you all don't have any. So, I'm sending you light-blue sky, wispy white clouds, yellow winter grasses and a warm stripe of sunlight. Just close your eyes and they will be with you!"

January 17th

Today, our friends gather for a press conference and prayer service in a nearby Lumberton church, followed by a march to the jail and a vigil outside it. In honor of the King holiday, we wrote statements in tribute to Dr. King to be read at the vigil. "The night before he was killed," I wrote, "Dr. King declared, 'The choice before us is no longer between violence and nonviolence; it's nonviolence or nonexistence.' He was right. That's still the choice before us. Dr. King passionately witnessed to equality, civil rights and economic justice, but it was his stand against war and killing that led the forces of death to kill him. Today, his voice calls us to speak out and act against these same forces of death.'"

"Dr. King knew his country," Phil wrote. "The half-truths and outright lies of the politicians and spin doctors in Washington did not fool him. He knew we were an empire and that empires exploit the poor abroad and ignore the poor at home. He knew that government in Washington represents not the American people, but rather the one/two-hundredth of our population, the rich and the super-rich who control 37% of our country's wealth. He knew that the American killing machine, which has kept us at perpetual war since Pearl Harbor Day, 1941, exists simply to enforce the status quo, to keep the poor poorer and the rich richer. He knew that we were 'the greatest purveyor of violence in history,' and that our violence threatens to plunge the world into nuclear destruction. Martin Luther King was a prophet and the bottom line of prophecy is this: Stop the killing! Dr. King spoke truth to power, from the streets, the courts, and the jails—by giving his life. Let us honor Dr. King's memory by sharing his prophecy, by becoming prophetic people ourselves. Our message is simply this, from the streets, the courts and the jails, 'Stop the killing!'"

*

We open our Gospel to the story of Jesus calming the storm. I understand this episode as a parable of the disciples' fear and faithlessness in the midst of nonviolent resistance, in this case, crossing the sea into enemy territory, to confront the imperial forces.

Christ stills the wind and calms the sea. Today, with our nuclear weapons, our nation stirs up firestorms and nuclear fallout and blows up the seas in hydrogen bomb tests. We reverse Christ's love and care for nature. We extend the fears and faithlessness of the disciples to their worst potential—the destruction of the earth itself.

January 18th

Tonight, we converse with Mike, one of the quieter, more mature men on the block. Originally from Guyana, Mike faces trial on conspiracy charges for drug dealing. We share our books with him. He knows that although he is innocent, he stands little chance of finding justice because "I am black and the system is rigged against me. It's all about power." Then, he quoted from memory Paul's letter to the Ephesians: "Draw your strength from the Lord and from God's mighty power. Put on the armor of God so that you may be able to stand firm against the tactics of the Evil One. For our struggle is not with flesh and blood but with the principalities and powers, with the rulers of this present darkness, with the evil spirits in the heavens. Put on the armor of God that you may be able to resist on the evil day and having done everything, to hold your ground" (Eph 6:10-12). "God gave Satan power to hurt Job's family, to destroy his health, and to test Job's faithfulness to God," he concludes. "We too have to hold our ground against evil." He works on his spiritual development each day, he tells us, by reading the scriptures and praying to God the Creator. We sit, quietly, amazed at his faith and wisdom.

Once again, I am evangelized by the poor. May Christ in the imprisoned teach us anew how to live in the Spirit and hold our ground against evil.

7

The Arraignment

January 18th, 1994

Jesus steps off the boat into the enemy territory of the Gerasenes. A raving man possessed by the spirit of militarism confronts him and Jesus heals him. He sends the evil spirit into a herd of 2,000 swine who then run off a cliff into the sea. The townspeople respond by begging Jesus to leave the region. This episode (Mk 5:1-20) captures Jesus' resistance to imperial Rome. Ched Myers writes about this event in an article from *Sojourners* (January, 1987), which someone sent:

> The setting is designed to suggest to the Jews the prototypically "unclean." The Decapolis ("Ten Cities"), one of the eastern frontiers of the Roman empire, was strongly pagan. The cemetery environment (the madman dwells "among the tombs") and the subsequent role of the herd of the pigs, reeks of impurity (Is 65:4). The demon's protest is directly symmetrical to the synagogue encounter (5:7). This time, however, Jesus is addressed not with the Semitic title "Holy One of God," but the very Hellenistic "Son of the Most High God." The clue to the social symbolism of the story of the Gerasene demoniac is its recurring military terminology. The powerful demonic hord identifies itself to Jesus as "Legion," a Latin term which had only one meaning in Mark's social formation: a division of Roman soldiers. Jesus drives Legion into a "herd" of pigs (5:11). This term—inappropriate for pigs, who do not travel in herds—was sometimes used to refer to a band of military recruits. Jesus' command, "he gave them leave," is a military order, and the word describing the pigs' rush into the

lake connotes troops charging into battle (5:13). Enemy soldiers being swallowed in the sea brings to mind, of course, the Exodus 14 narrative. It can hardly be incidental that the number of swine drowned, "about 2000" (5:13), corresponds to the number of soldiers in a Roman legion! Finally, when we read that Legion who is so powerful that no one can restrain him (5:4) "begged him earnestly not to send them out of the district" (5:10), the conclusion is irresistible that this is a symbolic representation of the Roman military occupation of Palestine.

Mark offers a powerful parable of Jesus' confrontation with the empire. Jesus liberates people from the demonic spirit of militarism. Such healing has economic consequences and is not well received.

I write this tonight at 11:15 after receiving some 25 letters from family and friends, many expressing grief, concern and disagreement with my action. I am disappointed by some of them. Yet I take comfort in the realization that Jesus was rejected time and again by his family, the crowds, his religious community and finally, his friends. The whole town asks him to leave at the end of this story. They prefer Roman military control. The people of the United States, including many of my family and friends, prefer to live under military control as well. I should not be surprised that many people object to my passionate anti-war stance. Tonight, I look to Jesus for solace.

January 19th

The possessed man in our Gospel text rages in violence and dwells amid the tombs. He throws around his chains and shackles, a prisoner of his own violence. He symbolizes what the military does to every human being. This parable sums up the military occupation of our world. Few people want the military disarmed, dismantled and driven away. I have seen entire communities possessed by the demon of militarism, from Subic Bay in Olongapo, Philippines to the U.S. base in Soyopango, El Salvador to the Bay Area's Livermore Laboratories and Goldsboro's Seymour Johnson Air Force Base. Jesus offers a great service: He tells us the truth about our demonic possession. We are controlled by militarism and he is eager to free us. When the possessed man regains his sanity, the townspeople are filled with fear. The Gerasene people place their security, not in God, but in the Roman military. We resemble them in many ways.

January 20th

What are the spiritual consequences of militarism? What happens spiritually to people in complicity with mass murder? As Mark's Gospel explains (5:3,5), people go insane. They do violence to themselves. Violence begets violence. Those who live by the sword die by the sword. They have no peace, like the possessed man who throws himself against the stones.

Military people go through a terrible torture to extricate themselves from military control. The vast majority are ruined by their experience of the military. They never get over it. So many veterans suffer imprisonment, alcoholism, drug addiction, homelessness and even suicide. Most never recover from violence. They are filled with self-hatred, hatred for others, cynicism, and a desire to dominate. Jesus indicts militarism and offers a way out. He still longs to heal us and return us to peace and sanity.

I shared a pleasant morning with Fr. Gene McCreesh, S.J., followed by a long afternoon visit with Lynn, Bruce, Phil, Patrick and another lawyer. Lynn went outdoors yesterday in the courtyard for 45 minutes and thoroughly enjoyed it. These visits lift our spirits and give us strength to carry on.

January 21st

The challenge inside jail is to practice the discipline of nonviolence. Teaching nonviolence here is a crucial ministry. Our cellmates practice overt personal violence. Their conversion to nonviolence can heal their lives and break the cycle of violence.

This afternoon, I spoke with Chuck about nonviolence. "I believe in 'eye for an eye,'" he said with a smile. "An eye for an eye only makes the whole world blind," I replied, quoting Gandhi. The right thing to do, I suggested, is to break the cycle of violence, not by retaliating with further violence, but by creative nonviolent alternatives. "If we did that there would be no more wars, no more greed, no more judges, no more big companies," he observed. "I essentially agree with you. I agree with your action but you need to do something that will capture everyone's attention. People don't know about the Plowshares movement. You have to get people to look again at how these weapons affect their money. You've got to get the public to realize that all their money is being wasted on weapons, not on improving society. You've got to wake people up!"

*

The military forces are doomed. The imperial legions will run themselves off a cliff and drown in the ocean of their own violence. Militarism today is similiarly doomed. The United States operates military bases in 77 countries. We need to close down each and every military base, installation and weapons center around the country and the world. The scriptures proclaim that the days of such military imperialism are numbered. Our task is to hasten that downfall.

The parable about the Gerasene demoniac ends with Jesus instructing the healed man to go and tell his family "what the Lord in his pity has done for you." The Greek word for "pity" speaks of compassion that erupts from one's guts. The most compassionate act God can do for humanity is to drive out the spirit of war and militarism.

January 22nd

It strikes me that prison bars grant clarity. Over coffee, we began to discuss the Pentagon. There has never been such an institution in the history of humanity. The Pentagon employees' mental talent, energy, time and money focus on preparing to kill people. The Pentagon is anti-life, anti-humanity, anti-earth, anti-God, and anti-Christ. It is the institutionalization of death. Death as big business. Death as patriotism. Death as empire. The building itself contains not only countless offices for the military, but several banks and chapels. There are more Masses going on inside the Pentagon than at St. Matthew's Cathedral in downtown Washington, D.C. The Pentagon sums up America: massive violence to protect our money—all in the name of God.

For years, Jonah House has been resisting the Pentagon's business. They block entrances, pour blood around the concourses and disrupt the religious services by reading from the Sermon on the Mount. Few other people speak out against the Pentagon. There should be a permanent nonviolent presence to keep vigil and protest the work of the Pentagon. Though it seems impossible to close down the Pentagon, as a people of faith and hope, we must call for its transformation.

God rejoices at every small step towards disarmament, justice and peace. After our arrest, Dan wrote to me that "Christ must weep tears of gratefulness for this Plowshares action."

January 23

The days go on and on with little variety. Restless nights, long bible study sessions, Eucharist, check-in, pitiful meals, naps, hanging out with the other inmates, pacing back and forth, and answering the stacks of mail. I try to take it one day at a time, yet they are all the same. I long to walk in a park, in the fresh air, in the countryside or at the ocean. I miss my privacy. I hunger for solitude. I yearn for music, for beauty, for a good movie and a delicious meal with friends. All these simple pleasures are over for now. Instead, I sit on my bunk and imagine that I'm held by God. A certain peace comes over me and I find the strength to endure for another day.

January 24th, 11:30 p.m.

This day may be the worst so far. All night and all morning, the other cellmates shout out abusive language towards one another and the trustees. I have not heard such mean-spiritedness since college. Their verbal violence not only kept me awake, it ate away at me, down to my bones. How cruel human beings can be to one another! How vicious the oppressed can be towards other oppressed people. The victimized so often create their own victims. All the horrors of violence play out before my eyes, right here in this cellblock.

We held a tense two hour discussion this morning about our upcoming trial, followed by Eucharist and bible study. We share Mark's account of the healing of Jairus' daughter and the woman with the hemorrhage. "Do not be afraid," Jesus tells us once again. "Just have faith." He heals the woman and delays his trip to heal the little girl. Word arrives that the little girl is dead. There is no hope. Commotion, weeping, and wailing fill the house. Jesus will have none of it. He believes. He is hope personified. Little girl, arise!

We too are called to live compassion for the poor who interrupt our ministerial work. Believe and have hope, we're commanded. With such faith and hope, we can resist and go to jail and keep on resisting, even when there appears to be no hope of change. As Daniel Berrigan writes, we resist because we believe and we believe because we resist.

I fasted today and felt nauseous. I didn't have the strength to write one letter. Instead, I lay on my bed all afternoon depressed. I wondered how I could take years of this slow grind. I suddenly remembered my elderly grandmother who complained the last ten years of her life about being locked in her apartment and not being able to get out. Now I understand what she went through. Like her, I am sick of day to day confinement and monotony.

I read the Psalms tonight and dwell in God's presence. I pray for strength and grace. I ask for a deeper faith and a renewed hope that somehow my action, my imprisonment and my suffering will bear fruit for disarmament, justice and peace. May Jesus raise my spirit too.

January 25th

As soon as I awake, a renewed strength comes over me. I do not know from where or how, but I am so grateful. I write over 40 letters and notes today. I walk and laugh with Bruce. My spirit has lifted.

"Do not be afraid. Just have faith." We ponder Jesus' command. If we were more faithful, more fearless, more active, anything would be possible—from the resurrection of a little girl to nuclear disarmament. If we believe and ask and act on our belief, then God will use us and God's reign will be revealed.

President Clinton gives his State of the Union Address as I write this. One of our cellmates shouts out, "That man is a liar!" Another responds, "They're all professional liars." Clinton speaks of fighting crime, combatting drugs and pursuing universal healthcare. Yet he speaks for the rich, for the multinational corporations, for the Pentagon, for Trident Submarines, for death rows and F15 fighter bombers. He does not commit himself to housing every homeless person, to ending the daily starvation of the masses, or disarming our nation. He is more powerful than the Roman emperor who threatened the early Christians. If he sought total disarmament, the abolition of hunger, housing the homeless, ending the death penalty, and promoting nonviolence, then perhaps I might listen. His power is an illusion. Wall Street and the Pentagon run this country. But God is not dead. God reigns and God's reign of peace will come.

A judge has issued an injunction against us, preventing us from meeting any more with lawyers. He declares that since we are pro se defendants, we do not need lawyers. This prevents us from meeting with Lynn. When our trial begins, we will tell the judge that we were not allowed to meet to prepare for trial and that we refuse to cooperate with the charade of justice in the courtroom when our basic rights have been so denied.

January 26th

All night long, our four cellmates shouted abusive language to the top of their lungs. They spoke about abusing women and shooting and how they would like to kill people. Each tried to outdo the other in a story of violence. Phil and I could not sleep a wink through it. At one point, Andrew, the loudest of the bunch, told Bruce off and Bruce snapped back.

This morning, we discuss the whole episode and how we can be more Christlike and nonviolent in the face of violent provocation. Phil and Bruce want to tell our cellmate off directly. I suggest that since he has approximately one week left, we ignore him and not give in to his violent provocations. Perhaps the best thing we can do for this brutalized and brutalizing person, besides keeping him in prayer, is to offer him the example of our nonviolence, our discipline, our humanity, and our prayerfulness.

May the God of peace help us to endure the fiery violence and dark spirits of this furnace.

*

"Fear is useless. What is needed is trust." Phil's translation of our Gospel text pushes us to examine again our fears and our lack of trust. "I should trust but I don't know if I trust God," Phil confesses. Trust comes with faith and a profound knowledge of the uselessness of fear.

The power of faithful nonviolence. In the 1970s, over 20 million Iranians marched in the streets every day for a week to demand the expulsion of the Shah. These masses faced tanks and machine guns every day, all day long, yet they remained determined. Many were killed but their steadfast nonviolence in the face of death brought the immediate downfall of the Shah.

At the Good News Plowshares' "Festival of Hope" last August in Norfolk, Phil spoke of the power of confrontative nonviolence. "When nine people burned A-1 draft files with homemade napalm in Catonsville, Maryland, the Vietnam war was doomed. When eight people hammered on a Mark 12A nosecone at the General Electric Plant on September 9, 1980, the nuclear arms race was doomed. As we continue this Plowshares movement, weapons of mass destruction are doomed. This we believe through our faith and trust in the God of peace. More and more people will come forward and dismantle these weapons. The world will be made right. God is determined. God will see to it."

January 27th

How do we practice nonviolence in jail? How do we deal with our own inner violence when we're behind bars? How do we invite our cellmates to walk the way of nonviolence? Prayer, community and discipline help.

This morning, Bruce shared more about his own inner violence. He is ready to slug Andrew. He could beat him up any minute, he is so angry. If Bruce actually started fighting, Andrew, who is huge, would surely not take it passively. It would be bloody. Andrew is a bully and itches for a fight.

What would Jesus do? I ask Bruce. Jesus never hit anyone. If anyone ever had a right to beat someone up, if anyone was ever so thoroughly provoked, it was Jesus. But Jesus is the incarnation of nonviolence. He tells his disciples, "Put down the sword. Love your enemies." He is beaten, punched, mocked, spat on, yelled at and tortured, yet he does not retaliate or even get angry. He forgives. He prays. He stays centered in God. He does not give in to violence. He breaks the cycle. "The violence stops here," he whispers, pointing to his own body.

We are commanded to practice nonviolence at every level, with our family and friends, with those who threaten us personally, and with our international "enemies." Nonviolence demands consistency, an active love that crosses the whole spectrum. Gandhi demonstrated that it is possible to live that spectrum of nonviolence. Prayer, peacefulness, forgiveness and a loving spirit, however, are all we may be able to offer to people like Andrew, consumed with hostility.

*

Today's Gospel tells how Jesus is rejected by his hometown people of Nazareth when he returns to speak in the synagogue. These townspeople have known Jesus since he was a baby; they cannot fathom that he is the messiah, the fullest image of the living God. "Jesus was not able to work any mighty deeds there. . . . He was amazed and distressed at their lack of faith" (Mk 6:1-6). How easily we too reject Jesus when he comes into our lives. How quickly we put down truth and goodness when it shines in our midst—especially among family and friends. How striking it is that faith is necessary if God is to work mighty deeds. We are challenged not to reject Jesus, but to trust him, to believe him, to permit him to do mighty deeds through us.

Tom Gaunt, S.J. and my brother Steve were here for visits today. A letter arrives tonight from the judge announcing that we will be arraigned on February 1st. We could be separated but we hope that they will simply take us to Raleigh and then bring us back.

*

Mark Danner has written a devastating account of the massacre of one thousand people in El Salvador on December 9th, 1981 ("The Truth of El Mozote," *The New Yorker*, December 6, 1993). One woman, Rufina Amaya, witnessed the entire massacre, snuck away just as her friends were shot and survived to tell what happened. The detailed account explains how the Salvadoran soldiers with U.S. guns raided the village, rounded everyone up, raped the women, chopped off their heads, shot them, and bayonetted the babies. Finally, the houses, buildings and bodies were burned. Everything alive, from cows to dogs to birds to humans, was killed. An Archdiocesan human rights report later read: "Some men who had been gathered in the church were decapitated with machetes by soldiers. The soldiers dragged the bodies and the heads of the decapitated victims to the convent of the church, where they were piled together." Rufina was in one of the last groups to be taken off for execution, after a dozen hours of listening to the killings. As her group was taken from its house to the plaza, they saw one house with "thick pools of blood covering the floor and, farther inside, piles of bloody corpses." Rufina fell to her knees, "crying and begging to God." While the soldier guarding her went up to the front of the line, she snuck off behind a bush. Seconds later, all her women friends were shot. Later, she heard her own children amidst a group of children being killed. "I prayed to God to help me," she said later about those terrifying hours hiding away. "I promised God that if God helped me I would tell the world what happened here." The article continues:

> Rufina could not see the children; she could only hear their cries as the soldiers waded into them, slashing some with their machetes, crushing the skulls of others with the butts of their rifles. Many others—the youngest children, most under twelve—the soldiers herded from one house across the street to the church sacristy, pushing them, crying and screaming, into the dark tiny room. There the soldiers raised their M16s and emptied their magazines into the roomful of children.

Rufina overheard some of the soldiers after that night discussing the faith of the people as they died. In particular, they spoke of one young girl whom they had raped many times all afternoon. She continued to sing hymns. They shot her in the chest and she kept singing. Danner writes: "She had lain there with the blood flowing from her chest and had kept on singing—a bit weaker than before but still singing. And the soldiers, stupefied, had watched and pointed. Then they had grown tired of the game and shot her again, and she sang still, and their wonder began to turn to fear—until finally they had unsheathed their machetes and hacked through her neck, and at last the singing stopped."

That night, Captain Salazar, head of the Salvadoran military, gathered his murderous soldiers around and addressed them:

> What we did yesterday and the day before, this is called war. This is what war is. War is hell. And goddammit, if I order you to kill your mother, that is just what you're going to do. Now, I don't want to hear that, afterward, while you're out drinking and bullshitting among yourselves, you're whining and complaining about this, about how terrible it was. I don't want to hear that. Because

what we did yesterday, what we've been doing on this operation—this is war, gentleman. This is what war is.

For 11 years, the United States government, the Salvadoran government, and the U.S. media denied that this massacre ever happened—until 1992 when the Truth Commission published the evidence
of an expert forensics team that had dug up hundreds of bones left in
the abandonned town. In the summer of 1992, I travelled with Fr. Bill
O'Donnell and Martin Sheen through this beautiful mountainous region, to El Mozote and beyond to Perquin on the Honduran border. I
saw the ruins of this war in the tortured faces and broken hearts of the
survivors. The article brought to mind all my trips to El Salvador and
the many people I knew there, including the six Jesuits, who were
killed.

El Mozote is a parable of the world. It is the story of Hiroshima
and Nagasaki. It continues today in Bosnia-Herzegovnia, Guatemala,
East Timor, Peru, Haiti, the Sudan, Sri Lanka, and many other places.
To read this article is to stare the reality of violence in the face. To
ignore it, to look the other way, to deny it—is to allow it to continue.

More than ever, we need to risk our lives nonviolently resisting
the killing machines of war. I am so glad to be in prison for hammering on a war machine. Given the atrocities that are committed in the
world today, and that are being planned at every military base and
facility around the country, I am saddened that more people are not in
prison for resisting imperial violence.

Besides unearthing the skulls and bones of 1,000 women, children, and men, the forensics team at El Mozote dug up hundreds of
bullets and cartridges. All of them said, "Lake City, Missouri." The
guns that killed the poor of El Mozote come from our own backyards.
We are responsible. We have to drop everything and stop the weapons
shipments and massacres that go on in our names. The blood of the
people of El Mozote, the blood of the crucified Christ, cry out to us.
Wake up. Stop the killing. If you are alive, then spend your life opposing death.

January 28th

This morning, we discuss the nonviolence of Jesus. He was neither passive nor quiet. He was confrontative but not violent. He prac-

ticed an offensive nonviolence for truth. He was mocked, assaulted, tortured and abused. Yet when a guard strikes him, he replies, "If I have spoken wrongly, testify to the wrong; but if I have spoken rightly, why do you strike me?" (Jn 18:23) Jesus insists on the truth.

We ponder how to intervene nonviolently if a fight breaks out. We share our struggles with community and family members who do not support our anti-war witness. Tonight, I meditate on the nonviolence of Jesus and the contemplative nonviolence required here. I believe our action was the fruit of contemplation and that we are invited to go deeper into that contemplation now that we are here in jail. Indeed, I believe that prayer is the only way we can learn how to practice the nonviolence of Jesus. This time in jail should be marked with contemplative prayer if it is to radiate Gospel nonviolence.

January 29th

Jesus sends the disciples out two by two and gives them authority over unclean spirits. He instructs them "to take nothing for the journey but a walking stick—no food, no sack, no money, no extra coat." They went off, "preached repentance, drove out many demons, and anointed with oil many who were sick and cured them" (Mk 6:7-13). Very quickly, Herod hears about Jesus and these activities. Herod is threatened by the hopeful, nonviolent resistance Jesus is organizing. The disciples comfort and heal people by transforming them into nonviolent resisters. The imperial officials will not let this go unchallenged.

*

Phil Land, a great Jesuit priest, scholar, and social justice teacher, has died. He entered the Jesuits in 1929 and spent his whole life humbly serving others. He was a real saint. During the 1960s and 1970s, he helped write many Vatican documents on social justice and then came to work at the Center of Concern, a Catholic social justice research center in Washington, D.C. I remember seeing him at the end of Mass at St. Al's on Thanksgiving day. He shook my hand and asked how I was doing. As always, he was smiling. May he rest in Christ's peace.

*

From Los Angeles, friends write that they will hold a public, prayer vigil in conjunction with our trial. From the San Francisco Bay area, friends write that they will hold a demonstration at Livermore Laboratories on Ash Wednesday in solidarity with us. Their support and their actions hearten me.

January 30th, the 46th anniversary of Gandhi's assassination

We spent the morning discussing the details of our upcoming arraignment and trial. Many questions linger: How do we act as a community since we are separated from Lynn? How do we respond if the judge pushes up the date and place of the trial and will not grant us a continuance? How do we have a good process through all this with such limited time to prepare and be together? How do we respect individual conscience yet at the same time uphold communitarian conscience? How do we best protest and resist the charade of the judicial system which defends nuclear fighter bombers? How do we proclaim the Gospel of Jesus through all of this?

We sort out the details as best we can. We recognize our poverty and powerlessness before the judicial system. Our hope is in the God of peace, not in the courts or the political system. We share in the cross of nonviolent resistance and pray that we may respond with peace, love, and truth.

At the heart of my new day to day life stands the cross. I am living it as never before. Being in jail for an act of disarmament is a 24-hour a day reminder of the world's systemic violence. These four walls and jail bars remind me of the domination system we live under. They also turn me back to God. I constantly think of Jesus and how he suffered under the empire and died on a Roman cross. I pray that I may be faithful, loving and compassionate in the days ahead.

*

Mohandas Gandhi once advised, "Recall the face of the poorest and most helpless person whom you may have seen and ask yourself if the step you contemplate is going to be of any use to that person. Will that poor person be able to gain anything by it? Will it restore her to a control over her own life and destiny? Will it lead to self-rule for the hungry and the spiritually starved millions of men and women? Then you will find your doubts and self melting away." For years, I've kept this quote always before me. I've been trying to take that next step of ultimate service and benefit to the poorest of the poor, the starving millions of the world. Though I've stumbled and fallen, I keep on walking, trying to follow that narrow path of nonviolence. Last December 7th, I took a crucial step on that journey. It has been one step at a time, from charity to justice to resistance and disarmament—in short, a spiritual journey.

How does one respond to the overwhelming evil of the world? Do we throw up our hands in despair and declare that there is nothing we can do, or do we take responsibility for systemic violence and enter the nonviolent struggle for justice and peace?

Recall the face of the poor. . . . Take the next step. . . .

January 31st, Thomas Merton's Birthday

It's 10 a.m. and Andrew is yelling at the top of his voice. "Attention! You are a United States marine!" he shouts. Earlier, he barked and growled like a dog. He is deeply disturbed. We pray for him and try to be present to him whenever he returns to coherence. Anthony, the young heavyset kid who is the father of four children, is being arraigned today for shooting two people in the back. Last night during the Superbowl, Anthony and Andrew kept making jokes about Chuck to humiliate him. Andrew and the others are incapable of listening to reason when they are in these violent moods (which is most of the time). We are all quite helpless. We do not let ourselves get provoked. We try to be human with everyone, to defuse the violence if we can.

February 1st, Arraignment Day

At 5 a.m., we wake, pack our papers, and sit ready to be carted off for a 10 a.m. arraignment in Raleigh, where we will enter a "not guilty" plea. Six o'clock, then seven, then eight, then nine, and still, no call. Bruce and I discuss discipleship to Christ. We take a long cold look at our own self-righteousness and absolutism. We conclude that we lack humility and openness and need to pray for these graces. At 10:15, we give up waiting and unpack our papers. Just then, we are called. We are led to a holding cell and sit there until noon. Another case of "Hurry up and wait!"

We are driven to the Raleigh Federal District Court. At 2 p.m., we are brought in chains and shackles into the crowded holding cell on the fifth floor. Bruce is called out alone. We wait for half an hour. He returns very upset. Judge Terrence Boyle, who has been appointed to our case, has denied all our requests. A Ronald Reagan appointee with close ties to Senator Jesse Helms, Boyle will not allow the four of us to stand together. He would not allow a lawyer to sit with us. He moved up the trial date one week to February 14th and changed the location from Raleigh to Elizabeth City (my birthplace and childhood home!). He would not permit the media to interview us. Lynn received the same harsh treatment.

When supporters stood silently as Bruce was led into the courtroom, Boyle said, "I don't know what's going on here, but everybody's going to be in jail by the end of the day if they don't watch out." When asked to enter a plea, Bruce replied, "I personally am not guilty of any crime. I believe the government is guilty of crimes against God and idolatry."

The Federal Marshalls shackle me and lead me into the courtroom. Judge Boyle sits in his robes behind a large panelled desk. We have heard that Judge Boyle is a Catholic. With me, he changes his attitude. He asks how I plead, guilty or not guilty. I look upward, lift both my hands in prayer and answer softly: "I plead for nuclear disarmament. I plead for the abolition of war and weapons of mass destruction. I plead for the starving peoples of the world. I plead for the victims of F15Es. I plead for justice and peace. I plead for humanity's conversion to the truth of nonviolence, God." I bow my head in silence.

After a long pause, the judge says, "I'll take that as a 'Not guilty.'"

He asks me how long I've been a priest and a Jesuit. Several times, he inquires if I am a person of peace. "Yes, I try to be a person of peace, like Jesus," I respond each time. "Yes, I have dedicated my life to the nonviolence of Jesus." Suddenly, he declares that he might release me. "That's the most caring and responsible thing to do," he says. "Jail is expensive, dislocative and unnecessary." He speaks about the good I can do outside of jail and how I do not belong in jail. He has not offered such a possibility to my friends. "I want to remain with my friends," I announce. "I'm not sure you have that right," Boyle replies. He dismisses me so he can think the matter over. They handcuff me. I smile to the crowded courtroom and am led out.

Later, Phil appears before Judge Boyle and is given the same deferential treatment. Ultimately, Boyle decides to keep us all locked up.

On the way back to Lumberton, in shackles and chains, the four of us resolve not to cooperate with the charade of justice. We will not participate with the trial under the pretext that justice is possible from the courts. It is not. The courts are the flipside of our militarism. A society which makes nuclear weapons is not going to dispense justice from its courts—especially to people who seek disarmament. Quite the contrary.

I am glad to be back in our cell. The cell in Raleigh was packed with tough men yelling and screaming at each other, and verbally abusing Lynn when she walked by. Our cellblock here seems tame by comparison.

February 2nd

Jim Douglass writes from an airplane on his way to Sarajevo where he will fast, pray and organize a pilgrimage for peace: "The Sarajevo fast and pilgrimage project has taken on a life of its own and seems to be taking my life with it. You have experienced the same in the Spirit's movement through your Plowshares action. I think it is hopeful, yet [I am] unclear where exactly it is going. Perhaps that, too, is hopeful. My bags are stuffed with letters, money, medicines, and seeds for the people of Sarajevo from their loved ones in the U.S. who have deluged me with hopes that I might somehow succeed in helping them live, perhaps even (in a few cases) enable them to leave the city. Each letter and story is one of deep suffering and tragedy in the midst of genocide. It is a great gift to carry these words and hopes, one entirely dependent on the grace of God." Jim will meet with Muslim, Jewish, Orthodox and Roman Catholic leaders in Zagreb and Sarajevo, as well as with the head of the Pontifical Council for Justice and Peace in Rome to encourage the Pope to make a pilgrimage to Sarajevo. "Pray for the miracle of the interfaith pilgrimage. And I thank God once again for the miracle of your life and of Phil's, Bruce's, and

Lynn's, for your Spirit-filled action and presence in your new jail community."

February 3rd

During liturgy, the guard shouts, "Dear, you gotta visit!" Off I go to see Tom Gaunt, S.J., who has driven three hours from Chapel Hill. We discuss the arraignment, the upcoming trial and what it means to take a stand for justice when we have no possible clue as to the outcome. Tom reminds me that Rosa Parks, Dr. King and other civil rights activists had no idea of the outcome when they made their stand, yet they stood anyway. We forget that they acted in darkness. In hindsight, it all seems so clear, yet it wasn't at all clear. A similar situation applies to us, Tom says. We have stood without any clue as to the outcome. The possibility of nuclear disarmament certainly doesn't appear to be on the horizon. Nonetheless, we take a stand. The standing makes all the difference.

The guards forgot about us. Three hours later, at 1:30 p.m., I return to the cellblock. Bruce and Phil were convinced that I had been carted off to Raleigh to appear before the judge. They were surprised to see me.

Earlier, we reviewed our plans for the upcoming trial. Tonight, after dinner, Steve came by for a visit, bringing my delightful two-year-old nephew, Patrick Dear. We laughed the whole time. Patrick and I spoke on the phone to one another and pressed our hands against the glass wall that separates us. It was a thrill and a joy to see them. I love them so much. I am elated.

Certainly this has been the most intense week of all. I am apprehensive and nervous about the move to Elizabeth City and the trial. I keep praying for strength, grace and guidance. I no longer have the strength to answer my mail, which is over 30 letters a day. I try to keep my eyes on the Lord, to dwell in his Spirit, to be mindful and peace-filled. The fact is: I could not endure this suffering and tiresome oppression without the abundant grace of God.

February 4th

We read the story of John the Baptist's beheading: how Herod had imprisoned him; how at a government party, in a drunken stupor, he promised his daughter anything; and how, at the prompting of her mother, she requested "the head of the Baptist on a plate." The scene brings to mind the brutal murders of other noble prophets and saints: Franz Jaegerstaetter, Edith Stein, Mohandas Gandhi, Martin King, Oscar Romero, Ita Ford, Maura Clarke, Dorothy Kazel, and Jean Donovan.

We are imprisoned by the government for speaking out against evil, yet we will not be decapitated or killed. But if disarmament is to be realized, many nonviolent people like ourselves will have to offer our lives for change. Someday, someone may be shot to death in a Plowshares disarmament action. I pray for the willingness to offer my life in this nonviolent Spirit for the coming of God's reign of justice and peace, as John the Baptist, Jesus and all the martyrs of history have done.

It is 9 a.m. on Friday morning and the cellblock is quiet. Bruce sits on his top bunk reading; Phil sits on his bunk writing. I write this across the room by myself at one of the steel tables. It is oddly quiet. Andrew is standing trial, so our cellblock is much more peaceful. He will most likely return to us and resume his regimen of provocation and foul language. I read the letters that come in and sit content thinking about my friends. I feel run down, and this oppressive jail is to blame. I will try to exercise, to pray and to transcend this place. It is hard, yes, but I am a Christian and I must not allow the system to take away my joy.

"Take hope," the Spirit of God says to me. "I am with you. You are not alone. This will not last forever. Lift up your heart. I am coming to you." It is time to give God thanks.

8

The Chowan County Jail

Friday, February 4th, 1994

We've been moved! At 10:30 this morning, while I was writing letters, the guard told us to pack up and be ready to leave in five minutes. We threw our things together and said goodbye to Anthony, Mike and Chuck. After two hours, we were brought up front to the holding cell where we sat for another hour. We were shackled, chained, handcuffed and led off carrying bags of mail and papers. The air was warm, the sky was clear and though I was in chains, I was happy to be with my friends driving through the Carolina countryside. Frankly, I was happy to be leaving the Robeson County Detention Center. We stopped first at the Smithfield Jail, south of Raleigh, and then drove east.

We drove across a bridge over one of the magnificent sounds leading to the Outer Banks. The sheer beauty of the water and the sky! This region is my home. I grew up in these beautiful surroundings. After two months locked in an ugly jail cell, I was speechless at the sight of creation—the deep blue water, the cloudless sky, the countless Carolina pines. Life is rich. The colors exploded after months of sensory deprivation. All creation sings the praise of God.

As we drove through Elizabeth City, a flood of memories came pouring in. I was born in this town. I have only been back once or twice since my family moved from here in 1967 to Washington, D.C. My father was the local newspaper publisher and a civic leader. We passed my kindergarten, the elementary school, and the church where I was an altar boy. I recall playing in the schoolyard, walking on Main Street, and going to church. What an irony that I end up back here as a notorious criminal. The finger of God is here, I believe. We dropped Lynn off at the Albermarle District Jail on the outskirts of town. Then, we were brought to Edenton, 30 miles away, and checked in to the Chowan County Jail. The large, African-American officer who drove the van said to me as he uncuffed me, "I know you. I knew you when you were a boy. I watched you grow up in Elizabeth City. I knew your family, your brothers, especially your father." I was dumbfounded. I take such encounters as a sign of God's presence in my life. My life comes full circle in ways I never dreamed! The Spirit is upon me.

*

The guards process me first. The officer tells me that our papers and property will be stored away and that we will be separated. I suggest that he might want to put us together. "We like to pray together each morning." After that, the guard arranges for us to be together. I am given a new set of orange prison clothes. The new cellblock consists of a room with a large steel table and a tv set. On either side off the main tv room is a hallway with four cells. I share a cell with Troy, a big burly guy from Chicago. My cell has tall narrow windows which open to a wall, a tree, and the sky.

One of the guards, Glen, recognizes Phil and is friendly to us. Phil was given a single cell and Bruce shares a cell with Norman. Miguel from Florida came over and introduced himself to us. The warmth and friendliness here, from the guards to the other inmates, strike an amazing contrast to our last jail. Even more shocking is the seven course meal we were served for dinner. We stayed up talking and reading. Eventually, Glen brought us our bibles and a few books, but most of our papers are kept. No pens are allowed. Instead, we are given small two inch pencil stubs to use.

I enter my cell and for the first time in months experience privacy and solitude. I go to sleep thanking God for this change.

Saturday, February 5th

Today marks our first full day in the Edenton jail. After a good night sleep, we ate breakfast at 7:30 a.m., and then Bruce, Phil and I meet to study Mark's Gospel. Chapter six tells how Jesus gathers his disciples after their work, saying, "Come away to a deserted place and rest for a while." The crowds prevent them from getting away, but Jesus clearly insists that the life of resistance and service requires contemplative prayer. We all need solitude, rest and prayer if we wish to accompany Jesus into Jerusalem.

Bruce and Phil are less pleased to be here. They would prefer to have pens and their personal papers. I am delighted with the small cell, at least for now. We are all glad to remain together. I spent the morning reading and the afternoon sleeping. After lunch, we read from the book of Joel about the consequences of human violence, then offered prayers, broke bread and passed the cup. All day long, as I've prayed, I have felt the consolation of the Holy Spirit. I am grateful to God for the blessings I've known in these past hours. Yes, in jail for resistance to war, I am granted a sharing in Christ's own peace.

Tonight, during dinner, we watch the evening news. A marketplace in Sarajevo was bombed today. Sixty civilians are dead. Hundreds of people are injured. Our hearts break at this insanity. May God forgive humanity. May this senseless war cease. May the peoples of the former Yugoslavia put aside their religious hatred, stop killing one another and be reconciled to the God of peace and thus one another. May we renounce war and embrace nonviolence.

Sunday, February 6th

The miracle of the loaves and fishes displays the politics of sharing. Jesus inspires the disciples and the thousands of poor to share their food with one another so that they will all have enough to eat (Mk 6:34-44). The miracle is not the magic of food produced out of thin air, but something more profound: the sharing of one's own food with total strangers. The disciples question Jesus' attitude toward the crowd, as well as his command, "Give them something to eat yourselves." If only the rich countries would obey this command and share our resources which really belong to the poorer countries of the world! Millions starve to death each year. The U.S. comprises 4.7% of the world's population but consumes over 50% of the world's resources. Forty thousand people, primarily children, die of starvation each day. Jesus longs for us to relinquish these resources, to disarm the weapons which protect our hoard, and to share our food with all the poor! We agree: Jesus still calls us to give the starving masses something to eat ourselves. Sitting here in jail is the best protest I can offer to this international hoarding.

*

It's 10:30 a.m. and I'm sitting in the common room while the others read or watch tv. This week will be slow—a time of rest, relaxation and prayer before we go to trial next week and move on to federal prison. As always, I place my trust in Christ. At liturgy this morning, we prayed that Christ might bless our witness, guide us, and make us faithful disciples. I believe God hears our prayers.

February 7th

From 11:00 p.m. until 6 a.m., the guards lock us in our cell. At 6 a.m., the door in my cell buzzes and I lean over from my bunk and unlock it. My new cellmate, Buddy, gets up and cleans himself for half an hour then leaves. I get up, clean up, look out the window at the trees and the birds in the early morning sky, and sit down to meditate until breakfast. An hour passes. The tv blares with cartoons and the other guys shout, but I sit peacefully on the lower bunk, contemplating the Lord as if he stands before me, encouraging me, smiling at me. I tell him my troubles and my desires. He rejoices that I am following him and asks me to trust him. A deep peace comes over me in my cell and I am content. These moments of prayer make all the difference.

Yesterday afternoon, I had a long talk with Troy, my cellmate, about his life and his faith in God. He was all set to go to Duke University, my alma mater, on a football scholarship but got into trouble and lost his chance. His father, a former professional football player, died last year after being shot when his car was robbed. Troy became a Muslim years ago but has stopped praying. I urged him to return to the discipline of prayer. An hour later, Troy was transferred to another cellblock and Buddy showed up.

*

Phil, Bruce, and I turn to the Gospel this morning and read the account of Jesus walking on water (Mk 6:45-52). He deliberately sends the disciples ahead in the boat to the other side of the lake, then he scales the mountain to pray. He stands on the shore and sees them at sea. He walks across the water in the dark morning hours. They observe him, believe he is a ghost, and cry out in fright. "Take courage; it is I," he says. "Do not be afraid." They had not understood the miracle of the loaves. Their hearts were hardened.

Peacemaking is like walking on water. The remarkable scene of Jesus walking toward a boat full of terrified disciples caught up in a storm encapsulates not only the life of Jesus and the experience of the early Christian communities, but our predicament today as disciples of Christ in an outwardly powerful, weapons-saturated country. For first century Palestinians, the sea symbolizes the division between Jew and Gentile and Jesus insists that false barriers be crossed. Reconciliation is his passion, because for Jesus there are no enemies. Today, the sea symbolizes all the divisions and barriers we have set up between us, between races, gender, classes.and nations.

This marvelous story sums up Jesus' faith and steadfast nonviolence. Jesus walks the waters of nonviolence. The disciples can not cross the sea in the storm and are terrified at the sight of Jesus. The same can be said of us. We are terrified and faithless. We get overwhelmed when we attempt to practice nonviolence, when we try to cross to the other side in a gesture of love toward enemies. I remember thinking of this passage as I walked over the fallen fence two months ago this morning at Seymour Johnson Air Force Base and proceeded for two hours through the woods, through a creek, across a tarmac, through war games, up to the nuclear fighter bomber. We were walking on water.

Matthew's Gospel builds on Mark's story: "Lord, if it is you, command me to come to you on the water," Peter declares. "Come," Jesus responds. Every one of us is commanded to get out of the boat and walk the waters of peace. When Peter takes his eyes off Jesus, he sinks. "Lord, save me," he implores. Jesus catches him and says, "O you of little faith, why do you doubt?" (Mt 14:22-33). Dare we step out of the boat at Jesus' command? Dare we keep our eyes on Jesus? Jesus shakes his head in wonder, "O you of little faith."

This scene captures our plight today: Jesus desires that we be peacemakers. He sends us in the boat toward the other side and tells us at the darkest, windiest, most terrifying moment to get out of the boat and walk (on water) with him. Jesus invites the peacemaking church today to make the same crossing, to weather the same winds. Every disciple is invited to get out of the boat and walk toward Jesus.

Resisting nuclear weapons and militarism in the United States is like walking on water—or being terrified as your boat tosses about in a storm. Either we get caught up in fear, start to despair and sink, or we believe and walk on water to the land of disarmament with perfect faith that the Lord is leading us and transforming our world.

The church and the peace movement are filled with fear as we get tossed about by the winds of the empire. The words of Jesus speak to us: "Take courage; it is I. Do not be afraid. Come on out. The water's great." Nonviolence is God's way, Jesus proclaims.

The key to walking on water is to "focus on Jesus." The startling fact is that Peter does get out of the boat and begins to walk on water. It is possible. But the moment Peter takes his eyes off Jesus and starts looking around at the storm, the wind, and the waves, at that instant, he becomes afraid and starts to sink. The same is true for us. Peace-making is only possible for Christians if we keep our eyes focused on Jesus. As we remain centered in the peace of Christ, we can proceed with nonviolence, confronting militarism and oppression fearlessly. The moment we take our eyes off Jesus in our struggle for disarmament, justice and peace, the instant we start to let the winds of persecution and cultural criticism affect us, then our fears overtake us and we begin to sink. In that moment, we will not just be paralyzed with fear, we will be drowning in the turbulent sea.

February 8th

At 8 a.m. each morning, they lock us out of our cells until 4 p.m. We take our bibles, books, papers, plus our blankets, and ensconce ourselves at the end of one of the hallways. Yesterday, we camped out there until we were allowed back into our cells, where we napped until our 6:30 p.m. dinner. Last night, Phil and I watched a dreadful movie on tv with the other inmates. I finished reading *The Trick of It*, a novel by Michael Frayn. This morning again, we nestled in our corner, Bruce reading on the floor, Phil and I sharing a corner bench. Phil is presently posed like "The Thinker," lost in thought. Now he grabs his bible, seeks out a passage, and starts reading again. So it goes.

Yesterday, I prayed throughout the day. This morning, after liturgy, sitting in this hallway, I feel uninspired. I think much about my lack of faith. If I were more faithful, all my trust would be in God and I would be convinced that God would be using these days for some great end. But I remain in the dark. All I have is my faith in God—I believe; Lord, help my unbelief.

February 9th

O God, be with us here in jail. Help us to see and feel your abiding presence and to know your peace. Help us to love one another, to love our neighbors, and to love our enemies. Help us to love you with full hearts. You are our God. No matter what they do to us, no matter what we endure, no matter how many people reject us, still, you are our God and we place our trust in you. Be our loving Mother, our caring Father. Be the Christ, risen, appearing to us in this dungeon. Be our guide and comforter, dwelling always in our hearts. O God, we count on you. With you, all things are possible. Please care for us.

*

The words of Jesus speak directly to our unfaithful generation: "You disregard God's commandment but cling to human tradition" (Mk 7:8). Jesus dismisses the piety, rituals, and legalistic, false worship of the devout Jews, the Scribes and Pharisees. Instead, he calls us to love God, our neighbors and ourselves. He commands us to seek peace and justice, rather than practice the routine of religious obligation which oppresses the poor. Mark quotes Isaiah: "This people honors me with their lips but their hearts are far from me. In vain do they worship me, teaching as doctrines human precepts" (Mk 7:7 Is 29:13). We are explicitly called to eliminate our oppressive religious practices and unjust laws and become people of faith and nonviolent resistance. If Christians in the U.S. followed Jesus, we would relinquish our possessions, renounce our complicity with injustice, form base communities like the Latin American poor, turn to the scriptures, and resist the evil around us. We would become a church of nonviolent resistance, like the church of the first three centuries. As long as we as a church continue to pay lip service to God while disregarding God's commandment of active nonviolent love, we live in disobedience to God. As long as we remain silent in the face of systemic injustice, we rebel against God. Discipleship to Jesus demands much more than Sunday church attendance. We are called to be a church of active resistance.

February 10th

It's 10 p.m. and I'm sitting alone in my cell. It's noisy with the
tv and the shouting next door, but I so appreciate this relative solitude.
Today was a full day. It began with breakfast and check-in. I spoke on
a phone conference call with my friends at Pax Christi—Bishop
Thomas Gumbleton, Marie Dennis and Dave Robinson, as well as
Pamela Meidell of the Nevada Desert Experience, about plans to mark
next year's 50th anniversary of the atomic bombings of Hiroshima and
Nagasaki. Then, I received a haircut from Willie, one of the other cellmates. We were supervised by an armed guard. We spoke at length
about peacemaking. During the haircut, Mike Chinsolo, the chief jailer,
came by and joined the discussion. I asked him to stop reading our
outgoing mail. He was friendly but refused my suggestion. Afterwards,
we held our bible study and Eucharist.

During lunch, Bruce begged five portions of spinach from the
other guys. This morning, he had six small boxes of Raisin Bran cereal. All this eating prompted the other guys to speculate that he has
tapeworm. Ha!

After lunch, I had a two hour visit with Jim Stormes, S.J., the
Assistant Provincial for Social Ministries of the Maryland Province.
We talked about the Society of Jesus, our action and imprisonment,
and the Society's ongoing support. He was very friendly and I felt
energized by his visit. I spent the remainder of the afternoon reading
The Brothers Karamazov.

We continue to discuss Jesus' charge that the scribes and Pharisees "disregard God's commandment" and "nullify the Word of God in
favor of human tradition." Jesus challenges the religious authorities,
the disciples and us to seek nonviolence in our hearts: "From within
people, from their hearts, come evil thoughts, unchastity, theft, murder,
adultery, greed, malice, deceit, licentiousness, envy, blasphemy, arro-
gance, folly. All these evils come from within and they defile" (7:21-
23). If we would disarm the world, we need disarmed hearts. Yet, we
agree, we cannot wait to be perfect while the Pentagon goes on killing.
The nonviolent life is a rhythm of resistance and contemplation. From
our disarmed hearts, our inner spiritual life of prayer and attention to
God, we go public with nonviolent action that disarms our world of
violence.

February 11th

A cold, icy February morning. Edenton has shut down. Last night's dinner and this morning's breakfast never arrived from the hospital a few blocks away.

Heavy discussion this morning about the upcoming trial. We spend many hours writing a trial statement that we will mail to Lynn and preparing for what will surely be a travesty of justice. I have been reading *The Brothers Karamazov* and Kurt Vonnegut's *God Bless you, Mr. Rosewater.*

February 12th

A restless night in a freezing cold cell. After breakfast, we sat in silence for a while then began our bible study. After the lights went out last night, I sat on my bunk wrestling with God in prayer, dealing with my inner demons, frustrations, anger, resentment, hurt feelings and ego. After a long while, I was able to let go of it all, accept God's help and go to sleep. Jail heightens my powerlessness and dependence on God. I paced for a while in the short hallway and thanked God for the grace of being here with Phil and Bruce; for the action, Lynn, my family and supporters.

We read Mark's account (7:24-30) of Jesus' encounter with the Syrophoenician woman (perhaps the most marginalized caste—both gentile and female—in Jesus' world). Jesus pompously declares that he is here to serve only the Jews, but she insists that he take pity on her and heal her daughter. Jesus is amazed at her faith and changes his mind. He learns compassion. This challenging story not only encourages me to a great faith—to persist with my insistence on disarmament and peace—but it calls me to be open to new possibilities, to be teachable, and to be as inclusive as I can possibly be.

I sit here on the cold concrete floor in the hallway. Bruce and Phil are sitting on a bench against the wall writing. Down the other end of the hall, Willie is on the phone. The jailer in charge has locked us out of our cells. Miguel argues with "Schoolboy." Others sleep or watch TV. They are a friendly bunch. They have read newsletters and articles about us and support our stand for peace. I am grateful for the spirit here.

Tonight, our friends and supporters hold a "Festival of Hope" to mark the approaching trial. We each wrote statements to be read. I wrote about Jesus' command to love our enemies:

"The U.S. government, from the Pentagon to the courts, tells us to hate our enemies, to bomb our enemies, to nuke our enemies, to pay for the destruction of our enemies, and to obey the laws which legalize their destruction. 'Do not mind that we kill your enemies,' the government says. 'Do not let it bother you that the F15E bombers at Seymour Johnson Air Force Base killed thousands of Iraqis, or are on alert to kill thousands of Bosnians, or stand ready at a moment's notice to incinerate millions of people in nuclear war. Do what we tell you,' the government insists, 'and you will have peace.'

"The Gospel proclaims exactly the opposite. Love your enemies! Do not kill them. Do not threaten to kill them. Do not pay for killing them. Do not obey orders to kill them. Do not obey the laws which legalize their killing. Do not kill them because you need the job. Do not kill them because you want to 'be all that you can be.' Do not be complicit in killing. Do not hoard property or possessions because the government may use them as its excuse to kill. Do not look the other way while 40 wars are waged, while millions starve to death and while preparations for nuclear war continue presently, quietly, in your name.

"For God there are no enemies. God sees no borders and no differences. God sees only love. God is not a god of war; nor a god of violence; nor a god of deterrence; nor an unjust, wrathful god, eagerly waiting to destroy us. God loves us all and wants us to love one another. "The first step towards loving our enemies is dismantling our weapons. We cannot rationally claim to love our enemies while we prepare to kill them. If we are going to obey God's command to love our enemies, we will have to risk disarmament. We ourselves will have to confront these weapons. The government will never disarm because it does not obey God. As followers of Jesus, we must begin anew this process of disarmament by beating our nuclear swords into plowshares of peace.

"Until we disarm, we mock God. Our weapons are aimed at God's heart. These weapons of destruction may destroy other human beings who our government labels as enemies, but our willingness to use them destroys our souls.

"As we disarm and love our enemies, we fulfill God's command. Perhaps then the question before us is: How much do we love God? How seriously do we take God? Will we obey God's command?

"With you, I want to love God, to love enemies, and to love every human being. And love is not passive; love is dangerous, provocative, scandalous, publicly disruptive. Love is concrete. Love summons us to place ourselves between these weapons of death and our enemies. Love leads us all into Seymour Johnson, the Pentagon and other such hateful and heretical places.

"Though our Plowshares action has landed us is in jail and disrupted our lives, the Spirit of Love encourages us. Here in jail, I feel the presence of God blessing us with peace.

"God is disarming our world and our hearts. We can join in the process or reject the invitation. I have discovered that not only is it urgent, costly and imperative that we join God's peace movement, it is beautiful and grace-filled. In our violent world, nonviolent love surely sparks persecution, rejection, division, arrest, jailings, trial and imprisonment. But here in jail, these sufferings seem small in comparison to the gain we receive in Christ. We are learning a beautiful lesson. We are filled with love. Come and join us."

February 13th

Visitors! My mother and father spent nearly two hours with me this afternoon. Before they left, my brother Steve and his wife, Janet, showed up, with our friends Patrick O'Neill and Jean Chapman from the support committee. How good to see them all and to catch up on the news. Last night over 125 people celebrated a "Festival of Hope" in Raleigh. Fr. Richard McSorley, S.J. and my brother Steve were among the speakers.

Meanwhile, I finished reading *The Brothers Karamazov*. The Grand Inquisitor scene and the character of Aloysha touch me deeply. The jail has been packed all weekend. I spent the day sitting on my blanket on the floor. The other inmates were furious that we were locked out of our cells today, a Sunday. Phil quietly inquired with the guards to see if we might be allowed back into the cells so that we could rest on our bunks.

This morning, we read the story of Jesus healing the deaf and mute man (Mk 7:31-37). We see it as a parable for our culture: We too need to have our ears and mouths "opened" so that we might hear and "speak plainly." As it is, few people really listen to God. And then we babble without saying anything real or truthful. I too need such healing. I too long to become a real contemplative, someone who listens to the voice of God and shares it with others.

It's after 9 p.m. and I write this on my bunk in my cell. The tv blares in the background. I am not looking forward to Tuesday and our courtroom witness. Bruce and Phil are eager, but I am never excited about confronting the system. I do it because it must be done. May God bless our witness with radiant grace—and grant me an inner spirit of peace as I stand up for peace.

February 14th

Tonight, we receive Daniel Berrigan, Elizabeth McAlister and a host of good friends. What a blessing and a joy! We share much laughter and storytelling. The Festival of Hope visits us! They renew my hope.

A good day. This morning, Bruce and I went to the exercise room and I went running for a while on a running machine. The rest of the day was spent reading, writing an article, studying the scriptures, and talking with the other inmates. Our Mark text (8:1-10) tells the story of Jesus feeding a crowd of 4,000 people who had been with him for three days and had no food. "My heart is moved with pity for the crowd," Jesus sighs. He asks the disciples to share their seven loaves and everyone eats and is satisfied. What do we learn from this episode? Not only the politics of sharing but the miraculous intervention of God. We learn who God is—God is present in Jesus—and we learn our vocation as disciples of the Lord—to do what he says and share our food with those who are hungry. What a good God we have: God feeds the hungry. In a world filled with starving people, our God, nonetheless, calls us as a nation to share our food with all the hungry.

We ponder the Gospel and share Eucharist with one another. We pray for God's blessing on tomorrow's trial. We are excited about it. We have no sense of the outcome. We will take our nonviolent resistance into the courtroom and speak out against injustice. As far as we know, this has never been done quite as we intend. The judge could explode and haul us out. It will be dramatic and daring. The outcome is in God's hands.

9

The Mistrial

February 15th, 1994

At 7:30 a.m., we head to Elizabeth City. Lynn fills us in on the tough guards and awful conditions at the Albermarle Jail. At 9:30 a.m., they lead us into a small courtroom with paneled walls and flags. Family, friends, and a row of Jesuits pack the gallery. Familiar faces, including my parents, my brother David and his wife Karen, my brother Steve, Bishop Walter Sullivan and Martin Sheen greet us with smiles. Another hundred people, unable to get in, gather outdoors with anti-war banners and leaflets.

A dozen federal marshals and armed guards surround us as we sit at the defense table. We are wearing the clothes we wore on "the night in question." Judge Terrence Boyle enters the court and everyone stands. The prosecutor, a conservative, African-American lawyer named William Webb, and F.B.I. agent Al Koehler sit at the table next to us. All morning we listen as the prosecutor interviews prospective jurors. We tell the judge that we accept the first 12 people. All but two prospective jurors have military backgrounds. Some have even worked at Seymour Johnson Air Force Base. One specializes in F15Es! They are all accepted. Two people out of the 20 or so questioned express sympathy for us. One speaks of the moral witness of priests, and another of the influence of Dr. King and the Berrigans. They are both removed.

Then, the prosecutor submits a "Motion *in Limine*." It is read aloud:

"Comes now, the United States of America, by and through its attorneys, and moves the Court for an order granting the Government's Motion in Limine, restricting defendants from commenting in opening argument to the jury and during trial proceedings on any of the following topics, which would be inadmissible as evidence, prejudicial to a fair trial, and inappropriate for the jury to consider, unless counsel first obtains permission of the Court after argument or hearing outside the jury's presence:

1. Possible sentence faced by the defendant;

2. The military activities of the United States;

3. International law as it pertains to the United States military and United States military armaments;

4. The "Necessity Defense" as it pertains to the alleged crimes committed;

5. Activities of the United States military or any United States Government agency relating to any person other than the defendants;

6. The "Nuremberg Defense," or other like defenses as to the alleged crimes;

7. Crime prevention as a reason for entering the military facility at Seymour Johnson Air Force Base;

8. Allegations of crimes committed by the United States Government, or its officials or agencies;

9. The United States Government's foreign or domestic policy;

10. The military or other use of aircraft alleged to have been damaged by defendants;

11. Divine or natural law or other religious teachings;

12. Alleged crimes which were or are being committed by the United States military and/or other federal officials at Seymour Johnson Air Force Base."

By 12:30, the judge has sworn in the jury and recessed for lunch. The four of us sit together in a small cell under watch by several armed guards who walk to a nearby restaurant and bring us lunch—spaghetti with Italian sauce, garlic bread, salad and iced tea. The best meal we've had in months.

*

The trial begins. The prosecutor speaks first. "On behalf of the United States, I will call a number of persons to the stand who will be sworn to tell the truth. Then they will tell you about the events that occurred on December 7th, 1993, in the early morning hours. They'll tell you a little bit about themselves and what they were doing. They will tell you about what they saw and what happened. They will tell you that at a certain point in time they heard some noises, hammering. They ran to the airplanes and saw the four defendants and what they were doing. They'll talk about the hammers. The government will introduce the hammers into evidence so you can see what it is that we've alleged caused the damage. Finally, there will be some pictures which will illustrate the kind of damages that was done to the F15 Strike Eagle jet aircraft. I'd like to read the indictment charge. 'The Grand Jury charges that on or about December 7th, 1993, in the Eastern District of North Carolina, the Defendants willfully and by means of a hammer did injure the property of the United States; that is, one F15 Strike Eagle jet aircraft, thereby causing damage to such property in excess of one hundred dollars. And did aid and abet each other in doing so.' And then it talks about the law that that violates. That's the issue that you'll be looking at. Whether or not the four persons the government has charged did, in fact, damage the property of the United States in excess of a hundred dollars."

Lynn stands and begins our statement: "Good afternoon jurors, friends and supporters, members of the press, Judge Boyle. On December 7th, 1993, the four of us walked onto the Seymour Johnson Air Force Base in Goldsboro, N.C. to nonviolently disarm one F15E Strike Eagle, a nuclear-capable fighter bomber which has already been used notably in the massacre of Iraqis during the Gulf war. Even as I speak dozens of F15Es are poised for yet another possible bombing, this time of Bosnia. We poured our own blood on one bomber to expose the

bloody warmaking of the entire U.S. military; we hammered on that
bomber to begin the process of disassembly and conversion. We acted
in the Spirit of Life and the peace of Christ to fulfill the words of the
prophet Isaiah: 'They shall beat their swords into plowshares, and their
spears into pruning hooks; nation shall not lift swords against nation;
neither shall they learn war anymore.' Each year, millions starve to
death while the people of the United States, who make up 4.7% of the
world's population, consume over half of the world's resources. One
F15E costs $40 million just to build. And the U.S. devotes over $500
billion annually to warmaking—a sum that virtually bankrupts the
country. We four are not guilty of committing any crime on December
7th, 1993. The real crimes have been committed by institutions, corporations. . ."

"I'm going to object to this part of the opening statement," Mr.
Webb stands and says, "and ask that you instruct the jury to disregard
it." The judge chastises Lynn but allows her to continue.

"The real crimes," Lynn declares, "have been committed by institutions, corporations, the U.S. government and its military and covert
forces that develop, construct, stockpile, and deploy genocidal weapons and conventional weapons at genocidal levels. It is no coincidence
that we acted on Pearl Harbor Day. The nuclearism of the U.S. government has surpassed even the murderous psychosis of Nazi fascism.
Lest you feel isolated from the truth of this reality, lest you feel safe
from this madness as you sit in the courtroom, consider closely what is
really taking place. The so-called criminal justice system (which includes this very court) offers legal sanction to the high crimes of the
government and its military for example, the U.S. slaughter in Iraq."

"I'm going to stop you right there," Judge Boyle interrupts.
"You're impugning the integrity of the court and the court system. I'm
going to stop you unless you have something to say about the charge
in this case."

"I do have something further to say," Lynn states.

"Limit it to what's involved in this indictment," Judge Boyle
says.

"This court indicts peace activists for a felony while intentionally
ignoring those who make nuclear hostages of us all," Lynn declares.

"Objection!" shouts Mr. Webb.

"Sustained," answers the judge.

"The criminal justice system," Lynn continues.

"Stop right there!" the judge shouts.

" . . . and the nuclear strike force are two sides of the same coin," Lynn speaks out, "the coin for which the survival of the planet is threatened."

"I'm admonishing you that you're in contempt," Judge Boyle yells angrily.

"This court, like all others, protects the interests of the national security state," Lynn goes on.

"Take the jury out," Judge Boyle interrupts. "She's in contempt right now."

". . . and uses its illegitimate power to suppress the truth. . . .," Lynn continues.

"She's in contempt. The jury is excused," the judge bellows.

". . . and to discourage further acts of resistance." The guards grab the statement from Lynn.

As they prepare to lead Lynn away, I stand and announce, to the shock and amazement of the judge and prosecutor, that I will finish reading our opening statement. "The four of us have been denied very basic rights supposedly guaranteed by the justice system," I say.

"You're in contempt," the judge cries out.

"We have been denied the means to represent ourselves," I continue.

"If you continue, you'll be in contempt," he continues.

"We have been denied meetings together to prepare a mutual defense," I point out.

"No, no," he yells.

"The date and location of the trial have been manipulated," I declare as a Federal Marshall lunges at me and tears the statement from my hands.

"This courts has made a fair trial impossible," Bruce continues.

"You're in contempt," Judge Boyle screams.

"We will not pretend that justice is possible here," Bruce continues. "From this point, we shall remain silent and and nonviolently non-cooperate with these proceedings."

"We invite all our friends here in the courtroom to join us by standing and turning our backs to the court," I say.

All four of us stand with our backs turned to the judge. The jury is being led out of the courtroom. The judge is shouting out contempt charges against us. Twenty-one people in the courtroom stand and turn their backs to the court, including Dan Berrigan, Martin Sheen, and my brother Steve. They recite the Lord's Prayer out loud. We are led out. Our friends break into song. We are brought back to the "cage" and sit guarded by the marshals. We can hear the singing.

Suddenly, we hear a friend of Lynn's, David Sawyer, an African-American musician from Baltimore, shouting. Six Federal Marshals and one F.B.I. agent throw him against the wall, pull on his long hair and grab his throat, in front of more than a dozen witnesses. They shackle him and charge him with two counts of felony assault on a federal officer, even though he had done nothing different than the 20 others who stood in nonviolent protest. We hear him screaming throughout the ordeal. After a few moments, he is brought into the cell with us and we introduce ourselves. He is okay, though extremely shaken by the police brutality.

The other 20 people eventually come before Judge Boyle and are offered a chance to leave or be sentenced. Fourteen leave. Six friends remain, are charged with contempt and sentenced to six months in jail: Greg Boertje-Obed; Michele Naar-Obed; Maureen Kehoe-Ostensen; Kathy Boylan; Brad Sjostrom; and Rosemarie Harper. They are brought into the cell with us.

"You intentionally, deliberately, and willfully undertook to disrupt United States District Court," Boyle told Brad Sjostrom. "You acted with total disrespect and indignity. I'm sorry for you." "I'm sorry for you," Brad replied.

*

Tonight, I sit here in the Edenton Jail, exhausted after one of the most intense days of my life. We carried the Spirit of the action into the courtroom. It was hard for all of us, but it was a day of truth-telling, nonviolent love in action, and steadfast resistance to injustice.

Ash Wednesday, February 16th

It will take me a while to recover from yesterday's ordeal, but one thing's certain: we will have plenty of time to reflect on this latest episode. We may not have another trial for months. We spend the morning reflecting on the mistrial, the judge, our friends, families and supporters. Last night, I spoke on the phone with Martin Sheen and Joe Cosgrove, my lawyer friend from Wilkes-Barre, Pennsylvania. This afternoon, Dan Berrigan and Earl Crow visit for a few minutes. Earlier this morning, Dan led an Ash Wednesday service outside the courthouse in Elizabeth City.

This morning, my friends in the Bay Area gather for a prayer service, vigil and nonviolent civil disobedience at the entrance to the Lawrence Livermore Laboratories. Fr. Bill O'Donnell, Fr. Steve Kelly, S.J., Sherry Larsen-Beville and others will probably be arrested for kneeling and blocking the entrance. No doubt they will mark each other's foreheads with ashes and speak of the Labs' work to reduce the world to ashes in a nuclear hellfire. Their repentance and nonviolent action encourage me.

The Pharisees argue with Jesus and demand a sign, we read in Mark's Gospel. Jesus "sighs from the depths of his spirit," and refuses to give them a sign. They want assurance and results because they have no faith in him. In our age too, people seek a sign. Jesus continues to sigh from the depths of his spirit as he looks upon the human race and its systemic injustice. We have already been given a sign, indeed two of them: a cross and an empty tomb. Jesus wants us to follow him on that journey of nonviolent resistance to the cross. I think I'm beginning to know the price of discipleship.

10

Days of Prayer and Faith

Thursday, February 17th, 1994

Jesus instructs his disciples to "watch out, and guard against the leaven of the Pharisees and the leaven of Herod." Neither the Pharisees nor Herod has faith. The same challenge confronts us—to guard against the hypocrisy of the institutional church and the warmaking government, to beware of idols and false gods, to believe in the living God.

Our seven friends remain in the Albermarle District jail. Perhaps they are with Lynn. They may be in jail for six months. We have begun to discuss our various options—what to say when we are brought before the judge for our contempt charges, how we will approach our individual trials if the judge separates our cases, and how we might call one another to the stand as witnesses.

February 18th

This morning, the local parish priest visited. The judge, Terrence Boyle, is not only one of his parishioners, but the head of the church hall building committee. We encouraged the priest to speak to the judge, to ask him to stop oppressing us, and to see if he would support our work for disarmament and refuse to try us.

This afternoon, my friend and Jesuit classmate, Frank McAloon, visited. He spoke of his parish work in Richmond, Virginia, and I told him about our action and life in jail. After laughing over old stories, we prayed together that we would be faithful "Companions of Jesus."

The chief jailer tells us that he plans to move us into a smaller area tomorrow. Phil and I are glad because this will mean that we can rest in the afternoons on our bunks in our cells, since the celldoors will not be locked. Meanwhile, we have been discussing the chief's racist behavior towards one of the inmates yesterday. "You have to show them who's in charge," he told Phil, after hauling a friend of ours into solitary confinement.

I am reading Annie Dillard's *Holy the Firm*, which Elizabeth McAlister sent me.

*

Jesus arrives in Bethsaida and meets a blind man (Mk 8:22-26). Jesus takes the man by the arm and leads him out of town; through a series of actions, Jesus restores the man's sight completely. The story thus presents the different stages which the disciples go through before they receive vision. It opens Mark's discipleship catechism section.

During Eucharist, we pray for vision, that here in jail we might see Christ's nonviolent reign, an unarmed world of peace. Like the blind man, we are being healed and invited to share the vision of nonviolence.

Later in the day, after writing some letters, I pray over this text. I imagine Jesus leading me (because of my blindness) and healing me. I ask that I might never leave his vision. My spirit is lifted and healed. I am consoled and grateful.

February 19th

Lynn's friend David Sawyer was brought before a judge yesterday. The Federal Marshalls took the stand and lied, calling him a violent threat. They hold him without bond. Patrick O'Neill and my brother Steve witnessed the hearing and were outraged. Meanwhile, Lynn and two of the women have been moved to the Hertford County Jail in the small town of Winton.

Bruce's mother, Rena Rae, told him on the phone the other day, "I completely support your judgment and trust you. If you're doing it, it must be alright." What a supportive, affirming person she is!

We were moved after breakfast into three small rooms: a hallway with a tv and a foot-wide table against the wall, with two cells off the hallway. Phil and I share a cell. Bruce shares a cell with Troy, my original roommate. The chief jailer says we'll be here for quite a while.

"Who do you say that I am?" Jesus asks the disciples (Mk 8:27-31). "You are the Messiah," Peter responds. Jesus rebukes him and orders him not to tell anyone. Peter has completely misunderstood Jesus. He believes and hopes Jesus will form an army, liberate Israel, and become their king like all the other dominating rulers. Jesus' lordship, instead, is based on nonviolence, suffering love, powerlessness, and resistance to evil. His great question includes an answer within it: "I am 'I am,' not just the 'I am' of the scriptures, but the 'I am' of the cross."

Who do we say Jesus is? Sitting in our dark, cold jail cell this morning, we declare Jesus is God—the God of the cross, the God of nonviolence, the God of resistance, the God of suffering love, the God who is Truth and Spirit, the All-Powerless God. Recognizing our Lord in such terms demands a sacrifice on our part. We too have to be people of nonviolence, resistance, suffering love and justice. We need to risk our lives in discipleship to Christ by resisting the murderous state. It is an uncomfortable, painful journey.

February 20th

Jesus proclaims that "the Human One will suffer greatly, be rejected, be killed and three days later rise." Peter takes him aside. "Heaven forbid, Lord, that you should suffer, that you should get in trouble, that you might provoke the authorities to kill you." Jesus rebukes Peter, "Get behind me Satan. You are not thinking as God does but as human beings do" (Mk 8:31-33).

We spent hours discussing this passage. I approach it from my own experiences in El Salvador and Guatemala. If a peasant organizer in northern El Salvador, in the countryside of Chalatenango, spoke out against war, called people to a faith that practices nonviolent resistance, and then walked to San Salvador where he turned over the tables in a symbolic act of transformation, he would be arrested, disappeared, interrogated, tortured and executed. Public peacemaking in the outskirts of the empire results in execution. Jesus outlines the inevitable. The disciples want results, success, good press coverage and political victory. But Jesus is God. And He knows that suffering precedes social change. He sees the deeper possibility of resurrection. Jesus goes to the cross telling the world, "The violence stops here in my body. If you want to follow me, you have to enter this process of confrontation with systemic injustice and take on the world's violence in a spirit of love. Hearts will then be converted and many will be redeemed." The logic of nonviolence is the logic of God.

We sit in our jail cell mulling over God's way of nonviolent suffering love, pondering our own effort to follow that way of the cross. "This is the least we can do," Phil says. Certainly this imprisonment is the closest I've come to taking up that nonviolent cross. I hope God may use our witness to spark not only the disarmament of my heart and others, but nuclear disarmament.

Many friends send me picture postcards. Using a little toothpaste as glue on the back of the cards, I hang on the walls surrounding my top bunk icons of Jesus, St. Ignatius, and St. Francis of Assisi, and pictures of Dorothy Day, Martin Luther King, Jr., Thomas Merton, and Archbishop Romero, as well as photos of Yosemite, the Grand Canyon and the Outer Banks. As I look at these pictures, the sunlight streams through our cell and I feel at peace.

February 21st

"If anyone wishes to follow me, they must deny themselves, take up their cross and follow me. Whoever wishes to save her life will lose it, but whoever loses her life for my sake and the sake of the Gospel will save it."

Slowly, in fits and starts, we try to deny ourselves, to take up the cross and follow Jesus. We speak of two ingredients for discipleship: community and resistance to evil. We resist violence through our Plowshares action, but some days community life feels harder to bear than the cross itself. Jesus was disowned, betrayed, denied and abandoned by his community. If he had trouble with his community, why should any of us expect better? Nonetheless, we are called to follow him, to live in community, and to resist injustice.

February 22nd

"It's all hope and none of it is optimism," Daniel Berrigan said last December, accepting the *Pacem in Terris* award in Davenport,

Iowa. "I think of Dorothy Day and Thomas Merton and Cesar Chavez and all these great people who have walked ahead with a light in the darkness. I think of people especially who are able to do good work without being attached to success in their work. I think if we look at the invisible writing of these lives, we see people who were doing the good and beautiful because it was good and beautiful, with a very intense understanding that the outcome was in better hands than ours. And that, it seems to me, is one clumsy way of putting the hope of all this, that we can continue without being attached to the outcome of what we do because we have gone deeply into the meditation on the worthwhile character of what we do. This is certainly a spiritual tradition that crosses all sorts of lines and borders. It was one great insight of Merton from Zen; Gandhi in the relationship between means and ends, I think is another angle. . . . But Merton and Dorothy especially, died without seeing anything happen, whether in church or state, except that things got worse; and that was not the issue. And it must not be the issue. So one sign of this kind of anonymous greatness is that people have been able to say, invariably with community help and with sacraments and with a discipline of prayer, this is the work to be done. It is Godly work. It will have outcome in God's good time. Meantime we belong at the work. Period."

February 23rd

Jesus climbs the mountain and is transfigured into a martyr wearing bright, white clothes (Mk 9:1-8). He speaks with Moses and Elijah, who represent the law and the prophets, about the way of suffering love. Peter, James and John do not understand. They want to stay on the mountaintop. They do not want to go down into the valley and up the road to the cross. They are terrified. Yet the voice of God comes upon them: "This is my beloved Son. Listen to him." Suddenly, they see only Jesus.

The glory of God's incarnate nonviolence shines like the sun before the disciples. As in the Hebrew scriptures, God comes in a cloud, casting a shadow over the disciples, who fall prostrate as if dead (according to Matthew's account, 17:1-8). God speaks to them about the beloved Jesus and commands them to listen to him. Jesus tells them to rise and not to be afraid.

The nuclear age offers, in Dorothy Day's words, "a counter-transfiguration." We have created a white light as bright as the sun and a nuclear cloud that disintegrates people and leaves nothing but their shadows. We fall prostrate in adoration of the nuclear bomb. This anti-transfiguration manifests humanity's effort to resemble God, to claim God's power. The bomb epitomizes not resurrection but destruction, the exact opposite of Jesus' glorious nonviolence.

Eventide. Mary Rider, on the phone tonight, whispers to me: "John, whatever comes from all this, one thing is for sure: God has all of this, all of us, in Her hands." Amen, sister, Amen. I spoke with Troy at length this afternoon about nonviolence. The whole world is watching Tonya Harding and Nancy Kerrigan skate in the Olympics. We sit here on ice, biding our time.

The outcome is in better hands than ours. Yes, and those hands, I notice, are scarred. They have been nailed to a cross. As we approach the Lord in glory, he will look at our hands for scars. Our hands will bear scars as well.

February 24th

Yesterday, after dinner, I lay on my bunk and prayed for the grace to listen to Jesus. I could hear nothing except the tv. I find it hard to pray with the tv always on. I miss silence. I have never been as faithful about prayer as I wish. Last night, when the lights and tv suddenly when out at 11:30, I was too tired to sit up and meditate and instead, before I fell asleep, I thought, "I wish I had the strength to pray." Yet, as I fell asleep, a voice whispered back to me, "You are not alone. I am with you. I love you. You are my friend, my disciple, and my companion."

*

"We think of prayer with words like formal, verbal, solitary, communal, and intentional," Elizabeth McAlister told last week's Festival of Hope. "We associate it with asking and with answers; or with being still and waiting. Above all, we think of prayer as something we are doing. We may even know this is bad theology, but still it is our habitual frame of reference. Such prayer feeds our obsession with success. It's an achievement. God or whatever we name the Holiness in life becomes familiar, manageable, reasonable. If we do the right things and follow the rules, everything will be alright. But the Holy cannot be contained. It erupts with energy and vitality when things are not as we thought or as we wanted them to be. Think of the prayer of tears. Or the prayer of rage that asks, 'How could you allow this to happen, God? How can you permit such suffering? Where are you?' There is another eruption of the Holy that we might call the prayer of laughter. . . . Laughter expresses a sudden, piercing view of how unmanageable God is. It opens us to a God that is both larger and less predictable than we guessed (Psalm 2). . . . Laughter is the prelude to faith. . . . Our God has a sense of humor, surprises up Her sleeve, if indeed she has a sleeve. Everything will be alright but not in any way any of us can predict. To believe that is the challenge of our faith."

*

Jesus charges the disciples not to speak about his transfiguration until after the resurrection (Mk 9:9-13). They began to question among themselves what that means. We speak of resurrection. Any nonviolent, illegal confrontation with systemic violence and death, we agree, can be a resurrection experience. For us, our actions at Seymour Johnson Air Force Base and in the courtroom last week were resurrection moments. Questions rise: How can I practice resurrection in jail? How can I live in the Spirit of resurrection?

Jesus speaks of Elijah and the persecution they both suffer and how Elijah has come again in John the Baptist. We turn to 1 Kings 19:2-14. Elijah begs that God take his life because everyone is out to kill him. He lies down under a broom tree to die. But the angel of God comes, gives him food and tells him, "Get up and eat else the journey will be too long for you." He was strengthened then to walk for 40 days to the mountain of God. God encourages us and strengthens us for the long haul. According to Jesus, the cross is not just inevitable: it is the only way God redeems us. May we be strengthened to face our cross.

*

From *The Washington Post* (Feb. 20, 1994): "This fiscal year outlays for defense will total $280 billion, almost as much as the rest of the world combined. . . . The next biggest military budget—that of Japan—is less than $40 billion while Russia spends still less. . . . The Pentagon points to the threat posed by such adversaries as Iran, Iraq and North Korea. But *Defense News* reports that fearsome Iran is struggling to find $7 billion for military spending over the next five years; the U.S. will spend $1.2 trillion on its military over the same period. As John Kenneth Galbraith commented, it is hard to argue against this level of military spending for it merits only ridicule. . . . The U.S. could maintain the strongest military in the world for $150 to $200 billion a year, freeing up more than $50 billion annually to meet new challenges at home and abroad."

The War Resisters League estimates that actual U.S. spending for war preparations, if every department is included (such as Veterans Affairs, the C.I.A., and the Department of Energy), would be not $280 billion but $588 billion for this year's budget.

February 25th

Thirty-seven letters arrive in the mail. Since all outgoing mail is read, I can't use my smuggled pen to write. I struggle to answer each letter with these pencil stubs. The local priest brought us communion this morning along with envelopes and notepads. Yesterday, Fr. Frank O'Connor, the new pastor of St. Aloysius' church in D.C., was here for a visit. Then, later this morning, an uproarious visit for the three of us with Frank McAloon, S.J. and Bob Curry, S.J. Frank loaned me his copy of Louis Fischer's *The Life of Mahatma Gandhi*, which I've started to reread.

Yesterday, another long afternoon talk with Troy our cellmate while Phil and Bruce took naps. He asked me about our simple life-style and I tried to explain the reasons for our voluntary poverty. This led to deep reflection on the presence of God in our lives. Troy feels God's presence but resists. I confessed the same response.

Our friends remain in jail though joyful news has arrived that Greg and Michele are expecting their first child. They are both in the Elizabeth City Jail and face six months for contempt, as well as three years for a peace witness when they spray-painted "Stop the bombing" on the Baltimore Federal Building (last June after Clinton bombed Iraq).

*

The demon of imperial violence possesses a child (Mk 9:14-29). The boy's father tells Jesus that the disciples were unable to heal him and pleads with Jesus to heal him. "If you can do anything, have compassion on us and help us!" the father cries. "If you can?" Jesus replies in shock. "Everything is possible for one who has faith." "Lord, I do believe; help my unbelief!" the father responds. Jesus heals the boy and raises him, as though from death. Later when the disciples press Christ about why they could not heal the boy, he declares, "This kind can only come out through prayer."

If we would expel the demon of imperial violence, we must be people of prayer and faith. We must immerse ourselves in daily prayer. We beg for faith. We have faith in God and act out of that faith. If we are people of prayer and faith, our own possession by demonic violence diminishes. In that contemplative nonviolence, we expel the demons of violence.

February 26th

"Everything is possible for one who has faith." What does that mean to us in this "faithless generation"? Perhaps it means first of all that we need to pray specifically and intentionally for nuclear disarmament and the abolition of war. How regularly do we pray these great intercessory prayers for an end to specific wars, nuclear weapons and injustices? From that regular prayer, we can then act more fearlessly and bravely, knowing that our prayer has been heard. In faith, we know that it will come to pass.

These daily bible studies impress upon me the critical imperative of faith. Faithlessness is the root of our violence, of the world's problems. If we did not believe in the idols of death, we would be nonviolent and just with one another, and God would reign on earth as God reigns in heaven.

*

We discuss the upcoming trials. We agree to ask for a jury trial, to forgo *voir dire* selection, to stand *pro se* again, to speak as best we can, and to subpoena one another to testify. Our own testimonies may be the best truth-telling we can offer.

At Eucharist, we offer many intercessions, break bread, pass the cup, join hands in prayer and offer each other the sign of peace. So simple, so healing, so beautiful, so crucial. A quiet, prayerful and profound Eucharist. The nonviolent Christ is present among us in this sacred moment and I am strengthened. Lord, I believe. Help my unbelief.

*

"If one thousand, one hundred, or if ten people whom I could name—if ten honest people only—aye, if one honest person in this state of Massachusetts, ceasing to hold slaves, were actually to withdraw from this copartnership and be locked up in the county jail, it would be the abolition of slavery in America," Henry David Thoreau wrote over a century ago. "For it matters not how small the beginning may seem to be: what is once done well is done forever."

Sunday morning, February 27th

Gandhi's life stirs me to deeper devotion. In South Africa, at one point, Gandhi inspired thousands of Indians to go to jail in acts of protest to racist immigration laws. In jail, Gandhi read and studied the scriptures. He prayed. He considered imprisonment for nonviolent resistance and adherence to the truth to be a great blessing, perhaps the best and noblest thing one could do with one's life. The Gospel offers this same logic of nonviolence. Jesus explains to the disciples that he will be killed and then rise from the dead. They do not understand him at all and are afraid (Mk 9:30-32).

Last night, we watched the movie *Sommersby*. I'm still plugging along with my correspondence. Outside our narrow window, the sky is bright blue.

My father visited me this afternoon. We talked of many things, from our life in North Carolina 30 years ago, to nuclear weapons, to my mother's pain over my imprisonment, to our faith in God. He was, as usual, solicitous, generous, and kind. Though I know it is hard for him to see me in jail, he is very patient and listens with interest to my plight.

February 28th

Good letters arrive from Daniel Berrigan, S.J. and Richard McSorley, S.J. Henri Nouwen sent me a new manuscript on the Eucharist, based on the story of the disciples' encounter with Christ on the road to Emmaus. Meanwhile, I'm correcting the galleys for my new book, *The God of Peace: Toward a Theology of Nonviolence*, and reading about Gandhi.

Instead of listening to Jesus, the disciples argue about who among them is the greatest. So Jesus instructs them, "If you want to be great, you must be the last of all and servant of all." Embracing a child, he continues, "Whoever receives a child, receives me, and receives not just me, but the One who sent me" (Mk 9:33-38). Like the disciples, an ambitious ego plagues me. I need to hear these words of Jesus. Part of me longs to be first of all and served by all. That part needs to die. I need to be reborn as last of all and servant of all.

Phil comments that a Plowshares action quickly shatters one's ego. In jail, one's ego turns upside down as one is barraged with humiliations.

The U.S. shot down four Serb airplanes over Bosnia-Herzegovnia this morning. We prayed in the silence of our cell for an end to the bombing, an end to war, an end to hatred. We broke bread, passed the cup and exchanged the sign of peace. All very simple but filled with hope and faith in the God of peace who hears our prayers.

March 1st

It's late and I'm exhausted. I spent the entire day writing over 30 letters and trying to answer another stack of 40 letters that arrived. My cousin Marry Anne Muller from Brooklyn, Patrick Atkinson from Guatemala, and Jim Gartland, S.J. from Chicago write fine letters. Martin Sheen writes, "I am deeply moved by your courage and commitment and saddened by the day's events [at the mistrial]. I have written Judge Boyle and asked him to reconsider the harsh 'contempt' sentences on yourselves as well as the supporters. I am returning to North Carolina next month to film a tv movie and I'm hoping for a chance to meet with him privately and discuss the matter. I am also looking forward to visiting all of you as well at that time."

We delve into the Gospel admonition not to prevent those who do mighty deeds in Jesus' name yet who are not members of the community. We reflect on non-Christians like our friend Lynn who teaches us so much about resistance, nonviolence and the struggle for justice. Lynn challenges me to a more authentic discipleship to Jesus. She writes marvelous letters about sharing a cell with Kathy and Rose and other inmates. "We normally have our 'check-ins,' business and discussions over lunch and dinner. We've managed to maintain good space by separating in between to our bunks to read and write. Kathy is the consummate peacemaker. Rose is doing great with her first arrest and incarceration ever. Good stories all around . . . May you be filled with loving-kindness," she signs off. "May you be well. May you be peaceful and at ease. May you be happy."

March 2nd

Last night, after lights went off and Phil turned in on the bunk below me, I sat up in the dark reflecting on the day, praying to God about it and for the Lord's presence in my life here and now. Slowly the mad determination to answer 150 letters melted away and I felt the presence of the Lord. I marveled at how easily I can give into my workaholism, even in jail, at how easily I can let go of the Lord's presence. And I thanked the Lord for his gentle presence in my heart. I asked that the days ahead deepen my awareness of God's heartfelt presence, that these might be holy days marked by transforming grace. The Lord is kind and gracious to me. Once again, I am disarmed by God's love.

Today brought a lighter spirit, a longer bible study, less mail, good conversations with Phil and Bruce, much reading, and a more reflective mood. Perhaps our inner life reflected the rain puddles and gray clouds we could see out our narrow window. It is chilly in the cell as I write this. Troy is fasting today in anticipation of his Friday release. I sit here like Buddha, covered in a blanket, next to my pile of mail, sipping my iced-tea, surrounded by picture postcards, a veritable cloud of witnesses looking over my shoulder. My soul is set in peace.

Our scripture text today admonished the community of disciples not to sin or to allow one another to sin (Mk 9:42-50). Instead, Jesus says take drastic measures within the community to remove whatever causes one another to sin. Luke expands on the passage, delineating forgiveness and faith as the keys to Christian community. "Everyone will be salted with fire," Jesus remarks. "Salt is good, but if salt becomes insipid, with what will you restore its flavor? Keep salt in yourselves, in your hearts, and you will have peace with one another" (Mk 9:49-50). Salt purifies and preserves. Jesus' salt is fire, the drastic burning that we need to do to correct and build our peacemaking communities. Mark writes that if we salt one another with nonviolent correction, then we will have peace.

Peace. It is strange that this glorious word is only now mentioned in Mark's gospel. Jesus intimates how communities can be at peace. He does not speak of the world, which John will later write, does not know peace. But the community of disciples will know Christ's own peace as they correct one another, forgive one another and continue forward in faith and nonviolence.

If the church today rejects violence, gets its house in order, renounces war, expels nuclear weapons manufacturers, and becomes a church of nonviolence, then perhaps we will see some serious change in our world. Jesus advocates this inner-community conversion as the first step to the liberation and transformation of the world. Albert Nolan comments in his book, *Jesus Before Christianity*:

> Jesus set out to liberate Israel from Rome by persuading Israel to change. Without a change of heart within Israel itself, liberation from imperialism of any kind would be impossible. . . . Jesus saw what no one else had been able to see, that there was more oppression and economic exploitation from within Judaism than from without.

Gandhi believed in the same dynamic of transformation. Throughout the 1920s, he insisted that the only way India would be liberated from Britain would be if the Indian people renounced their violence, the injustice of untouchability and the division between Hindus and Muslims; then, they would be free. Britain would recognize that India was already free, and leave.

What does this mean for us? At least this: the churches in our country need to renounce war and every form of injustice which we reflect among ourselves (including sexism, racism, homophobia, and violence). When the churches do this and start practicing Gospel nonviolence, we will be disarmed and liberated and be able to offer disarmament and liberation for all.

March 3rd

Bishop Walter Sullivan, president of Pax Christi, visited today and he told us of his recent journey to El Salvador and the upcoming elections there. We spoke of the latest horrors in Haiti, and in Israel where 50 Palestinians were shot dead in the Hebron mosque on Saturday. He believes that "peace movement" people have lost their direction. I urged him to call people back to the urgent work of nuclear disarmament and active nonviolence.

Troy was allowed to leave a day early so it's just the three of us now in this three room suite. Mike Chinsolo, the chief jailer, came in this morning and asked how he could order books which Phil and I have written. By this afternoon, he had ordered them. "Now don't go writing bad things," he told me today. "And be sure you get a thin person with alot of hair to play me in the movie." Mike has been friendly with us lately, though we have seen him be harsh to other inmates.

March 4th

We enter a monastic rhythm. With only the three of us sharing three rooms, we control the tv and thus the noise. We now eat our meals in silence. Tonight, after dinner, we read and write letters and it is actually quiet. The silence heals our spirit. This quiet can change at any moment. We might be hauled off to another jail. We might be split up. We might be put back into the large cellblock. We might be joined by other inmates. We enjoy the peace and quiet of the moment while we can.

The cell has been cold all day. Since I wear only this orange jump suit, I wrap myself in my blanket most of the day. While reading the life of the Mahatma on my bunk, I feel and look a bit more like him.

Jesus observes, "Whoever does not accept the reign of God like a child will not enter it" (Mk 10:15). How do we become more like an accepting child? The Word instructs us to be more trustful, open, dependent, and vulnerable. Our action and jailing help us to accept God's reign like children. We are more vulnerable, helpless and dependent here in jail, as we were when we hammered on the nuclear bombers and were surrounded by guns. But we have farther to go, especially in the areas of faith and trust.

God our doting parent, help us all! We are your children.

March 5th

"I fought the government from inside jail," Gandhi proclaims at the end of his life. "For me, jail is a palace." I ponder these words and summon all my strength to adopt the same noble attitude. Though ignored by the country, the media and the mainstream church, nonetheless my friends and I remain in jail, fighting the government through steadfast nonviolence. I feel helpless, rejected and ignored; still I trust that God has brought me to this "palace" and that I am serving God best here.

This morning, we discuss the great story of the rich man who confronts Jesus about entering eternal life (Mk 10:17-27). Jesus lists the commandments and adds, "Do not defraud." The rich man insists he has kept these all his life. Looking at him with love, Jesus issues the great invitation which has haunted me all my life: "You are lacking in one thing. Go, sell what you have and give to the poor and you will have treasure in heaven; then, come, follow me." The rich man goes away sad. He is attached to possessions. "How hard it is for the rich to enter God's reign," Jesus exclaims. "All things are possible for God."

The call to discipleship demands a renunciation of possessions. I remember applying to the Jesuits, writing that I wanted to do what the rich man was unable to do: to renounce my wealth, to give it all away and to follow Jesus for the rest of my life. I have tried to do this. With this Plowshares action and my imprisonment, I feel that I am plunging even deeper into the radical discipleship Christ demands. The freedom and union with Christ which I know are infinitely more valuable than any worldly possession. Here in jail, I am free. In this poverty, I am rich. This Chowan County Jail cell is a palace and I am a prince for I am blessed to share in the Spirit and life of Jesus.

March 6th

"There is no one who has given up house or brothers or sisters or mother or father or children or lands for my sake and for the sake of the Gospel who will not receive a hundred times more now in this present age—houses and brothers and sisters and mothers and children and lands, with persecutions, and eternal life in the age to come" (Mk 10:29-30). Thus, Jesus teaches the dynamics of discipleship to his unbelieving disciples. In our bible study, Phil remarks that the disciples, though they thought they had given up so much, in reality, had not given up anything, for everything belongs to God.

In the last decade, as I have traveled around the country to speak at churches and conferences, I have been taken in and welcomed by hundreds of families, churches and communities. The piles of mail that I continue to receive attest to the solidarity of Christian life. As I renounce all, I receive it all back—and a hundred times more.

As we enter this Christian dynamic, we challenge the imperial culture which persecutes us. Persecution becomes then a measure of discipleship, as Dorothy Day noted. If we have never suffered persecutions for the sake of the Gospel (for denouncing war, injustice and death and announcing peace, justice and new life in Christ), then we have not begun to walk the way of the cross. Sitting in this jail cell illuminates this truth for me. The Gospel remains political, dynamic and costly.

March 7th

"They were on the way, going up to Jerusalem, and Jesus went ahead of them. They were amazed, and those who followed were afraid" (Mk 10:32). Jesus marches on, like Gandhi on his salt march, to act in the Temple and accept the consequences. Jesus risks resurrection. He has his eyes set on God. His faith is perfect. The disciples do not have a clue. They cower in fear.

Today marks three months in jail. We speak of the passion of Jesus, of his torture and suffering, the fear he must have known, the total offering of his life. Everyone opposed him. In light of his suffering and death, our three months behind bars are nothing. We have a private, three room suite; good food; tv; and a phone. Today I received 60 pieces of mail. We have great friends and supporters. Surely, this is where we belong. Our presence here is the best service we can offer God. I pray that we will be better contemplatives, more loving to the guards and court officials, more centered. If we could plunge the depths of nonviolence within, then we will touch more people through Christ's spirit. I hope that we do not misuse this graced time.

God of the cross, transform us that we might radiate your spirit. Keep us centered in you. Let these days be a true sharing in your passion, death and glory.

11

Keeping Watch

March 8th, 1994

Jesus explains the cross and the resurrection to his disciples. They have no idea what he's talking about: they demand that he do "whatever they ask" (Mk 10:35-45). They want to control Jesus. They want him to be obedient to them. For 2,000 years, the church has suffered from the same egotistic desire. Nonetheless, Jesus puts himself at their service: "What do you want me to do for you?" When he asks that question to the poor, blind beggar, Bartimaeus responds correctly, asking for vision which Jesus grants. The blind disciples respond egotistically, asking to sit in glory and power. As Thomas Merton once remarked to Phil, the ego is our predominant idol. Our egos rule us. We must constantly deny our egos if we would serve others and God.

Resistance to evil disrupts our egotistical desires. Resistance turns our egos upside-down. Jesus responds to the disciples with the challenge of the cross: "Can you drink the cup of suffering I must drink? Can you be baptized in blood? Are you willing and able to suffer arrest, jail, torture, and execution for nonviolent resistance?"

Mark sums up the life of Jesus: "You know that those who are recognized as rulers over the Gentiles lord it over them and their great ones make their authority over them felt. But it shall not be so among you. Rather, whoever wishes to be great among you will be your servant; whoever wishes to be first among you will be the slave of all. For the Human One did not come to be served but to serve and to give his life as a ransom for many" (Mk 10:42-45).

*

The chief jailer, Mike Chinsolo, interrupts our bible study to ask me to autograph my book, *Disarming the Heart: Toward a Vow of Nonviolence*. We ask him about racism and he confessed that once, he attended a Ku Klux Klan rally of 10,000 people in the 1960s. He decided he did not believe in hate and never returned.

March 9th

Saying Yes and saying No, as Robert McAfee Brown explains in his book, makes all the difference. In our culture, many say Yes, but too few say No: No to war, No to nuclear weapons, No to militarism, No to violence, No to racism, No to sexism, No to injustice, No to greed, No to domination, and No to imperialism. In order to say Yes to life, love, nonviolence and peace, we have to say No to death, hatred, violence and war. St. Paul writes that Jesus is the Yes of God. Phil comments this morning that Jesus is also the No of God, the clearest No in history. "If he had not said No, he would not have served humanity." But he said it—strongly, powerfully, clearly. Jesus gave his life saying Yes and No. We must too.

We read about the blind beggar, Bartimaeus, who keeps calling out to Jesus despite the disciples' orders otherwise. "Jesus, Son of David, have pity on me." Instead of the flattery and the inappropriate title, 'Good Teacher,' which the rich man used, the blind Bartimaeus recognizes Jesus as the Messiah. When Jesus calls him, he throws his begging cloak aside. He gives up his livelihood, his entire possessions. "What do you want me to do for you?" Jesus asks. "I want to see," he responds. "Go your way, your faith has saved you." Bartimaeus receives his sight and follows Jesus "on the way" to the cross.

Blindness plagues us all. We do not see the violence we do to one another. We are the blindest of the blind, Dorothy Day once wrote. And we prefer our blindness. Once we see Jesus, as Bartimaeus experienced, we recognize God in our midst and drop everything to follow the way of the cross. Once we see Jesus, we gladly risk our lives to be with him, even if he heads for trouble. If we see Jesus, we recognize that we must change the way we live.

"What are we blind about?" Phil asks. We are blind to the meaning of the cross. We do not recognize God in our midst. We do not see the violence we do. We do not envision the duties of disarmament. We are blind to the spiritual requirements of peacemaking, especially detachment from results. Blindness is essentially a spiritual matter. We as a people have no imagination because we have no vision. Jesus offers vision. Nonviolence is his remedy to our cultural, imperial blindness.

March 10th

Mark describes Jesus entering Jerusalem as a nonviolent warrior, like Gandhi marching to the sea to pick up the illegal salt (Mk 11:1-11). This procession into Jerusalem is classic street theater, a nonviolent political demonstration with symbolic overtones. Instead of riding a warhorse as the imperial conquerors do, Jesus rides in on an ass, a humble symbol of peace. A conqueror, yes, but of an entirely different sort! The only blood shed is his own.

Yesterday, all our supporters were released from jail, except Brad, who was sentenced to several more weeks.

March 11th

Jesus commits nonviolent civil disobedience in the Temple by turning over the tables in a symbolic act of transformation. Along the way, he curses a fig tree, biblical symbol of Israel (Mk 11:12-13). This "parable in action" portrays Jesus looking for fruit from the faithful people and not finding it. Instead, he finds the Temple of God turned into a "den of thieves."

Likewise, today, Jesus curses the structures of war, beginning with the Pentagon, because they do not bear the good fruit of justice and peace. Additionally, Jesus curses the institutional church for not resisting injustice. We need to recognize our complicity with injustice and begin the process of conversion—so that we might become an authentic church that reflects the revolutionary life of Jesus.

March 12th

Seventeen years ago today, Salvadoran death squads assassinated Jesuit priest Rutilio Grande as he moved between Eucharist in one village to Eucharist in another village. Rutilio had publicly condemned injustice and poverty. His death sparked the dramatic conversion of Archbishop Romero and the transformation of the Salvadoran church. Rutilio, pray for us.

Jesus turns over the tables in a dramatic act of nonviolence (Mk 11:15-19). He does not hurt or kill anyone, but he significantly disrupts business as usual. He stages a sit-in, a nonviolent blockade. Instead of religion and empire collaborating together to oppress the poor, Jesus calls for real worship, "a house of prayer for all peoples."

This passage serves as the basis for my presence in jail. I went to Seymour Johnson Air Force Base because Jesus went to the Temple. Jesus confronts the Temple through active nonviolence and suffers the consequences. He insists on God's reign, and through his civil disobedience, remains obedient to God. Trying to be faithful to Jesus, we go to the nuclear weapons centers and announce the coming of God's reign. Now, we suffer the consequences of our action. Our suffering does not compare to the crucifixion of Jesus. Nonetheless, we struggle to follow. I pray that we might take God even more seriously and be faithful to the disruptive Jesus.

March 13th

The fig tree withers. Jesus tells the disciples, "Have faith in God. I say to you, whoever says to this mountain, 'Be lifted up and thrown into the sea,' and does not doubt in her heart but believes that what she says will happen, it shall be done for her. Therefore, I tell you, all that you ask for in prayer, believe that you will receive it and it shall be yours. When you stand to pray, forgive anyone against whom you have a grievance, so that God may in turn forgive you your transgressions" (Mk 11:20-26).

The mountain stands for the Roman empire. Jesus admonishes the community to trust in God, not the idolatrous Temple system and its empire. Faith, prayer and forgiveness interconnect in Jesus' transforming nonviolence. Pray to God, forgive one another and act out of your faith that injustice will be overcome.

After our bible study, we share Eucharist in this Temple of the Spirit, here in jail. We stand in faith, prayer and forgiveness. We hope and trust that our suffering and imprisonment will bear fruit for disarmament. Despite our failings, God is in our midst.

March 14th

Jesus encounters total opposition to his action in the Temple. Mark presents four confrontations with the chief priests and Scribes over the respective questions of authority, taxes, resurrection and the commandments. When the religious leaders question his authority, he retorts: "I will ask you a question." He questions them as to whether John the Baptist's baptism was of God and reduces them to silence. He reveals their ignorance. They do not speak with authority. He tries to solicit a change of heart, to help them see themselves, but they remain trapped by pride and prestige.

"Who gives you authority?" people ask us. "Who gives you the right to hammer on government property?" We hear these questions often. We answer by invoking the Spirit of life and the Word of God. We find our authority in Jesus. We act in the name of Jesus. We believe in Jesus and trust him; we take him at his word; we try to do what he says. Jesus is the center of our lives.

March 15th

"Jesus' nonviolent action in the Temple," Phil comments, "kicks out the legs of the empire and pinpoints the place where we internalize the empire." Jesus' political act binds the strong man. He calls for an end to the entire system. Jesus follows his action with teaching. Citing Hosea, Isaiah, Jeremiah and even Malachi, he explains that the Temple is no longer about sacrifice, atonement or prayer: it is robbing the poor. As the fig tree story symbolizes, the Temple system is rotten to the core and needs to die.

Abandon faith in the Temple, Jesus declares, and place your faith in God. The mountain of imperial violence can be turned upside-down, Jesus proclaims. The world's injustice can be overturned. All that is required is faith in God. For faith, we need to pray. The one condition of prayer is forgiveness of those who have hurt us. Without forgiveness, we can have no faith.

What is the nonviolent alternative which Jesus offers instead of the corrupt Temple state? The community of faith, prayer and forgiveness succeeds the Temple as the site of true worship. We can worship God anywhere, as long as we are in community together, praying and forgiving one another, even in jail.

Today, for us, the Temple of our times is the Pentagon. At one point in the Cold war, the Pentagon administered over 300 U.S. military bases around the world. People have internalized the spirit of the Pentagon. Not one institution has seriously challenged the Pentagon and its nuclear weapons system. And, the churches are called to do just that.

Tonight, a new cellmate joins us. He was yelling and cursing for a while, then ate dinner, got some sleep and finally began to inquire about our predicament. We told our Plowshares story and after a few questions, he concluded, "That's cool, man." I marvel how this fellow, picked up off the streets of Edenton, so quickly grasps the meaning of our action, when many well-educated, privileged, religious people actively oppose it.

March 16th

Waking up in jail each morning is a shock. I confess that at some subconscious level, I deny that I'm here or that I'll be here long. Then I wake at the sound of the jailer or the lights coming on or when I almost fall off my top bunk—and reality strikes: You are in jail! You are "a danger to the community," a threat to national security. You are—a disciple of Jesus.

I reach for a cup of coffee and awake to the new day; and I thank the good God for my life, for the grace of being here, for trying to be a voice for peace.

*

We open our bibles to the parable of the tenants (Mk 12:1-12). The tenants who guard a vineyard keep beating up and killing the owner's servants who come to inquire about the vineyard. When a beloved son is sent, the tenants kill him, hoping to gain the entire vineyard. In the end, the owner returns, the tenants die (as a consequence of their own violence) and the vineyard is handed over to others.

Though the parable capsulizes the story of the martyred prophets, Jesus and the early community, it is our story, too. From Haiti to El Salvador to South Africa to our own land, prophets of justice and peace have been killed defending the vineyard and speaking out for the God of the vineyard. Martin King, Oscar Romero, Jean Donovan, Ita

Ford, Steve Biko, Mohandas Gandhi, Maura Clarke and Dorothy
Kazel—these prophets call us to the prophetic ministry of defending
the vineyard of the earth. The urgency of the parable cries out. But the
concluding note rings with hope: "The stone rejected has become the
cornerstone." The house of God, the house of peace, stands on the
martyred faithful, beginning with Jesus.

March 17th

The Pharisees and Herodians try to entrap Jesus by flattering
him. "Teacher, we know that you are a truthful person and that you are
not concerned with anyone's opinion, that you do not regard a person's
status but teach the way of God in accordance with the truth" (Mk
12:14). When we contrast this description of Jesus with the modern
day all-American, we are shocked by the distance we have drifted.
How rare to find someone who speaks the truth regardless of the consequences. The Pentagon and the government are founded on lies. As a
people, we are very insecure. Jesus knows himself. He is secure in
God. Our entire culture is founded on status, on getting ahead, on making it, on becoming successful. Jesus is so free. He lets go of status.
He is not impressed at all with the upper class, the privileged, the elite.
He has a preferential love for the poor and marginalized. He will soon
be one of them. He teaches about God in accordance with the truth.

The confrontation builds. Should we pay taxes to Caesar? The
question of paying imperial taxes was at the heart of first century politics. It became the key issue of the Jewish revolt which led to the
destruction of Jerusalem in the year 70. Jesus responds to their test
with a challenge: "Bring me a denarius. Whose image and inscription
is on it?" The Pharisees should not have had any coins. Jesus exposes
their complicity in Roman occupation. They profit from the imperial
exploitation of the poor, whereas Jesus does not have a denarius to his
name. Worse than that, the coin declares, "Caesar, the Divine One."
They are guilty of idolatry.

The punchline explodes like dynamite. "Repay to Caesar what is
Caesar's and to God what is God's." If Israel is in complete debt to
God—and it is—they owe God everything. As Dorothy Day said,
"Once we give God what belongs to God, there's nothing left to give
to Caesar." Not only are we not to pay taxes to the empire, we must
resist the empire's killing machine. We give our lives to God and

God's struggle for peace. Our allegiance is to God, as Jesus demonstrated, by dying on Caesar's cross.

*

The NBC-TV show *Dateline* interviews Phil this morning. They pummel him with questions: What difference has your life made? What good does it do to be in jail? How effective are you? Phil responds patiently. Meanwhile, our other cellmate was released this afternoon.

March 18th

Pressed to speak about the most intense political issue of the day, the question of paying taxes to Caesar, Jesus turns the question to God. Where does God fit into this political question? I find this dynamic instructive and wish to apply the same theological urgency to every question of our times. How does God fit into our culture and political system?

Such questions challenge my own life: Where is God for me in jail? I have not been outdoors in three and a half months. It is pouring rain outside and beautiful lightning fills the sky; it is followed by thunder. I sit in these ugly rooms. Phil writes letters next to me on the table. Bruce reads on his bunk. Where is God for us? Where is God in my day to day life? First of all, God resides clearly in our sharing of the Word, in the breaking of the bread and the passing of the cup. Also, God is present to us in each other, in our struggle toward patience and kindness to one another. God is present in all the other inmates. God is present in our souls, where Jesus leads us by the hand, trying to heal us of our blindness. The inner experience, even here in jail, offers the deepest peace, the consoling presence of God. In that inner space, sitting up long after the lights went out the other night, it occurred to me that I would not want to be anywhere else in the world than right here now in jail with these friends. I was shocked by this realization. And I remember moments in El Salvador, Guatemala, Nicaragua, the Philippines, Haiti and Israel, my work among the homeless poor and visiting people on death row, the years teaching and studying—and I recall the many times when I felt that the greatest deed I could do with my life would be to go to jail for a nonviolent protest against war. In this place, I feel the gentle presence of Jesus in my life. He leads me into new spiritual territory. A deeper spirituality beckons me. This deepening is a great grace and I want to pursue it.

March 19th

A quiet Saturday afternoon. The cell is freezing. Phil sleeps soundly. Bruce rests in the cell next door. In the small common room, a new cellmate watches basketball. He is catatonic, completely unresponsive. We try to be human with him, but find it difficult since he does not respond.

Because we seek God, we taste an inner freedom beyond anything the world offers. Suffering in the nonviolent struggle for peace is redemptive. We are being pruned, purified, and healed. The living God tests us in the furnace of life—through our confrontation with death at the military base, through the courts, and through the day to day survival in jail. We survive because we read the Gospel, break bread and pass the cup. We survive through God's grace in the spirit of contemplative love.

In this jail, I find Jesus in my friends and cellmates, in the guards, the FBI agents and Federal Marshals, in my relatives and supporters who visit. God comes to me in those still, silent moments when I am least aware, beckoning me, blessing me. My task in jail: to let go, to go deeper, to let Jesus lead. In this journey, I taste freedom.

March 20th

"You shall love the Lord your God, with all your heart, all your soul, with all your mind and with all your strength. And you shall love your neighbor as yourself" (Mk 12:29-30). Thus, Jesus joins two central pieces of the biblical puzzle (Dt 6:4-5 and Lv 19:18) and calls them the greatest commandment. We love God by loving our neighbor. The scriptures boil down to this. Our neighbors are made in the image of God—in them, we find God. But who is our neighbor?, the Gospel asks. As Jesus explains by the parable of the Good Samaritan, the enemy is our neighbor. To love God, we must love our enemies. Jesus loves himself, the neighbor, his enemies and God. Jesus fulfills these commands. He loves God so much that he denies himself, takes up the cross, and offers his life as a ransom for humanity. He invites us to follow.

Here in jail, I find these commands hard, a struggle to fulfill. I strive to love others. But I find myself selfish, mean, egotistical, even hate-filled. I find it hard to love others. Yet this is the only thing asked of me. Love, love, love beyond measure.

March 21st

Good letters today from Tom Gumbleton, Joe Sand, S.J., Shelley Douglass, Brother Patrick Hart, Lynda Ward (a theology graduate student at Duke), and Professor Stanley Hauerwas also from Duke. Henri Nouwen writes that his L'Arche Daybreak community in Toronto held an evening session to reflect on our action and "to unite our way of peacemaking with yours."

Yesterday, Phil recounted the stress-filled weeks in 1970 while he was in prison while Dan traveled underground. Later, in 1972, Phil endured over five months on trial in Harrisburg, Pennsylvania. At the end of one long day, he returned to the jail cell to the news that Nixon had resumed carpet bombing of North Vietnam. He broke down and wept. All the terrible bombings that Nixon ordered! "How am I to love Nixon?" Phil asked himself. "By nonviolently resisting the war," came the clear reply.

March 22nd

Our poor cellmate—quiet, catatonic, helpless—was dragged off to court today. Yesterday afternoon I was interviewed by a probation officer: Would I kindly give out all the "pertinent information" on my parents and brothers—where they can be reached, their political views, their line of work. No thank you, I replied. Would I please list my previous arrests and trouble with the government. Thank you, no. Instead, I spoke about my work with the poor and my discipleship to Jesus. Why is it, this friendly young African-American woman asked, that God is close to prisoners? God is always close to those who suffer, to the oppressed, to the victims of systemic injustice, I replied. God is close to us prisoners. God exudes a preferential option for the poor, the oppressed, the imprisoned. I offered her a question: what is

God's position towards those who work for brutal governments, including its judges, jailers, police officers, and probation officials?

*

Jesus denounces the religious establishment for oppressing the poor, accepting extolment in the market place, accepting predominant seats in the synagogue and places of honor at banquets—while devouring the houses of widows! (Mk 12:38-44) He sits down in front of the bank at the Temple and watches poor, oppressed women handing over their last coins. He is livid; the system crushes the poor who pay their last penny. The elite profit from this robbery under the pretext of long prayers. The passage challenges my complicity in the institutional injustice of the church, which oppresses the poor in the name of Jesus. We Jesuits are very much like the Scribes. The solution, for me, is to follow Jesus to the cross, to stay in the church and resist, to join Jesus in liberating the oppressed poor.

March 23rd

Henri Nouwen sent me his new book, *Our Greatest Gift*, a meditation on dying well and caring for one another. He writes:

> Is death something so terrible and absurd that we are better off not thinking or talking about it? Is death such an undesirable part of our existence that we are better off acting as if it were not real? Is death such an absolute end of all our thoughts and actions that we simply cannot face it? Or is it possible to befriend our dying gradually and live open to it, trusting that we have nothing to fear? Is it possible to prepare for our death with the same attentiveness that our parents had in preparing for our birth? Can we wait for our death as for a friend who wants to welcome us home? . . . People are dying. Not just the few I know, but countless people everywhere, every day, every hour. Dying is the most general human event, something we all have to do. But do we do it well? Is our death more than an unavoidable fate that we simply wish would not be? Can it somehow become an act of fulfillment, perhaps more human than any other human act? . . . We can choose to befriend our death as Jesus did. We can choose to live as God's beloved children in solidarity with all people, trusting in our ultimate fruitfulness. And in so doing, we can also

become people who care for others. As men and women who have faced our mortality, we can help our brothers and sisters to dispel the darkness of death and guide them toward the light of God's grace.

Tonight, news arrives that an F16 has crashed at nearby Pope Air Force Base, killing over 15 people, injuring over 75 people. We mourn the loss of life, pray for the families of the victims, and look for the coming of disarmament.

*

We read Mark 13, the apocalyptic sermon of Jesus, offered as he sits on the Mount of Olives overlooking Jerusalem. Mark wrote this text during the turmoils of the 60s, during the Roman occupation and Jewish insurrection. "Do not be deceived," Jesus orders. "Do not be alarmed" (Mk 13:3-8). He opposes the oppression of Temple functionaries and Roman occupiers as well as the violence of revolutionaries. He envisions the end of the Temple-based world and the beginning of God's reign of peace, God's domination-free order. He warns against joining the violent revolutionaries who would wage a messianic war in defense of the Temple. Jesus teaches an eschatology of nonviolence, the nonviolent coming of God and the politics of nonviolent resistance. Today, we are to follow Jesus and reject revolutionary violence, imperial oppression, mainstream church domination and exclusion and the false prophets of the culture (from academia to media). We must resist evil and practice nonviolence.

March 24th, the Fourteenth Anniversary of the Martyrdom of Oscar Romero

Keep watch, Jesus warns. There is no better place to keep watch here in the United States at the end of the 20th century than in this jail. We sit here, on ice for our resistance, and watch the culture. Our presence here is a profound witness against our culture's violence. Keeping watch means living as contemplatives, people of prayer who listen to God and look for God's presence in the world. Such is our task.

March 25th

What is the peace of Christ? As we reflect on this question, we turn to the Gospel of John: "My peace I give you, but not as the world gives." After Jesus is executed for his peacemaking activities, he appears to the peacemaking community which is gathered behind closed doors in great fear. "Peace be with you," Jesus says. Then he shows them his hands and his side. "Peace be with you," he says to them again. What are we to learn from this breathtaking scene? For Christ, the gift of peace comes only through the cross. He offers them his peace, shows them his wounds and invites them to follow him. If we want to know his peace, we must take up the cross and follow.

March 26th

We talked into the night about the upcoming court trials: how do we respond to the *in limine* order from Judge Boyle? Do we accept the court appointed lawyers? Should we use any lawyers as stand-by counsel? What stance should we take in the courtroom—vocal confrontation or silent non-cooperation? What is the main purpose of our presence in the courtroom? How do we witness to Christ, expose the systemic injustice and speak the truth?

After the cataclysmic last days of tribulation, when the powers will be shaken, "the 'Human One' will come in the clouds with great power and glory" (Mk 13:26). This climactic moment in fact occurs when Jesus dies on the cross, the most spiritually explosive moment in history. At the point of Jesus' complete powerlessness, the domination system topples and death is overcome. So too in jail, in our powerlessness, in our Christian weakness, we are most powerful. We become instruments of God's transforming grace. In this place of powerlessness, Mark writes, keep watch. And so we sit here, reflective, chastened, beloved, keeping watch.

12

Holy Week

Jail provides the appropriate context for meditation on the Passion of Jesus. Thus, we begin Holy Week reflecting on the cross. Politics, spirituality, and life itself are best understood from the perspective of the cross, the prism of nonviolence.

Today, Phil, Bruce, and I mailed a letter (with Lynn's agreement and signature) to Judge Boyle: "We write to register our total opposition to the *in limine* order. We feel it removes any prospect for justice when we come before you. All people are called to work for an end to injustice, oppression and war, Judge Boyle. This is what it means to be human. War and preparations for war will eventually go the way of slavery and the only path to this eventuality is the road of nonviolence and voluntarily accepted suffering. As our trials approach, we request that you ponder your own role in bringing about a world free of injustice, a world free of weapons and greed. . . . We urge you to join us in the struggle for justice and peace, by declaring our indictments invalid and indicting the government for preparing omnicide."

*

My brother Steve and his wife Janet visit this afternoon, along with Patrick O'Neill. Then, Martin Sheen arrives at 5:00 until 6:30. Mike allows this special visit and offers the plush sheriff's office, on condition that Martin would visit with Mike's mother and others after. Twenty-six people show up. Martin was buoyant as ever, filled with good humor and stories about his work. He leaves soon for filming in Zagreb, in the former Yugoslavia. His presence boosts my spirit immeasurably.

March 28th

We begin the day by reading Mark's full account of the passion of Jesus. Then, we sit in silence.

Today, we discuss the religious authorities' plot to kill Jesus (Mk 14:1-9). At the house of a leper, a woman approaches and anoints Jesus with oil—as if to prepare him for burial (or ordain him king). The disciples are furious. "That money could be spent on the poor and you waste it on Jesus," they complain. Thus, they insult Jesus: No one serves Jesus, except now this good woman. Indeed, she is portrayed as the ideal disciple: she accepts his impending passion as victory. She anoints him. The male disciples don't have a clue about Jesus' impending death and its transforming nonviolence.

March 29th

We discuss today the theme of betrayal vs. intimacy (Mk 14:10-21). Mark portrays Jesus as a fugitive: undercover authorities plot against him; his community meets underground (as the secret signals and anonymous network used to find a safehouse for passover indicate). And betrayal comes from within the community: Judas is one of Jesus' most intimate friends. He turns on Jesus because, as a zealot, he rejects Jesus' nonviolence. When Jesus predicts this imminent betrayal, each disciple asks in shock if they are going to betray him. They all incriminate themselves. They are all complicit. In a few hours, they all abandon him.

And how does Jesus respond? He neither betrays nor denies them. At the moment of betrayal, denial and abandonment, he moves in with even greater intimacy! He offers himself completely, as bread and wine, to be their food and drink. Everyone is against him yet he responds with pure nonviolence, intimate love, complete forgiveness.

We too, like every disciple, betray Christ. We ask ourselves where, when and how we have betrayed Christ in our lives. How have we betrayed our communities, our friends, the poor? How have we been betrayed? How has the church betrayed us? Most importantly, how have we responded? Have we retaliated or have we responded like Christ with even greater, intimate love? How do we share Christ's intimate love with others? Where do we feel Christ offering us his intimate love and forgiveness?

March 30th

The Eucharist offers the clearest sign of God's intimate love for each of us. "This is my body. Eat it. This is my blood. Drink it. Do this in memory of me" (Mk 14:22-26). Jesus updates the Passover memorial meal. He invites them into the struggle here and now. He offers us a way to remember him. At the hour of betrayal, abandonment and arrest, he reconciles us, transforms us, sustains us and missions us in the Eucharist. This humble meal remains the ultimate peacemaking gift.

When the lights go out, I sit up late, trying to create a space for Jesus in my life. Come into my heart, Jesus. Be present here. Come, share your intimate love with us.

*

My friend Patrick Atkinson, who runs a center for homeless youth in Guatemala, was shot at by government death squads the other day as he was driving a van filled with children through the countryside. He had recently called for a government investigation of an unmarked mass grave of children discovered in his backyard, left there by the previous owner.

Holy Thursday, March 31st

Today, we discuss Peter's denial of Jesus. We confess that Peter's denial is sadly understandable. If Peter had acknowledged his friendship and faith, he too would have been crucified. Who among us would risk our lives in similar circumstances? With this action, I have risked my freedom for the Gospel: yet, like Peter, I would be afraid to risk my life by being associated with the revolutionary Jesus. I still have a long way to go on the journey of fidelity.

Our publisher friend Frank Fortkamp visited this morning. Later on, Bishop Walter Sullivan celebrated Eucharist with us. This afternoon, I worked on an article, wrote letters and took a nap. Tonight, we finished watching the film series *Jesus of Nazareth*. The trial, torture, crucifixion and resurrection scenes brought the human Jesus to life for us. They inspire a new consciousness of Jesus' life.

Good Friday, April 1st

There is no better place to be on the day marking the execution and death of our Lord than here in jail for nonviolent resistance to evil. Though we are not tortured, we are imprisoned by the United States government for opposing war and nuclear weapons. We are trying to follow Jesus and to share his determined Gospel proclamation. Today, I share in Jesus' cross and taste his resurrection.

We read of Jesus' agony in the Garden of Gethsemani. Jesus calls his disciples to community. He commands them to remain awake, to keep watch and pray. He prays to God, "not my will but your will be done" (Mk 14:32-42). He is terrified, but he can face the cross because he prays to God. Prayer is the only way to undergo suffering and death and still remain nonviolent, faithful, and loving.

How prayerful are we? How obedient to God? How awake? Do I pray that God's will be done, not mine, even if that means I must suffer?

I think of the millions today who remember the suffering and death of Jesus. I pray that we might all have the courage to follow Jesus on the way of the cross. I think too of our many friends who march for justice and peace in Washington, D.C., New York City, the Bay Area and Los Angeles. This day challenges us to resist the state nonviolently and accept the consequences in a spirit of forgiving, transforming love. Are we willing to risk our own Good Friday?

Holy Saturday, April 2nd

These small, stone rooms feel like a tomb. Yet we claim to live in the resurrection, so we try not to give jail or death power over us. Bruce and I talk for a few hours about life in jail. I work on an article, write some notes in preparation for our trials and read some of Merton's *Zen and the Birds of Appetite*, which Brother Patrick sent me from the Abbey of Gethsemani. During bible study, we reflect on the betrayal and arrest of Jesus, and how he exposes the state's violence. He lives nonviolence and the empire can only respond by sending out hundreds of armed men to arrest him. Violence, as Gandhi observes, is the sole recourse of government. It is inherently coercive.

We see our arrest as a sharing in the arrest of Jesus. We entered Seymour Johnson Air Force Base in a spirit of nonviolence and were met with hundreds of armed soldiers. A government which sees militarism as a solution to famine and execution as a solution to murder could not respond otherwise.

Yesterday on Good Friday and April Fool's Day, Fr. Carl Kabat dressed up as a clown and disarmed a missile silo in North Dakota. Though he hammered for a short time, he may well receive a long prison sentence. We rejoice in his witness for peace.

Easter Sunday, April 3rd

What does the resurrection mean in a world of death and destruction? To us, it means being hopeful in the face of despair, being faithful in the face of faithlessness, being nonviolent in the face of worldly violence. "Resistance to death epitomizes the resurrection," Phil states. If we fail to resist war and systemic violence, we implicitly practice despair, faithlessness or apathy. Wendell Berry concludes one of his poems with the admonition to "practice resurrection." Look death and destruction in the face and still insist on life and peace. Living the Spirit of resurrection requires living life to the full. Sharing in the resurrection means confronting death with the fullness of life. And so, we try to be people of love and hope.

This morning, I sense the risen Jesus in our midst. We see him in each other, in the breaking of the bread, the passing of the cup, and the exchange of his peace. As we have shared in Jesus' cross of nonviolent resistance, so too we glimpse his resurrection. The blessings continue. Praise God.

It has been a good morning, and I sense a new dawn. I want to experience the new life of resurrection, to know the risen Jesus in our midst, to have that mystical experience of freedom in jail. This morning, I have hope. Death does not have the last word. Nuclear weapons, war, F15Es, the Pentagon, injustice, and the culture itself are not in control. They do not have the last word. God does: Jesus is risen.

*

Jesus' trial is a complete farce (Mk 14:53-65). The Sanhedrin railroad him: they meet at night; they issue an *in limine* order; they gather false testimony; they convict him; they spit at him, mock him and hit him. As we face trial next week, we pray that we might share in the trial of Jesus. Mark invokes Daniel and portrays Jesus as the judge in charge, as the "Human One" coming in the power of nonviolence, in the glory of God. We hope to stand trial in this spirit, as witnesses to the resurrection, to denounce death and proclaim the way, the truth and life of nonviolence.

*

Bruce and I stay up talking about the meaning of the resurrection in our lives. I recall my first real Easter, in 1981, after my conversion and decision to enter the Jesuits, when I joined Catholic students at the Duke University Newman Center for an Easter Sunday picnic in the Duke gardens. That afternoon in the sunlight was a moment of idyllic peace and joy. I remember the Easter at the Jesuit novitiate in Wernersville, Pennsylvania in 1984, talking late into the evening with another novice about the meaning of resurrection, when suddenly, an earthquake struck! This Easter, in jail, I sense Christ in our midst and rejoice in his resurrection. May the days ahead be filled with alleluia!

Monday, April 4th, the 26th Anniversary of Martin Luther King, Jr.'s Assassination

We celebrate Eucharist at 6:30 a.m. and shared John's account of the resurrection. Then, we continue our regular bible study, today about Peter's denial of Jesus (Mk 14:66-72). While Jesus is inside being tortured by the authorities, Peter sits outside in the courtyard warming himself by the fire! Peter emphatically denies knowing Jesus three times. This great disciple boasted only hours before of his loyalty, and now he curses and swears that he does not know Jesus. Then, he "remembers Jesus' word." He breaks down and weeps. His tears begin his conversion back to Jesus.

In order not to deny Jesus, we need to deny America and its power over us. We need to set aside our fears and seek God's reign. It's one or the other. We are going to have to deny the state in order to remain faithful to Jesus.

We ask: How do we deny Jesus and how can we serve him? How do we seek the warmth and comfort of the authorities who torture the poor? How does the church deny Christ and support killing? Do we break down and weep over our denials?

*

A quiet, uneventful day spent reading mail (including an original poem from Denise Levertov), writing to friends, and meditating. I think of Martin Luther King, Jr. and pray that he may intercede for me and help me to be an instrument of Christ's peace and justice.

Tuesday, April 5th

Time slows to a standstill. Mainly, I am tired and feel claustrophobic. We cannot leave these cramped quarters. We can not go out for a walk or fresh air. We can not have a cup of coffee or see a friend. We can't even sit in contemplative silence. Our two cellmates keep the TV going all day long. Sometimes, I just manage to survive.

This morning, we discuss Jesus on trial before Pilate (Mk 15:1-5). Jesus stands silent. He is the Suffering Servant portrayed by Isaiah (chapter 53). He denies the illegitimate power of the Romans. Indeed, he is the real judge. Jesus is helpless, powerless, defenseless, trusting solely in God, not in Roman power. His pure nonviolence inspires me to stay centered in the Spirit of nonviolence as I stand trial next week: Jesus, may my standing in court be a sharing in your courtroom witness. May I testify to your way of peace and inspire conversion of heart—just as you did.

April 6th

Jesus is condemned. Scourged. Tortured. Crowned by a ring of thorns. Mocked by the guards. Jesus is abused, hurt, humiliated, and finally sent to death. We comment that though jail is not easy, we do not suffer as Jesus did. Jesus is brutally murdered. We are merely jailed. He responds nonviolently, keeps his eyes on God and his heart overflows with love and forgiveness. How do we respond to our jailers? To the judge? To the police? To the federal marshalls? Can we radiate pure, nonviolent love to those who oppress us? Jesus commands that we do just that.

"If Jesus teaches us anything, it is not how to kill, but how to die," the late theologian John MacKenzie wrote. How prepared are we to undergo suffering and death? I recall how miserable I felt after I had my wisdom teeth removed a few years ago. I never wanted to be sick again, much less respond with love towards others in the midst of my suffering. I have a difficult time when I'm well being kind towards those around me, including my family and friends. I'm not always successful by any means. In the sufferings and crucifixion of Jesus, I learn not only resistance to the state and fidelity to God, but peaceableness and nonviolent love. Jesus' kingship is a reign of nonviolence. His nonviolent suffering love overcomes empires, nuclear weapons and death itself. Throughout it all, he radiates forgiving love. May I have the courage and strength to follow him into that martyrdom of love.

*

This afternoon, Carol Brothers, a local friend, and our friends at the Norfolk Catholic Worker, pay visits. The most remarkable moment of the day occurs when the chief jailer, Mike, comes by for a talk. With all sincerity, he pleads with Phil to get out of jail. "Let the young lions stay in and continue the protest," he says, looking to Bruce and me. "You're 70-years-old and should get out." He says we may well be in prison for ten years.

"What better place to be than in jail for peace?" Phil asks with a smile. "I can't think of a better place to be these days." The chief is completely astounded by this statement. "God will take care of us," I say to the chief. "I know," he replies, "but you can do so much more good on the outside." "This is where we need to be in order to oppose preparations for war," I say. "It's the greatest good we can do with our lives."

April 7th

It has been four long months since our Plowshares action. Perhaps for the first time, I'm thinking seriously of the possibility of years in prison. Maybe Mike is right. I quake at the thought. I pray for the grace to accept it in peace. I long to be an apostle of Gospel nonviolence and that requires that I be willing to suffer, as Martin King and Mahatma Gandhi recognized. The evil we oppose towers over humanity and can only be overcome through voluntary, suffering love. Some lives will have to be spent in prison and some will have to be offered up in the martyrdom of nonviolence. Why should I assume that only others must undergo this crucible? I offer myself for that sacrifice of love. I accept ten years if that is our future. I thank God for whatever lies ahead. It is a sharing in Christ's cross.

The cross is so objectionable! It is Jesus' insistence that social change comes about through suffering that is intolerable. Revolutionary nonviolence to the point of death is unacceptable, not only to passers-by, the religious authorities, and the disciples, but to most everyone who has ever lived. "Who of us is really prepared to accept that by remaining (on the cross), Jesus shows the way to liberation, to acknowledge that in this moment, the powers are overthrown and the kingdom is come in power and glory?" Ched Myers asks. "Do we not share that rage that the promise of a new order of justice and peace doesn't happen?"

The cross is the ultimate deterrent to those who would threaten the Roman empire. In Jesus' time, only political subversives were crucified on the empire's cross. We are summoned to join Jesus on the cross, to be at his right and left for our own revolutionary nonviolence. As we each go through the crucible of nonviolence—results, success, despair, abandonment, and our own violence get turned over and God uses our steadfast love to transform the world. Yes, the way of the cross is the only way to true liberation. It demands the ultimate price and that is why we are so scandalized and horrified.

*

After our bible study, the chief took all 25 inmates out to a drive-through garage. It was my first time outdoors in four months. On either side of the garage, chain link gates were lowered in place of garage doors to keep us in. We did not stand in the sun, but we could look outside at the green lawn, the magnolia trees, the birds, and the sky. Most of all, we felt the cool breeze. I am refreshed. I spent all 30 minutes looking through the metal bars up at the sky. My spirit was lifted and I offered a prayer of thanksgiving. Like Elijah, I found God in the gentle breeze and was granted new strength.

April 8th

At 5 a.m., I wake and pray for an hour and feel consoled by God's presence. In this spirit, I am filled with faith. I believe that my action and imprisonment will help contribute to nuclear disarmament and global transformation. I trust in God.

At 6:20, we held a short bible study on the death of Jesus (Mk 15:33-40). "My God, my God, why have you forsaken me?" Jesus cries out. Mark invokes Psalm 22 which begins in despair but concludes with triumphant hope. "You, O Lord, be not far from me; hasten to aid me. Rescue my soul from the sword. . . . My soul shall live. Let the coming generation be told of the Lord that they may proclaim to a people yet to be born the justice God has shown" (Ps 22:1, 20, 30-32). Jesus dies and at the moment of his death, the Temple veil is torn in two: the dominant order falls. The nonviolent suffering love of Jesus brings it down. Likewise, nuclear weapons will be dismantled. War will be abolished. Justice and peace dawn upon humanity. The earth turns a corner into the light. God be praised.

*

Yesterday afternoon, I had a great visit with my brother Steve. Today, Patrick O'Neill came by with a briefcase full of illegal food: prunes, figs, bananas, juice, peanuts, cheese, crackers and chocolates. Patrick told hilarious stories of his felonious peacemaking adventures. I felt nervous the whole time eating contraband food in a room with a big window where every few minutes a guard passes by and looks in. Patrick also brought mail, newsletters, pens, pencils and paper. I wrote letters and read the fourth volume of Thomas Merton's letter, entitled *The Courage for Truth*, which my mother sent.

April 9th

I dread the upcoming court appearance. I want to speak openly and to persuade the authorities to join in our efforts for disarmament. I long to be open to the Holy Spirit. Yet I expect the Judge to silence me immediately, even to haul me out. I do not relish this confrontation, yet I know this stand must be taken.

Joseph of Arimathea asks Pilate for Jesus' body. Without anointing the body, as Jewish custom demands, he lays Jesus in a tomb and rolls a stone in front of it (Mk 15:42-47). Mary Magdalene and the other Mary (Jesus' mother?) observe where the body is laid. Until the end, they keep watch. They are faithful.

What can we conclude? A lesson, perhaps, about being faithful to the end and beyond; about loving Jesus, serving Jesus, staying with Jesus; about looking despair and death in the face if we want to witness resurrection. The women were faithful. Because they saw that Joseph was concerned only about burying the body before the sabbath began and thus did not anoint it, they come back after the sabbath to anoint Jesus. They encounter the risen Jesus. Their love leads them to the risen Jesus. Our love must also look death in the face while remaining faithful if we wish to meet the risen Jesus.

April 10th

"Jesus is risen! He is not here. He is going before you to Galilee. There you will see him, as he told you" (Mk 16:1-8). The stone has been rolled away. There could be no more hopeful image than the risen Jesus standing outside the empty tomb.

We continually ask ourselves: What does the resurrection of Jesus mean in the age of Auschwitz, Hiroshima, Vietnam, El Salvador, and Iraq? What does it mean that our survival is guaranteed? Where do we encounter the risen Jesus? What does the fear of the women tell us about our own fear, and about the meaning of resurrection? Are we willing to go through crucifixion to share in Christ's resurrection? In a culture of death, how do we announce the good news of resurrection?

Ched Myers writes that the Gospel is "a never-ending story." The only way, according to Mark, to truly see the risen Jesus is to start the narrative again in our own lives. The only way to resolve it is through our own participation in the cross of resistance. "For Mark the resurrection is not an answer, but the final question," Myers writes. "There is only one genuine 'witness' to the risen Jesus: to follow in discipleship. Only in this way will the truth of the resurrection be preserved."

13

The Trials

Monday, April 11th, 1994

Phil stands before Judge Terrence Boyle, Prosecutor Bill Webb, and Assistant Prosecutor Christine Hamilton. "How can we consider ourselves not guilty of an action that we admit doing?" Phil asks the jury in his opening statement. "Did we disarm and damage an F15E Strike Eagle on the morning of December 7th or didn't we? Of course we did. If there was any doubt about it we would shout it from the housetops. Then how can we consider ourselves not guilty? The government's approach to our 20,000 nuclear warheads is one approach; ours is radically different. The government couldn't care less about the command 'Thou shalt not kill.'"

"Objection, Your Honor," Webb shouts. The judge calls Phil to the bench. They discuss his statement. The judge orders him not to violate the *in limine* order.

"I'll take the stand to testify as to why I came to Seymour Johnson Air Force Base on December 7th," Phil continues, "why I switched from fighting in World War II to being an aging peacemaker facing ten years in prison."

"Your Honor, I'm going to object," Webb exclaims.

"Sustained," the judge answers.

"You're the conscience of the community," Phil tells the jury. "Before you begin deliberation at the end of the trial, Judge Boyle will tell you what the law is. But beyond that law, there's another factor, and that's your conscience."

"Your Honor, I'm going to object," Webb says. They prevent Phil from explaining why we went to Seymour Johnson Air Force Base. The government's case begins. Ten Air Force personnel testify. "There was a lot of banging going on," one young airman says. Phil asks him to read the inscription on the hammer. "This one says, 'Disarm now. No more war. Christ lives. Love your enemies.' This other one says, 'Repent. God's kin-dom is at hand. No War, No More War, War Never Again. For the Spirit of Life, Resistance and Creation, Disarm and Live. Seek the Disarmed Christ.'"

Throughout the morning, they object to Phil and threaten him many times with contempt charges. Former US Attorney General Ramsey Clark sits next to Phil and quietly advises him. Meanwhile, Bruce and I remain back here in the cell, reflecting on these past four months. Eventually, the Federal Marshals call for us. They drive us to Elizabeth City where we are led to the holding cell.

It is two o'clock in the afternoon. Phil and Ramsey ask me to take the witness stand to testify on Phil's behalf. I agree and the guards lead me into the courtroom. The clerk tells me to raise my right hand and put my left hand on the Bible to swear me in. I ask if I may affirm instead. Then, following Phil's questions, I introduce myself. "Objection," the prosecutor shouts. "His character and life background are irrelevant." The judge agrees. Finally, Phil asks me to give "a thumbnail sketch of what happened on December 7th." I respond:

> On December 7th, 1993, I saw Philip and two other friends along with myself enter the Seymour Johnson Air Force Base. We walked onto the base. At one point we crossed a creek and we sat down and we prayed. We prayed for disarmament and for an end to war. We came to some trees, and then we came to a little bluff where we overlooked the whole of the Seymour Johnson Air Force Base. It was kind of a God's eye view of Seymour Johnson because you could see everything before you in a great panorama, perhaps over sixty F15 nuclear-capable bombers laid out before us. It seemed like hundreds of people roaming around, along with tanks, bulldozers, and trucks moving everywhere over hundreds of acres. The place was very well lit because they were on alert to bomb human beings in Bosnia. And they're always on alert for nuclear war. So this is what we saw. And we spoke of this, and we prayed for a day when this place, when these weapons would be dismantled. And we walked on further, to a tarmac, the air-

strip. We went further and came to one F15 plane. Two of our friends approached the plane first, and then Philip and I came up to the side of it. I approached it before Philip did and, knowing what it stands for and knowing God's command that we beat swords into plowshares and learn to practice nonviolence and disarm so that we live in peace, I began to hammer on the plane. Philip was in front of me. But immediately we were surrounded. I know that Phil was not doing anything willfully injurious that was destructive towards anyone. Indeed, Phil was preventing willful and injurious destruction of property and human life. We were arrested. We were ordered to come around the plane. I told the guards how we are nonviolent people.

"Your Honor, I'm going to object," Webb declares.
"Overruled," the judge answers. I continue:

I explained to the soldiers with the machine guns aimed at us that we are nonviolent people, that we are unarmed, that we have no intention of hurting anybody, indeed, that Philip and all of us have dedicated our whole lives to the nonviolence of God and to disarmament. I was saying this on behalf of Philip, Bruce and Lynn. For a moment, the guards who had their weapons aimed at us listened and maybe they did not kill us because they heard that we had no intention of hurting them or anybody. Indeed, that's why we were there—to stop the killing and stop the hurting. As I was saying this, I saw Phil unfurl a banner which said, "Disarm and Live." Phil also helped Bruce hold another banner which said, "the Pax Christi-Spirit of Life Plowshares." This is what I saw on December 7th, 1993: you trying to prevent the destruction of human life.

"What is the meaning of this banner 'Disarm and Live'?" Phil asks.

We were saying that the whole point of the F15 is to kill. To kill. It sums up what has happened to our society. Our society is completely militaristic, with over 20,000 nuclear weapons. It engages in . . .

"Objection!" Hamilton shouts.
. . . in wars around the world," I finish.

Phil asks several more questions, all of which are shot down by the prosecutors and the judge. Finally, he asks, "What did we intend by this action on December 7th? What was the intent?" I reply:

> Our intent was the exact opposite of willful and injurious destruction. It was a prayerful, peaceful, nonviolent, even spiritual response to the destruction of life, which these weapons are all about. So we went in, if you will, to try to offer a symbol to the country about the only way out of the madness of violence in our world, to say, we all need to disarm. We had no intention of going in there and hammering on every plane there or trying to commit any kind of vandalism or intending to hurt anybody. Exactly the opposite. Our whole life is dedicated towards love, nonviolence, justice, disarmament, trying to address the real questions of the world. So the intent was to stop the killing in a very simple human way and to offer a symbol of disarmament. We were trying to follow the commands of God, "Thou shalt not kill. Love your enemies. Beat swords into plowshares. Be human with one another." These weapons are aimed in complete disobedience to those commands of life and justice and peace. So we were trying to do something very noble and human for society, for the world, in our own humble, human way, as best we could.

"Objection, Your Honor," Hamilton declares.

"Sustained," the judge agrees.

Phil has no further questions for me. The prosecutor stands. "Who drove the car?" he demands to know. "I refuse to incriminate anyone," I say. "I take full responsibility for my own action." The judge orders the jury removed and lectures me on the duty of answering the question. Webb asks why I affirmed the truth instead of swearing on the Bible. He has prevented us from quoting from the Bible, I think to myself, and now he wants me to keep my hand on a closed Bible, as if to make sure that it stays closed. I tell him that the Sermon on the Mount forbids us to swear, that we are to "let our Yes be Yes and our No be No, to always tell the truth." Of course I will tell the truth, I assure him.

Both the judge and the prosecutor insist vehemently that I say who drove us to Seymour Johnson Air Force Base on December 7th. The judge threatens me with criminal contempt charges and more years in prison if I do not answer the question. I look at him and the prosecutor. They are furious. It seems they have waited for months to find out who else might have been involved in our action. They want to arrest others on conspiracy charges.

Yes, I tell them. I will answer the question. I will announce who drove the car.

The jury is called back. "Who drove the car?"

"Thank you for insisting that I answer this question," I explain. "You have helped me to articulate the truth about what we did on December 7th. We've spoken a lot about affirming the truth and speaking the truth, and I want to speak the truth. In all seriousness, in an effort to speak the whole truth, the one who drove the car was—THE HOLY SPIRIT!"

All hell breaks loose.

"Answer his question in terms of a temporal person," the judge screams at me. "Who drove you there?"

"The Spirit," I tell him.

"Who drove the automobile?"

"The Spirit," I repeat.

"Is that going to be your answer?" the judge asks.

"It's not an easy thing to go to Seymour Johnson," I submit. "Only God could drive us there."

"You're not going to tell who drove you?"

"I'm telling you honestly, Judge."

The judge orders the jury removed immediately. The prosecutor and the judge argue with Phil. They practically tear their hair out over my answer. The jury returns. The prosecutor asks me again. "I stand by my answer," I declare. The judge threatens me with criminal contempt. Then, he strikes my testimony from the record. I am brought back to the holding cell.

If I had been able to continue, I would have tried to explain myself further. "Do not be surprised," I would have told the judge. "The Holy Spirit can drive a car easily. Our God can not only drive a car, but can make a car and make a human being and make a bird. Our God made the universe and all humanity and the stars and the sun and the sky. Driving a car is nothing," I would have said. "What's harder is changing human hearts so they will stop killing one another and renounce war. Think about it," I would have urged him. "We were going into the deadly force zone of a military air force base to hammer on a nuclear bomber. Unarmed, nonviolently, prayerfully, we were facing armed soldiers and their weapons of mass destruction. Our act could only have been an act of God."

Phil gets halfway through his own testimony, but after countless objections to his personal life story, he gives up and rests his case. They whisk us back to our jail cell.

April 12th

This morning, we share Eucharist together and then Phil leaves to finish his trial. After an hour, the jury finds Phil guilty of destruction of government property. He returns before lunch.

This afternoon, I am allowed a long visit with my father. On Sunday, we visited with Steve and Patrick. Later that day, we visited with Dan, Liz, Jerry Berrigan, and Ramsey Clark. Tonight, I speak with Joe Cosgrove, who will be my legal advisor. I work on my statements and pray for strength and peace.

Wednesday, April 13th

The marshals drive me alone to court in the early morning hours. They take Phil and Bruce separately to the Albermarle District Jail. I look out the window at the little town where I was born and raised. We pass the kindergarten, the school and the church I attended as a boy. The weather is beautiful. The day belongs to God.

One by one, the judge calls potential jurors to the jury box. Nearly every one has a military background. One has worked at Seymour Johnson. Another flies F14 fighter bombers out of Norfolk. Judge Boyle calls me up to the bench and threatens me with criminal contempt charges if I violate his *in limine* order. I am not to discuss the US government, US nuclear weapons, the US military, international law, the Nuremberg Principles, God, Jesus, or any religious principles. I ask him if my supporters could please be allowed in, and point to the empty rows in the gallery. The judge launches a tirade against Patrick O'Neill and my supporters and the prosecutor argues against allowing anyone in besides my family and few friends, who are present already. "I know all about you," the judge declares as he squints in anger. "I know you are an expert at civil disobedience and well educated and that you know what you're doing." "I just want to invite some more of my friends in to see my trial," I respond to him.

The prosecutor speaks to the jury. Now it's my turn.

Judge Boyle, sisters and brothers of the jury, sisters and brothers in the courtroom, good morning. My name is John Dear and along with my friends, Philip Berrigan, Bruce Friedrich and Lynn Fredriksson, I've been in jail for over four months now since we witnessed at Seymour Johnson Air Force Base on December 7th, 1993. As you've just heard, the government has indicted me and charged me with, as I understand it, willful, injurious destruction of property, of a an F15 nuclear-capable bomber. I'm not a lawyer. I am just an ordinary human being like yourselves. During this trial, I will testify and the evidence will show that I'm not guilty of this charge. I will ask you to point out the real guilt by finding me not guilty of this crime. The question is, Did my friends and I hammer and disarm the F15 nuclear fighter bomber or not? If the answer is, yes, I am guilty. If the answer is no, I'm not guilty. This trial, as I understand it, will point to a third alternative, to a deeper understanding of what happened on December 7th, 1993, to a deeper understanding of reality, truth, responsibility, the basic laws of conscience and so forth. The evidence will show that I did hammer on the F15E nuclear bomber and thus symbolically attempted to disarm it and that I'm not guilty of any crime. I did it and I'm not guilty. I am not guilty of the crime of willful injury and destruction. The prosecution will call witnesses against me who will show that, in fact, we were nonviolent; that we did not hurt anyone or do any injury to anyone; that we unfurled a banner which read "Disarm and Live"; that we were peaceful and prayerful; and that we left a signed statement declaring that our willful intent was not about destruction, damage, or injury but exactly the opposite.

As we examine the question of intention, the question of will, the evidence will point to the deeper issues in this case—the real crime and the real guilt. . . . The evidence will show that my work, my life, my community is not about injury, willful destruction, or willful damage toward anything. I've spent my life writing and speaking and promoting non-injury, willful non-destruction, what Gandhi called nonviolence. Through my travels around the world's war zones where I've lived and worked with poor people, I've seen with my own eyes willful injury, damage and destruction. I have been dedicating my whole life to stopping willful injury, damage and destruction. I'm trying to stop the destruction of life with all my will, with all nonviolence, in the tradition of Jesus, Gandhi, Dorothy Day and Martin Luther King, Jr.

Testimony will show that my friends and I have tried to stop willful destruction. We have tried to stop whatever is destructive and injurious to human beings or to the planet itself. Underlying all of this, the evidence will show, will be my faith, my Christian passion, my commitment to the truth of nonviolence, which are, I think, very much at the heart of this case, this trial and the charge against me. I am trying to follow the consistent ethic of life which teaches "love your enemies," "thou shalt not kill," and "beat swords into plowshares." This commitment of nonviolent opposition to willful and injurious destruction of life, the evidence will show, brought me to Seymour Johnson Air Force Base on December 7th and brings me here to you this morning.

The government speaks about destruction, injuring, killing, and doing violence. I am not about any of these; my life is about nonviolent transformation, nonviolent enhancement of life, the sanctity of all life, the law of nonviolence. . . . Your responsibility as the jury is to seek and decide the truth of the matter. You are considered the conscience of the community. I ask you to follow your conscience, to consider deeply the truth of the matter, to find me not guilty, and in doing so, to say who or what is truly guilty of destruction of human life. Thank you very much.

The prosecutor objects four times. The judge argues about my understanding of the charge. Eventually, the government calls nine witnesses, most of them Air Force personnel who were taking part in war games on December 7th. I question them as best I can. At one point, I ask an officer to read the list of equipment on an F15E from a chart he brought with him. I ask him to explain what a bomb rack is. The prosecutor jumps to his feet. "A bomb rack is a bomb rack," he screams. "Everyone knows the plane is a military aircraft," the judge snorts. I try to let the military explain how the purpose of their work is to kill other human beings. The prosecutor and the judge keep trying to shut me up. A frustrating morning.

After lunch, I call Bruce to the stand. He talks about December 7th. After I question him, the prosecutor launches his attack: "Who drove the car? Whose car was it? Whose hammer was it? Isn't the person who drove the car in this courtroom? How did you get from Washington, DC to Seymour Johnson Air Force Base?" His questions reveal his hostility for Bruce and all of us. Bruce refuses to incriminate anyone. When it appears useless to continue, I strike Bruce's testimony and he leaves the stand. I rest my case.

As we recess, while the jury is leaving, the FBI agent stands and says to the prosecutor, in front of my parents and a row of Jesuits, "Makes you ashamed to be Catholic." The prosecutor replies, "Well, they're all just slime anyway."

The prosecutor and the judge hold such venomous anger towards me, I reflect, that if the death penalty were allowed as a sentence for hammering on one of their nuclear fighter bombers, they would insist on it. They care more for these idols than for human beings.

At 4 p.m., I offer a closing statement.

> Much has been said and much has not been said. There are more questions here than answers. . . . The government says that it has proven that I hammered on an F15E. I've said over and over again that of course I hammered on the bomber. If this charge is just about hammering then I'm guilty, but that's not what this is about at the deepest level, the deepest level of all human morality. We were not there to destroy. We were there to promote life. As one Air Force officer said on the stand this morning, his 'opinion' was that I had done damage. Opinion is one way of looking at this. I think it's far more than opinion. Am I guilty beyond a reasonable doubt of having hammered and damaged an F15 Strike Eagle nuclear-capable bomber, or was I about something deeper, something good, something just and nonviolent, not for myself, but for the whole of humanity, for the love of God. I'm very limited here today in what I can say. All I can ask you is to reflect on this, to follow your conscience, to follow your heart and to take a stand for peace and justice and disarmament for the love of God. Thank you for listening.

Within 30 minutes, I am found guilty. Like Phil, I will be sentenced on July 5th. The sentencing guidelines suggest 33 months in prison for me. Though this feels like the most oppressive day of my life, I know too that it will stand as one of the greatest days for I have tried to speak the truth of peace as best I could.

*

In the 1960s, Thomas Merton wrote to Daniel Berrigan: "On the day a given general or chief of state decides to push the button on the human venture, we must understand that his act will lie within the law. For we must understand that the end of the world will be legal."

April 14th

A two hour visit this morning with my parents, my brothers David and Stephen, and Richard McSorley, S.J. My parents are furious at the FBI agent and the prosecutor for their hateful remarks yesterday. My parents spoke out to the press about it. The marshals nearly arrested them for confronting the prosecutor about his comment. When reporters asked Mr. Webb about his statement, he denied it.

While I am still shaking from this confrontation with "the principalities and the powers," my brother Steve tells me heartbreaking news. My friend, Mev Puleo, a young writer and photographer who has traveled throughout Latin America to report on the life of the poor and their struggle for liberation, was diagnosed four days ago with a malignant brain tumor and may only have days to live. Tomorrow she will undergo brain surgery. There is a very small chance that she will survive the operation. The cancer covers half her brain. This afternoon, I spoke with her for one minute on the phone. She says she has had a good life and has no regrets. She tells me she supports me. I tell her I love her very much. Afterwards, while Phil naps and Bruce reads in his cell, I sit down and cry.

Mev Puleo is one of the greatest people I have ever known. She has done more in her short life than most people do in a long lifetime. Her photo-journalism reports on the life and death of the poor in Brazil, Guatemala, El Salvador, Nicaragua, Peru and Bolivia. Her new book, *The Struggle Is One: Voices and Visions of Liberation,* will soon be published. I think of our trip together to Haiti in October, 1992. I recall our weekly prayer meeting and discussions with our Pax Christi Oakland group. Along with her husband Mark Chmiel, she has begun to speak out and organize against US military aid to East Timor. She returned only a few weeks ago from Chiapas where she photographed the Zapatista uprising. Her laughter, dedication, photography, brilliance, great love, determined faith, and sharp mind are such tremendous gifts. I cannot imagine life without Mev. I weep and I pray. Bruce joins me in a fast that she will survive the operation and live longer. We sit in silent vigil several times throughout the day for her. Everything crashes to a halt here in my cell. I am totally powerless. I know that hundreds of people gather throughout the Bay Area praying that God will heal our beloved Mev. I struggle just to write this. I am numb. I keep repeating to myself, Mev, Mev, Mev. Jesus, hold her close.

*

This afternoon, I hear word that Mev has survived the surgery. The surgeons removed half of the tumor, the size of an orange. She may live six more months. She has asked for her glasses and chapstick. Bruce and I pray a prayer of thanksgiving to God.

April 16th

Mev is alive and facing her death. We are in jail. Martin's mother-in-law, Bruce's grandmother, and Phil's brother-in-law are dying. Over 20,000 people have been killed in the last week in Rwanda, according to today's news. On Wednesday night, just hours after I was found guilty, a US F15 fighter bomber shot down two US helicopters in Iraq, killing 26 people, including 19 Americans. Everywhere we look, death surrounds us.

We spend the morning reflecting on the resurrection of Jesus. Mark offers several ingredients for discipleship to the risen Christ: repentance, resistance, nonviolence, community and faith. In light of the killings and the dying around the world, from my friend Mev to the anonymous people of Rwanda, Christ invites us to live and love one another. We sit in silence. We share Eucharist.

Today, I speak on the phone with Steve and David, Steve Kelly, S.J., and Martin Sheen. I read Merton's *The Courage for Truth*. Our two cellmates, Robert and Stephen, left. A young African-American named Johnnie joins us. He stands trial on May 23rd and claims he's innocent. But as someone told us the other day, 95% of all prosecutions in the United States end in conviction. We greet him and invite him to make himself at home.

*

The richest 2.5 million people in the US, one percent of the population, have as much income as the one hundred million Americans with the lowest income. In the 1980s, while the military budget increased by 46%, the Federal budget for housing decreased by 77%; healthcare by 49%; and job training by 48%. For every dollar paid in income taxes, one cent goes toward housing, two cents to food, three cents to education, and fifty cents to the military.

The 1990s began with 18,000 megatons of explosive energy available in the world's nuclear arsenals. By comparison, 11 megatons of explosive energy were released by all the conventional weapons used in World War II, the Korean War and the Vietnam War combined. In those three wars, well over 60 million people were killed, to say nothing of the wounded or refugees.

April 17th

Phil offers a biblical reflection this morning on the role of women in Mark's Gospel. Mark depicts women as the faithful few who side with Jesus on the cross and encounter the angel at the empty tomb. In light of this scripture study, we examine our sexism and patriarchal attitudes, and speak about the women in our lives who inspire us to faith. I speak of Mev Puleo, Shelley Douglass, Kathy Shields and Elizabeth McAlister. They each fight patriarchy and practice Christian feminism with gentle love, humble service and quiet faith. They stand against the Pentagon and its wars. They point to the compassionate, peacemaking Christ. As Joan Chittister says, the women went to the men and announced the resurrection of Jesus, but the men refused to believe it. Two thousand years later, the women still announce the resurrection and we men still don't believe it.

*

An 18-year-old, soft-spoken man named Chris has joined us. They charge him with bank robbery. Given his long history of misdemeanors and previous felony convictions, Chris faces at least 15 years in prison. The inmates in the larger cell nearly beat him up last night, so the guards moved him in with us.

Monday, April 18th

Early this morning, they shackle us and bring us to Elizabeth City. I sit in a tiny cell between Bruce and Phil in the Albermarle District Jail. We may be called to testify at Lynn's trial. Our cell is four feet by seven feet long. One side has the standard jail bars and door. Down the hall, Gospel music plays on some radio. Sunlight pours in from a window across the hall.

Last night, nightmares kept me awake. Today, I am tired. I enjoyed riding through the countryside this morning, and right now I am content.

*

This morning, Lynn gave one sentence of her opening statement before the judge ordered the jury sent out. "We poured blood on the F15E to expose it as a tool of death," Lynn said in the presence of the jury. She gave her full statement to the judge and concluded that she would not cooperate with the trial. "I refuse to sanction the illusion that I am being allowed an adequate defense for my actions." She sat silent throughout the entire trial. She was quickly found guilty. We return at 5:00 p.m. After dinner, we share a simple Eucharist and give thanks for Lynn and the day's witness.

April 19th

This morning, after Eucharist, we discuss Mark's interpretation of Christian community. Communities center themselves on Christ, the evangelist writes. We disciples live in the Spirit of the risen Jesus. We announce the Gospel and denounce demonic violence. We speak again about our own experiences in community and how hard, yet how crucial, community life is.

My sister-in-law Karen Dear has gone into labor ten weeks early. The baby may be born any minute. My heart and prayer go out to her in the hospital tonight, that the labor may be stopped, that the baby may live, that Karen may be well. May the God of love be with them.

April 20th

Phil and I sit here in this little one bunk holding cell at the Albermarle District Jail in Elizabeth City, while Bruce stands trial. Phil has one foot resting on the jail bars and is reading Ched Myers' new book. The sun streams in through the window and the bars. A radio blares down the hall.

Last evening, I was able to meditate over John 20 for an hour before dinner. I imagined being outside the empty tomb, despairing, angry, hurt, wondering if Christ's life and suffering love were worth it. A surge of emotions welled up within me. It dawned on me painfully that I do not even have the love of Mary Magdalene to ask, "If you know where he is, tell me and I will go and take him." What good comes from suffering and death? I found myself asking. I tapped into my pain and anger and finally, sat in prayer in the garden outside the empty tomb, with Jesus.

Here now, on this bunk, I don't see how I can pray over this with Christ, between the noise and the lack of space. I feel helpless and powerless.

Allow me the right to complain this morning. These trial days have been the most trying days of my life. I have never felt such a demonic violence aimed at me. This ordeal hurts. I do not enjoy it. I want to get out of jail—today! There is nothing romantic about it. It is a cross. No wonder Christians are not flocking to the jails, as Dorothy Day urged. Who wants to suffer? Where is the redemption or the glory in this?

My faith is weak. It is tested every single minute in this fiery furnace. I only hope it will be purified and strengthened from this ordeal. God, heal me and help me.

A Gospel station plays on the radio. We use this hymn for our communion meditation back home at St. Al's: "Give me a clean heart so I might serve thee. Lord, fix my heart so that I might be used by thee. For I'm not worthy of all these blessings. Give me a clean heart and I'll follow thee." The song ends. The radio announces Bruce's trial has begun.

April 21st

Webb objected 14 times during Bruce's opening statement and Boyle himself objected once. All objections were sustained.

"This trial is not so much about what will be said, . . . " Bruce began.

"Objection," Webb declared.

"You will find my participation rather limited," Bruce continued.

"Objection," Webb said.

"Keep an open mind," Bruce concluded.

"Objection," Webb said.

In his closing statement, Bruce compared our Plowshares action with the Underground Railroad. "Have a seat," Boyle told Bruce. "Disregard that part of the argument."

"I ask you to follow your heart," Bruce concluded.

"Objection," Webb said.

"Sustained. You're to follow the law," Boyle said.

The jury found Bruce guilty in six minutes. We are relieved that the trials are over.

We were eventually brought to the courthouse and held a grand reunion with Lynn who was in very good spirits. We will be sentenced together on July 5th.

As we leave the courthouse, a group of 25 people sang and clapped. We were shackled and handcuffed and tightly secured in the government van, but we smiled at our friends and our spirits soared. After dinner, we prayed and shared Eucharist. I went to sleep early, exhausted.

Today, I await further news from Karen. Mev Puleo has been told that she has the most aggressive type of cancer you can get. We have been praying also for the healing of Mike Chinsolo's granddaughter, who has leukemia. Now today Mike tells us that she does not have leukemia after all, but instead a treatable blood disorder. Thank God.

Today, we discuss community, nonviolence, resistance and lifelong commitment to peacemaking. Richard Nixon is dying, the US sends troops into Bosnia, and congresspeople are arrested at the White House for protesting US government policy in Haiti.

In the mail, friends send us chocolates, pencils, a walkman and even a jug of maple syrup, but Mike will not let us have them. The jailers still treat us inhumanly. Nonetheless, we love them and try to be human with them. We will probably be with them for months to come. We must make the best of the situation. Our trials may be over for now, but our tribulations continue. How long, O Lord, how long?

14

Breaking Bread, Passing the Cup

April 23rd, 1994

Yesterday, we began to discuss the Gospel of John and its themes, like the Word, the signs, the hour, glory, the light of the world, life, resurrection, the Good Shepherd, the bread of life, and the way. Immersion in this text will sustain us in the months ahead.

Last night, Richard Nixon died. The media portrays him in glowing terms. We remember him for leading the slaughter of the Vietnamese people, developing U.S. nuclear policies, and committing the lesser crimes of Watergate. I look at Phil, sitting in jail, and marvel at Phil's perseverance all these years in and out of jail since Nixon was president. Though the country focuses on Nixon, it should turn and listen to Phil. Instead, he is ignored and forgotten. We pass a quiet, monastic day, and focus on God. We pray for Mev Puleo, for Karen Dear, for Judge Boyle, the prosecutors, and for Richard Nixon.

April 24th

"John was sent from God to testify to the light. . . . The true light enlightens everyone. . . . The world did not know him. His own people did not accept him. To those who did accept him, he gave the power to become children of God, to those who believe in his name" (Jn 1:6-13). God sends every Christian on a mission of peace in Christ's name. God asks us to testify to Christ. Jesus was on trial all his life, and he's still on trial. He needs witnesses, people who will take the stand on his behalf. Having just taken the stand for Phil last week, I know what that means: to be objected to, interrupted, disbelieved, threatened with contempt, mocked, and stricken from the record! In some places, witnesses get killed.

As I reflect on the Beatitude, "Blessed are the peacemakers, they shall be called sons and daughters of God," I recognize that I am a son of God. This is my fundamental identity: I am John, a beloved son of God. God calls me to follow Jesus and to share in his life of nonviolent love and resistance. God calls everyone to their true identity, their true selves as God's daughters and sons.

Here in jail, I do not see where I am going. Yet I believe in God and I trust that I might be used to testify to the light and be a lamp for the light of peace. From jail, I can be a light in the culture's darkness. I witness to the light of nonviolence amidst the dark night of violence.

I read Merton, Thoreau, Gandhi, and Joan Bondurant's *Conquest of Violence*. This afternoon, Carol Brothers from the local St. Anne's church visits. She encourages me, telling me that I am filled with grace and that God is doing great things through me. She is filled with life, vigor, faith, enthusiasm, and grace. She lifts our spirits.

April 25th

"And the Word became flesh . . . " (Jn 1:14) If we accept and believe in the incarnation—that God became a human being—then we have no choice but to obey God's teachings. Christ is clear: "Love one another, love your enemies, put away your sword, sell your possessions, give your money to the poor, render to God what is God's, and follow me." And we know where Jesus goes: to Calvary. Christ was born into the world of the poor and died on the empire's cross as a criminal, an enemy of the state—and this is God. We too must undertake that same journey. I find such thoughts frightening, yet liberating.

*

The Raleigh *News and Observer* has called for our release. "Any prison time at all would be utterly senseless," an editorial in yesterday's paper said. "The usual purposes of prison—deterrence, punishment, rehabilitation—just have no relevance to this case. The protesters acted on firm religious convictions. They believe that war is wrong. To attract attention to their cause, they attacked an instrument of war. No one was injured. In fact, the property damage was minimal. If they had intended serious harm, they would have equipped themselves with tools more powerful than hammers. . . . Activism of this sort is the 70-year-old Berrigan's calling, and the former Catholic priest has been at it for decades. Prison won't 'reform' this man. Indeed, he may have something to teach the rest of us about giving purpose to life. The criminal justice system has plenty of genuinely bad guys to worry about. Let it concentrate on the ones who inflict real damage on the world, not on those who are trying to save it. What to do about Berrigan and the others? Easy. Let these people go."

Tuesday, April 26th

Jim and Shelley Douglass visit this morning after driving since Sunday, all day and all night from Birmingham, Alabama. Their car broke down outside Atlanta. Shelley just finished a lively retreat with the black parishes of Birmingham. She speaks of Mary's House, the Catholic Worker house she founded. They will be taking two homeless families in on Friday. Jim looks thin after his 51-day fast for peace in Bosnia-Herzegovnia, a fast which ended on Easter Sunday. He fasted during Ramadan (when he drank juices in the evening) and then only on water with the Great Fast of the Orthodox church. He travelled to Sarajevo and to Rome, meeting with religious leaders to pave the way for a religious pilgrimage of repentance into Sarajevo that would include the pope. He says the Serbs have used the Croats' collaberation with the Nazis as historical justification for their mass murder and that the Muslims are caught in the middle of all this killing. Essentially, he concludes, it's a Christian crusade to kill Muslims.

Jim and Shelley are two beautiful, holy, remarkable people. Their precarious life of voluntary poverty keeps them on the edge. They struggle and suffer for justice and peace. Jim has spent two years in jail for his nonviolent resistance to the Trident submarine and Shelley six months. Their books and essays call Christians to embrace nonviolence as a way of life. I see the Holy Spirit of nonviolent love through them, and their visit is one of the great blessings of this whole ordeal.

I feel like I've been visited by the cherubim and seraphim.

*

We read about John the Baptist who claims to be "a voice crying out in the desert, 'Make straight the way of the Lord'" (Jn 1:19-28). God invites us to be that voice from the desert of jail, crying out to the churches, "Prepare the way of the Lord. Reject the culture of violence and greed. Repent and disarm. Embrace nonviolence. Come back to the God of peace."

April 27th

Jim Percival died at the Lumberton Jail. He had been complaining to the guards that he needed to see the doctor because he was having spasms. He kept pestering the guards until finally they threw him alone into "the hole," a tiny cell. His body was found two days later.

Dozens of people have died mysteriously at the Lumberton, North Carolina jail in recent years. That institution shows total contempt for human life. Jim was a beautiful spirit who had made peace with God and was beginning to walk with Christ. Bruce met him one day at the canteen. He was later moved into the cell across the hallway from us. We used to wave to each other through our windows. We started writing letters to each other. He drew Christian artwork as gifts for us and would ask for our prayers. Christ receives him into paradise.

*

God tells John the Baptist, "Whomever you see the Spirit come upon and remain on, that is the one." John sees the Spirit like a dove come upon and remain on Jesus. This dove symbolizes the new creation after the great flood (Gn 8:8) and also the return of Israel from exile (Hos 11:11). John proclaims his faith and testifies, "Behold the Lamb of God who takes away the sin of the world. He is the Son of God."

I remember preaching on this text at Mission San Jose in Fremont, California days before the Gulf War began. I believe that we too have difficulty recognizing Jesus, because, as the Lamb of God, he practices the nonviolence of God. We refuse to recognize Jesus' nonviolence. Instead, we go on waring. As I preached at each of the Masses that Sunday, people got up and walked out. Today, God still calls us to recognize the nonviolent Christ, to testify to him with our lives, to listen to him and obey his commands, even as we are ignored, laughed at, disparaged, jailed or killed.

April 28th

Fr. Ed Glynn, my Jesuit provincial, was here yesterday for a visit. I asked him if he still supported me and my public stand for peace. "We've very proud of you," he replied. "Of course, we all support you." Then, putting his hands up as if to frame a picture, and looking at me through the glass window, he said, "You're right where we want you." We both burst out laughing.

*

Jesus asks the disciples, "What are you looking for?" (Jn 1:38). We wonder, What are we looking for? We look for God, for Christ, for the coming of God's reign. Phil looks for the kin-dom, for the sisterhood and brotherhood of humanity breaking through around us. Bruce longs for "a life of experiments in truth." The disciples spend a day with Jesus and realize that he is the Messiah. They search for Peter. "We have found the Messiah!" they announce. And we ask ourselves how often do we reach out to others and invite them to meet Jesus, to follow Jesus, and to walk his way of peace?

*

Though my friend Mev Puleo continues to be ill, she has apparently moved back home. Last week, Jean-Bertrand Aristide, president of Haiti, was speaking in the Bay Area, and went to see her in the hospital, but the hospital staff would not let him in to the intensive care unit to see her. My heart is broken over Mev's illness. I feel so helpless. And so, on her behalf, I sit with Christ and intercede for her and all suffering humanity. And suddenly, I do not feel so powerless.

April 29th

We read of how Jesus calls Philip to "follow," and then Philip calls Nathaniel. When Jesus sees Nathaniel, he calls him a true Israelite, free of duplicity. Nathaniel asks, How do you know me? And Jesus replies that he saw him sitting under the fig tree (a symbol of Israel and God's reign of peace). Nathaniel calls Jesus the Son of God and King of Israel. But Jesus says, "You believe because I say I saw you. You will see greater things." (Jn 1:43-52). Likewise, when we meet Jesus, he reveals our true selves to us.

Phil speaks of finding God in acts of nonviolent resistance. He says we only see God and the face of Christ in our neighbor. This love for our neighbor must include the pursuit of justice or it is false and sentimental love. "A spirituality which promotes a vertical relationship between God and me is heresy," he concludes. True spirituality must include the nearly six billion people on the planet. As we love and serve other human beings, we see "greater things"—the face of Christ in our sisters and brothers.

April 30th

"Mute prayer is my greatest weapon," Mohandas Gandhi once wrote. I long to be a person of prayer, a mystic, a person who seeks God. I long to go to a quiet mountain place to pray (Lk 6:12) and I have done that during annual retreats and days of recollection. But I find prayer is a struggle. It requires release of my false self and coming before God as I really am, with my many flaws and concerns and infidelities. My struggle to pray, more often than not, comes down to the basic plea, "Lord, I believe. Help my unbelief" (Mk 9:24). I know I cannot remain faithful or even survive as a Christian without this struggle. Prayer fortifies my life.

I pray through the Eucharist, read the scriptures, take quiet time for meditation, offer intercessory prayers for sick friends and for the coming of God's reign, and ask for blessings of love upon my enemies and persecutors (as the Sermon on the Mount advises, in Matthew 5:44). Prayer describes my basic relationship with God. Jesus taught his disciples, "When you pray, go to your inner room, close the door and pray to your God in secret. And your God who sees in secret will repay you" (Mt 6:6). John's Gospel puts it this way, "Whoever loves me will keep my word and my God will love them and we will come to them and make our dwelling with them. . . . As God loves me, so also I love you. Remain in my love" (Jn 14:23, 15:9). In my prayer, I try to close the door of my inner room, to sit in silence, to let my heart and soul be at peace, to rest in God's love and then, to listen. This is my intention. It has taken me ten years to come to this point in my spiritual life. For years I spent my prayer time venting, ranting, complaining and arguing with God about the world. I would tell God what God should be doing. Over time, I've come to realize that this is not how we speak to someone we love. In a true, loving relationship, each side take turns speaking and listening. Sometimes, both parties sit in silent peace. Nowadays, I want only to listen to God, to learn how God feels these days, to be a friend to whom God can talk.

I imagine sitting with Jesus. For years now, I hear the same basic words from the risen Christ: "I love you. I am with you. I want to share my peace, my love, my joy with you." Such words sustain me. I feel sent to share the spirit with others, to proclaim God's reign of peace. As Christ touches me in my poverty, I want to touch others in their poverty. As Christ disarms my heart, I want to disarm others and the world. Prayer makes all things possible. During these days, I hope to deepen my prayer life, my awareness of God, so that these times can be transformed and filled with grace.

*

This morning, our cellmate Johnnie explodes in anger at the heavyset young guard who was collecting the breakfast trays. As we begin our bible study, Johnnie proceeds to talk to us for two hours, first about his plan to kill the guard, and then about the pain he's in. Slowly, he confesses that he has never recovered from his experience as a marine in Vietnam where he killed at least 100 people and saw hundreds of others killed. Once, he tells us, he was part of a mission of a dozen helicopters, each with 47 men inside, who flew into a combat zone. Eight helicopters were shot down around him. On another occasion, he was dropped off in the jungle with 115 American men. They were immediately ambushed. Only eight survived. Many U.S. soldiers died at the hands of other U.S. soldiers, he claims. Since the war, he confesses that he has committed many violent crimes and has attempted suicide. He is ready to kill. I speak of nonviolence and prayer and he agrees that he needs both, but continues his threats.

*

Dan Berrigan writes from DePaul University where he is teaching for a semester:

At least one thing is past: those horrid days in court and your noble selves up against the carnivores. Now I know why I've always detested lions: the perfect imperial symbol and fact. I got a secret for you, which is probably no secret at all. Jawe departed that pseudo temple, in fury. It was the carnivores who were on trial. So were all high authorities of the air force. They were self-condemned, convicted, shamed before the world. They await sentencing. The judgment may possibly be mitigated, but only on the plea of the four, whose expert testimony was taken seriously and attentively and at great length by Judge Jawe. Then he departed the court for chambers. Disgust and anger on his face bodes ill for the defendants. Can the Judge be placated? The four Noble Experts will plead night and day for those 'dwellers on the earth' who 'worship the works of their hands,' who 'abuse the widow and the orphan,' whose deeds are 'the works of death.' They may perhaps prevail and win mercy, the Judge so loves them.

*

In Cana, at a wedding, Jesus orders that the ceremonial jugs be filled with water and then turns them into wine. In one revolutionary act, he does away with Jewish ceremonial washings and rituals—indeed, the whole law. The abundant wine fulfills Amos and Hosea's vision of God's reign. Jesus wants us to live life to the full. His reign resembles a wedding feast with unlimited wine. As the first of John's seven signs, this story calls us to believe in Jesus.

*

It's 9:30 p.m. and I'm bored and depressed. Today, I read and sorted through my unanswered mail and felt so overwhelmed by it all that I put it all away and just lay on my bed, unable to think or pray. My inability to pray has been my greatest disappointment. I thought I could be a great contemplative in jail, a mystic. Alas, for my dreams. I'm lucky if I sit still and say simply, "Lord have mercy, " or "Lord, I believe; help my unbelief." How I wish I could realize in myself that great inner unity which Gandhi and Merton write about and lived.

Sunday, May 1st

I speak with Mev on the phone. She remains very sick. She asks me to offer up my suffering for her and I do. I tell her I love her. My day is one long prayer for her healing. It is a quiet day here. This evening, it rains and the power goes out twice. Johnnie is calmer. Bruce reads as Phil and I write stacks of letters.

We discuss John's account of Jesus' cleansing of the Temple (Jn 2:13-25). Thus, John opens his Gospel with a vivid portrait of Jesus engaged in nonviolent civil disobedience in the Temple. This is the Jesus we follow: bold, daring, subversive, peaceful and revolutionary, prayerful and dangerous, actively nonviolent. It is only natural that followers of Jesus end up in jail. But I ask again: what about my heart? How peaceful, faithful, loving is it? I have a long way to go.

This evening, I sit alone here in my cell. My thoughts turn to Mev and Jesus.

May 2nd

Jesus sees through every human heart (Jn 2:25). We share our struggle to allow God to disarm our hearts and agree that prayer offers the only way to deeper faith and love. We speak about our day to day experience of prayer. Phil reads the Bible every morning, gets on his knees when he can and repeats the "Come Holy Spirit" prayer throughout the day. Bruce concentrates on his breathing, tries to center himself, and prays for a deepening of personal nonviolence. I sit and listen for the voice of God in Christ, and if I hear it, settle into his presence. Today, I take time to sit with Jesus and I feel more at peace.

Last night, I had a strange dream. I was sharing a room at Duke University with friends; the situation was not unlike this cell. In our midst, suddenly, stood Jesus. In his presence, I felt liberated, full of joy, at peace, happy to be in his presence. A deep reverence and adoration of Christ came over me. This rare spiritual feeling returned this afternoon in my prayer and as I write this, I realize that I have been blessed with a consoling sense of the Lord's presence in our midst.

Meanwhile, time passes at a snail's pace. Every day lasts two to three weeks for me. Our bible studies and my prayer experiences help a great deal and offer the assurance that my days are not wasted. I know that if I can focus on Christ, all will be well. Jesus controls my life. All praise and glory to Jesus!

May 3rd

I stumble through the story of Jesus and Nicodemus. We ask the question: What does it mean to be born from above? (Jn 3:1-8) Nicodemus approaches Jesus at night because he does not want to be seen with Jesus during the daytime. If Nicodemus publicly associates with this subversive, he may lose his powerful position. Jesus challenges him to be a person of the Spirit, to extricate himself from corruption and power. We ponder the scene and the invitation.

*

In jail for peace, we are on the edge of society—on the edge of politics, faith, government, reality, spirituality, and the culture. I feel like a pioneer, pushing the boundaries of human behavior in a society caught up in fear, consumerism and violence. We are not counter-cultural; we are a-cultural. We retreat from society like desert fathers into the wilderness. We cling solely to the book and the sacrament. We are ignored by many but not by God. God is with us, so what of society and its violence? What of us? Again, I write the words to engrave my belief; the outcome rests in God alone. And so we sit and offer our message to the country: "Stop the killing. Snap out of these murderous delusions. Be human," for God's sake.

May 4th

"The light came into the world but people preferred the darkness. . . . Those who live the truth come to the light and believe so that their deeds may be seen as done in God" (Jn 3:19-21). I like to think of myself as a staunch believer. I delude myself with the egotistic fantasy that I am a perfect disciple. But I am wrapped in sin and disbelief. And so, with Phil and Bruce, I pray to be with Christ, to dwell in the light, to believe and live in the truth.

Time passes second by second. Phil answers his mail with patient determination. Bruce reads the anthology *Voices from the Catholic Worker*. Johnnie watches tv. My dream from the other night lingers, and the unrestricted adoration of God that it unleashes in my heart leads me to a new wholeness. The dream becomes a grace. Slowly, slowly, like time itself, God answers my prayer and Christ transforms me.

Carol Brothers, our Edenton friend, visits with Bruce and me this afternoon. She throws her hands straight up in the air. Her mouth opens wide in a huge smile and her eyes bulge. "God is so great! God is moving in the world! Grace is everywhere! You all are so blessed!" Her visit is like a shot of new life, new energy, and boundless hope. Talk about faith! Bruce and I leave speechless, amazed, bolstered by this humble, enthusiastic Christian woman who read about us in the local paper and decided to come cheer us up. Like the Gospel, she calls us to great faith in the face of the world's (and our own) faithlessness.

May 5th

The Gospel paints John the Baptist as Jesus' best man and John's joy, even though he hangs on the verge of imprisonment, is complete. "I must decrease; he must increase" (Jn 3:30). John's role has been to stand and listen for the Messiah's voice. We must do the same here in jail—stand and listen for the voice of Jesus; announce his Word to the nations.

The slaughter in Rwanda continues. The Hutus have murdered tens of thousands of Tutsis. In Bosnia, Guatemala, Haiti and East Timor, the killing continues. Israel grants Palestine self-rule over Jericho and Gaza. Nelson Mandela will soon be president of South Africa. We bow our heads and pray for all these peoples, for the entire human race, that God may have mercy on us all and help us to have mercy toward one another.

May 6th

"Whoever accepts Christ's testimony certifies that God is trustworthy" (Jn 3:33). What does it mean to be trusthworthy, to believe that God is trustworthy? Why do we think that God is not trustworthy? We fashion God after our own image and because we are not trustworthy, we presume God can't be trustworthy either. If we could trust one another and trust God, we would have no need for our weapons. We would renounce our violence. Nonviolence, as Thomas Merton wrote, demands total reliance on God and God's word. God is trustworthy; we can be as well.

May 7th

Today marks five months in jail. The action seems like it occurred light years ago. Phil confesses that he feels in "the doldrums." We are in a holding pattern, he observes. We look at one another. None of us has any energy to write meaningful treatises on the peace movement or moving letters to convert the masses. I barely have the strength to scrawl these words.

So here I sit. Bruce speaks on the phone with his parents in Oklahoma. Phil takes a shower. Johnnie watches the blaring tv. We feel the effects of not getting outside and not exercising. We are lethargic. We live now in slow motion. Yesterday, for example, I tried to sit in the presence of Christ. What happened? I fell asleep. So much for keeping watch with Christ in Gethsemane! Disciple? Apostle? Yes—sleeping like the rest of the them! Over and over again, I say it: Have mercy on us. Help us. Strengthen us. Don't leave us alone.

Our bible study addresses all of this. Jesus goes to the holy well and asks for a drink of water from a Samaritan woman (not only a member of the marginalized, oppressed gender, but as a Samaritan, one of the hated enemies of the Jews). In the end, he offers her "living water which will spring up within to eternal life" (Jn 4:4-18). So we pray at Eucharist that Christ's spirit might be living water for our thirsting souls, that we might live these next two lonely months (until our sentencing) to the full. Though we are hidden away, vulnerable, and forgotten, we pray that Christ will satisfy within us the fullness of life.

May 8th

"The hour is coming, and is now here, when true worshippers will worship God in Spirit and truth; and indeed God seeks such people to worship her. God is spirit and those who worship her must worship in Spirit and truth" (Jn 4:23-24). What is true worship today? How does our worship differ from the imperial Judeans who built the exploitive Temple while ignoring justice? Do we not spend billions maintaining chuches across the country while ignoring the evils of war, injustice and poverty? True worship requires that we give our lives entirely to God and God's reign of justice. Nonviolence and justice signify the authenticity of our faith. If we are violent, if we support injustice, then our worship remains false. Yet we are all violent, all sinners, every one of us complicit in war and injustice. We journey toward nonviolence and truth. We try to worship God with our whole hearts, souls, minds and lives, and our neighbors as ourselves. True worship entails much more than going to church for an hour each Sunday; of course, communal gatherings do stand as beginnings, sign posts of our day to day, moment to moment, life in the Spirit of nonviolence and truth.

May 9th

To an oppressed woman, a Samaritan, the arch-enemy of the Jews, Jesus confesses that he is the Messiah, the Anointed One. "I am he, the one who is speaking to you" (Jn 4:26). What a profoundly intimate moment, a vulnerable revelation. She reveals her life; he does the same. Just at that moment, the disciples arrive. This pair scandalizes them. Imagine! The Master alone with a woman of her reputation. She leaves her water jar, runs off to the town and invites everyone to come and meet Jesus. She too is an apostle. She evangelizes her whole town fearlessly. She tells people, "He told me everything that I have done." For once, she understands her life. She has found new meaning in Jesus. The (male) disciples do not have a clue about what is going on; they try to get Jesus to eat (they themselves have been off feasting). "I have food you know not of. . . . My food is to do the will of the One who sent me and to finish that One's work." Jesus tells his disciples to look out into the Samaritan fields, into enemy territory, and with love to see that the harvest is at hand. The Gospel tells us to reap and to sow like Jesus himself—beginning in enemy territory.

*

This morning, Phil and I call Dan Berrigan on his 73rd birthday. His back has been bothering him, but he continues to teach and speak around the country. He amazes us. "The best theologian in the country," Phil says of Dan. His life and friendship are a great gift to me. Here in jail, we celebrate his life.

Yesterday, Phil and I spoke on the phone with Liam Neeson, star of the movie *Schindler's List*, and his fiance, the actress Natasha Richardson. They are friends of Dan, are making a movie called *Nell*, here in North Carolina, and support us in our plight.

May 10th

South Africa inagurates Nelson Mandela as its president. Clinton reverses his unjust policy toward Haitian refugees. Randall Robinson ends his fast for justice in Haiti. Meanwhile, the horrors continue in Rwanda, Bosnia, Haiti, Israel, Guatemala, East Timor, Peru, Yemen, Sudan, Iraq, El Salvador, Northern Ireland—and our own country. Last night, serial killer John Wayne Gacy, who murdered 33 men, was executed in Illinois. We train people like Gacy to kill (as I saw at Seymour Johnson Air Force Base and as our cellmate Johnnie knows from Vietnam)—and then we turn and kill those who kill to show that killing is wrong. If only we would embrace the consistent ethic of life. Will we ever become a people of nonviolence? I don't know. We need to undergo a nationwide conversion of heart.

May 11th

Before healing the royal official's son, Jesus observes, "Unless you people see signs and wonders, you will not believe" (Jn 4:46-54). We discuss how in our lack of faith we seek signs and wonders and how we as a people might be more faithful. Bruce confesses that he would not mind if the heavens were to open and God comes down and shows herself in a great sign. Phil speaks of the ordination of women, the abolition of celibacy as a requirement for priesthood, and the rejection of the just war theory as signs he looks for. I look for massive conversions, widespread disarmament and acceptance of nonviolence as a way of life. Instead, Jesus calls us to faith in the darkness, where there are no signs and no wonders. For the Christian, there are only counter-signs: persecution, arrest, imprisonment, rejection and crucifixion. From Gandhi to Romero, the faithful ones face obstacles but carry on in faith.

I hope we are plunging the depths of faith. We walk onto the base and into custody, into the courts, into this cell—and all we have is our faith in Christ. We have no signs and wonders to guide or con-

vince us. We are not able to satisfy the public's desire for signs and
wonders. We are unsuccessful and ineffective—as Jesus dying on the
cross. We will not win the Nobel Peace Prize. We will not precipitate
total nuclear disarmament next week. Rather, we experiment with our
faith and walk by faith alone and cling to faith in the God of peace. I
hope that we live the kind of faith Jesus desired, the faith he said that
God is seeking (Jn 4:30).

May 12th

Bill Finlator, a remarkable Baptist minister, visits this morning.
Bill has lived a long and full life. His journey took him full circle from
conservative, Southern politics to the prophetic vision of the Gospel in
these his twilight years. He speaks out and writes on our behalf. This
wise and holy man blesses us with his presence.

Today we discuss Jesus' cure of the sick man on the Sabbath.
Instead of celebrating the great feast, Jesus hangs out "with the ill, the
lame, the blind and the crippled" (Jn 5:1-18). He notices a terribly ill
man and asks him simply, "Do you want to be well?" How modest
Jesus is! He does not impose himself on anyone. "Rise, take up your
mat and walk," he declares. Such words connote resurrection (Rise!),
crucifixion (Take up your cross!) and discipleship (Follow me!). The
sick man obeys. Immediately, the authorities prowl about for the
healer. Healing is illegal. Liberating the oppressed is a crime. Resurrection and discipleship threaten the authority and power of those in
control. They accuse Jesus of breaking the Sabbath law. Jesus slips
away to avoid the crowd. He knows they want either to make him king
or kill him. He goes underground. He does not act for the crowds, but
one on one, out of love for suffering people. Jesus looks for the healed
man who had been interrogated and like a good shepherd, tells the
man, "Look, you are well. Do not sin anymore so that nothing worse
may happen to you." He connects healing with sin, forgiveness and
justice. Jesus ignores the growing hostility against him. "My God is
working up until now and so I am at work." Jesus obeys God, acts like
God, fulfills the law—and what is the response of the Judeans? They
try to kill him "all the more." Their murderous hearts are revealed. His
crucifixion is inevitable. As is his resurrection.

Peacemaking heals people, yet is not well received. All governments benefit from wars and division. They do not want us to get well.

They do not want us to recognize that, under God, we are all equal, already reconciled. "Look! You are well," Jesus tells the healed man. We too are healed but we do not know it and we go on hurting ourselves and others. Living out the healing already granted to us requires that we disarm, live in peace and love our enemies, even if it costs our lives.

May 14th

George Anderson, S.J. and Frank McAloon, S.J. visited yesterday. George has just left his position as pastor of St. Aloysius' church and heads off to work for *America* magazine. Frank will soon leave for the Jesuit School of Theology in Berkeley to begin doctoral studies.

Today, we break from our bible study schedule and share a simple Eucharist. We spend a quiet day, reading and writing letters. I am reading Albert Camus' *The Fall.* Though I hunger for silence and solitude, I still feel like a hermit or a desert father, living in some cave, pondering our scripture, living a solitary life, looking heavenward for consolation. I do Yoga exercises and they center me in peace, a great help.

May 15th

Jim Dolan, a Jesuit retreat director from New York, sends me his book of prayers, called *Meditations for Life*, based on St. Ignatius' *Spiritual Exercises.* His opening meditation offers the voice of God affirming me with unconditional love:

> I have come that you may have life. When you were young, you were the apple of my eye. When you were growing up, clumsily searching and getting lost, I delighted in your every move. I want you to know that nothing you could ever say or do could ever separate us—no sin, no judgment, no failure, nothing inside you or outside you, no evil, nothing in the future or in the past. With all of your limitations, selfishness, self-righteousness and jealousies, I have loved you with an everlasting love. I loved you when you were angry, sad, pompous or depressed. Do you know my love has no bounds? I love you the same whether you turn your back to me or to my people. Yes I am always on your side and I am always at your side. I would like to wipe away every tear and

every fear you could possibly have. I am with you and I am
yours, always.

These words reassure me on this lonely, Sunday morning in jail. In my
solitary, celibate life, I hang on such words. With St. Ignatius I pray:
"God, give me only your love and your grace. That's enough for me."

At Eucharist, we remember friends who are fasting on the steps
of the U.S. Capitol for the closing of the School of the Americas,
Georgia's military training institution for Latin American death squads.
We pray for Haiti and Rwanda, for my sister-in-law Karen and Mev
Puleo, for Bruce's grandmother and Lynn, for our friend Brad Sjos-
trum, and for Judge Boyle, Bill Webb and Christine Hamilton. Today,
we keep watch and keep the faith.

May 16th

In the early morning hours, again I dream of Jesus. For an hour
before I arise, while semi-conscious, I talk to Jesus. I tell him my troubles, my loneliness, my fears, my sadness, and my disappointments
and beg him to help me. Later on, while Bruce works out in the weight
room, Phil reads, and Johnnie sleeps, I sit in silence in the small tv
room (with the tv off for once!). Again, I look to Christ. "Take heart,"
he says. "I am with you. I love you. Yes, your life will bear good
fruit."

We read about Jesus as the new Moses, crossing the sea in a new
exodus, climbing the moutain as a new lawgiver, giving out his body
as bread in a new passover, offering his life on the cross as the new
and ultimate sacrifice. Jesus takes barley loaves (the bread of the
poor), gives thanks and distributes them to the masses (Jn 6:1-5). The
crowds, unfaithful as usual, eat it up: "This is truly the prophet, the
one who is to come into the world." They want to make him king,
their own emperor, a Davidic Messiah who will wage a holy war
against the empire. Jesus smells this infidelity and flees to the mountain alone. He will have none of it. He turns his back completely
against power politics, imperial domination or messianic warmaking.
Eventually, the crowds reject him. He ends up alone on the cross.

May 17th

This morning, a box of homemade cookies and lemon poppy seed muffins arrives from a friend at Duke. The chief jailer barges in, makes me open the box in front of him, and then confiscates them. You are not allowed to have food, he insists. Who knows what drugs could be smuggled in that way, he asks. We offer the gifts to him. He gladly accepts!

Today, a warm letter arrives from Peter-Hans Kolvenbach, the General Superior of the Society of Jesus, based in Rome: "Thank you for your pencil-stub letter, more consoling to me than many of the more elegant and formal missives I receive. Be sure that I am aware of your situation and of the blessing of obedience you had for the events leading up to it, and know that you are in my prayers, as I am glad to be kept in yours. We say about one of our aged and infirm members: 'orat pro Soc.': I am glad that you are using your enforced confinement for that end as well, and I am sure that the Lord will bless your concern for the Society as well as for the poor and the victimized. . . . Should the occasion arise when I might visit you, I will try to do that. In the meantime I invoke on you the blessing of the God of peace."

A fifth cellmate, George, joins us. Meanwhile, our friend, Brad, has been released by the judge. He has been ordered back to his hometown in Illinois under one year's probation. He was told to "disassociate himself from the Plowshares." We rejoice in his liberation and pray for the judge's liberation.

May 18th

I found myself telling a reporter from the *Chicago Tribune* this morning that though jail is not easy and I do not like it, though I wake up some mornings wondering how the hell I ended up here, I find myself looking at the reality of the world's wars and reading the Gospels about Jesus' crucifixion and concluding that this is the best place I can be and the best sacrifice I can make with my life. Maybe I believe it.

Jesus tells the crowds that they should "not work for food that perishes but for the food that endures for eternal life." This Bread of God is Jesus. The Gospel summons us to "the work of God," that "you believe in the one God sent." Bruce comments that eating the bread of

God and doing's God's work means sharing in the cross of Christ. The Eucharist, he notes, entails a sharing in Jesus' crucifixion and a summons to take up the cross in our own lives. Phil reflects that the Bread of Life is the bread of liberation, the new manna for our journey out of slavery into God's reign of justice. We break bread and find ourselves, as promised, strengthened and free.

May 19th

"I am the Bread of Life," Jesus declares (Jn 6:35-50). "Whoever comes to me will never hunger and whoever believes in me will never thirst. I will not reject anyone." Though he was and is rejected by everyone, Jesus rejects no one. This great promise of Christ reveals his kindness, mercy and generosity. "I do not do my own will," Jesus tells us, "but the will of the One who sent me," that "everyone who sees the Son and believes in him may have eternal life and I shall raise her on the last day." The text alludes to Jesus' crucifixion (19:37). It invites us to believe in Christ crucified and thus to follow him to the cross. The bloody road of nonviolence still repulses many. The Gospels explain that, as the Israelites "murmured" because they did not want to be in the desert, the Judeans grumbled over faith in the crucified Christ. "Stop murmuring," Jesus commands. The Word chastises us to start believing. "Everyone who listens to my God and learns from God comes to me," Jesus explains. Eucharist empowers us to reconciliation and the fullness of life. War and consumerism, on the other hand, are anti-Eucharist. They destroy our spirits, divide us, and turn us from God. The key for us is sharing the Bread of Life.

May 20th

Jacqueline Kennedy Onassis has died of lymphoma. The news reporters call her a symbol of the rich and sophisticated. Her death touches the whole country. We pray for her that God may rest her in peace. I am moved by her death, knowing the horror she must have gone through over the two assassinations.

In the past two months, over 500,000 people killed in Rwanda. Their suffering has not received the attention and interest that the death of this one, wealthy woman has. All this news of death sets my mind thinking about death and the meaning of life. First, perhaps the greatest gift we can offer with our lives is defending the helpless poor from the powers of death. To that end, what I admire about Jackie Kennedy Onassis was her eventual opposition to the war in Vietnam. It is reported that at a dinner party in 1964 or 1965, she turned to Robert McNamara, head of the Pentagon, and started pounding on his chest saying, "Stop the killing! Stop the killing!"

Secondly, my thoughts turn to the haunting voice of Jesus, who asks, "What good is it to gain the whole world but to lose your soul?" "If you would save your life," Jesus declares, "you must lose it." We are all going to die. The question is: how will we spend our lives, in the selfish pursuit of money at the expense of the poor or the selfless pursuit of life and dignity for those who suffer? We sit, in jail, trying to practice the downward mobility of the Gospel. The trick lies in renouncing wealth, power and prestige and getting lost in poverty, powerlessness and humiliations. On this downward journey, I meet the poor Christ, who was rich but who did not cling to riches and instead became poor, even dying on a cross. We long to follow Jesus on that difficult journey to the cross and into the risen life of God's reign. So our lives become a daily dying to self. When we eventually do die physically, it will be a quiet, peaceful event that we have been preparing and undergoing all our lives.

This morning, we pray for all those who have died. I see out the tall, thin window that the skies are grey. Johnnie and George, even Bruce, are sleeping as I write this (late in the morning). Phil writes in his journal with an open bible beside him, like St. Jerome himself or Abbot Agathon of the desert. I sometimes think if Christians understood the Gospel correctly, they would flock by the thousands to this jail cell to support him, to learn from him, even to join him. Instead, we sit "waiting on the Lord," serving God in silence.

*

Mohandas Gandhi, quoted in Joan Bondurant's *The Conquest of Violence*:

> Nonviolence in its dynamic condition means conscious suffering. It does not mean meek submission to the will of the evildoer, but it means the pitting of one's whole soul against the will of the tyrant. Working under this law of our being, it is possible for a single individual to defy the whole might of an unjust empire. . . .

Suffering injury in one's own person is . . . of the essence of nonviolence and is the chosen substitute for violence to others. . . . Just as
one must learn the art of killing in the training for violence, so
one must learn the art of dying in the training for nonviolence.
The votary of nonviolence has to cultivate the capacity for sacrifice of the highest type in order to be free from fear. . . . The one
who has not overcome all fear cannot practice nonviolence in per-
fection.

May 21st

I awake this morning thinking of Christ. I approach this evening,
meditating, imagining Christ before me, sitting on the floor after doing
yoga. The rest of the day, however, is not as centered. We share a
good reflection on the Eucharist, based on our text from John: "Whoever eats my flesh and drinks my blood has eternal life and I will raise
her on the last day" (Jn 6:54). Sharing Eucharist means sharing in the
suffering and death of Christ. It means confronting the forces of death
which kill the body of Christ today. Sharing Eucharist has consequences. We too will be crucified. We too will share our bodies and
our blood with others for the sake of humanity's redemption and transformation.

I want to be out of this cell—roaming the beach, walking in a
park, enjoying the company of friends, savoring a good meal, laughing
with my community. Though I struggle with this confinement, still I
am grateful to be here, grateful to be sharing the lot of the poor, grateful to be in trouble for opposing the government's weapons, grateful to
be reading the Gospel, grateful to be sharing Eucharist in jail.

Thank you, brother Jesus, for leading me here.

15

Pentecost Days

Pentecost Sunday, May 22nd, 1994

I dream of a future without war; a day when the killings stop; a time when all weapons will be dismantled; a new society where everyone loves everyone else; a new humanity where everyone shares everything equally—the reign of God on earth. To dream of that day ensures its coming. Here I sit, on the feast of the Holy Spirit, and pray for the coming of the Holy Spirit upon us all, that the risen Christ might lead us into that new reign of paradise on earth. A world without weapons, prisons, hunger, greed, or fear is worth suffering for, even dying for. The Spirit of Jesus leads us into that new world.

We read from John's Gospel how many people were scandalized by Jesus' teachings and did not believe him. "Many of his disciples returned to their former way of life and no longer accompanied him" (Jn 6:66). With hurt and pain in his voice, Jesus asks a heartbreaking question: "Do you also want to leave?" The disciples assert their faith in Jesus, but he counters that he had chosen them and that one of them will betray him (all deny and abandon him). "It is the spirit which gives life while the flesh is of no avail," Jesus explains. The flesh and its desires—its sinfulness, its violence and its dominating will—lead to death. The Spirit within guides us. The Spirit of God will lead us to new life. The Spirit will transform us into people of loving nonviolence. The Spirit behind our actions is more important than our actions themselves. We must act for justice and peace, but if such actions are not done in Jesus' spirit of nonviolent love, they lead to death. The depth of love in the Spirit in our actions makes all the difference.

*

Holy Spirit of love and peace, come upon us this Pentecost. Jesus, send the fire of nonviolence into our minds and hearts; let our lives be turned upside down by your illegal, troublemaking Spirit. Help us to take the nonviolent offensive, to confront the structures of war and injustice with your own powerful love; to tear them down. Root out every trace of violence within us, which keeps pushing us to risk an anti-Pentecostal, nuclear hellfire. Send forth your spirit that we might believe in God and be willing to suffer the cross for walking your way of nonviolent resistance to evil. Guide us to our own cross and into the risen life of your reign where finally our spirits may be one as you and God are one.

May 23rd

The Jesus we meet in our Gospel is surrounded by people who want to kill him. His own brothers, we are told, do not believe him and encourage him to go to Jerusalem for the great Feast of Tabernacles, to make a name for himself, to be effective and to get some "results." Jesus declares that he is hated because he speaks out against the world's evils. Later, in hiding, he goes to the Holy City. Halfway through the feast, he speaks out publicly and calls for faith.

I meditate on the turbulent life of Jesus—hated by the world, rejected by friends, hunted by authorities, used by many, abused by others. I embrace the Lord and feel a calming spirit come upon me. This deep peace heals me, draws me out, and transcends my cell. For a few minutes, I know the peace I have been seeking.

*

Johnnie was taken to court this morning. Bruce, George and I sat on the floor playing cards with Johnnie for hours last night. He hopes to be released today, but we know that the courts are typically unfair. The judge will probably not believe his innocence. Nonetheless, we pray that he will be released and that he will be healed of his inner violence. For weeks now, Johnnie has led us in our dinner-time grace, a rambling prayer that always took a personal note of gratitude and hope. His prayers were one of the great blessings of our time together for they voiced the prayers of all the prisoners we have met so far. Surely, God hears these prayers, the cries of the poor for liberation. May God keep an eye on Johnnie and help him rebuild his life.

May 24th

Though everyone seeks to kill him, Jesus stands publicly in the Temple and stirs the crowd with his teaching. He holds nothing back: "My teaching is not my own but is from the one who sent me. Whoever chooses to do God's will shall know whether my teaching is from God or whether I speak on my own. Whoever speaks on their own seeks their own glory, but whoever seeks the glory of the one who sent them is truthful and there is no wrong in them. Did not Moses give you the law? Yet none of you keeps the law. Why are you trying to kill me?" (Jn 7:16-20) "Stop judging by appearances, but judge justly" (7:24). The Gospel connects lying with murder and Jesus charges the people (including us!) with both. Though the crowds shout that he is possessed, truly they (and we!) are possessed with lying and demonic violence. Indeed, what culture is more obsessed with appearances than our own? Jesus exposes our delusions. For truth-telling, he is executed. His word beckons us to sanity.

May 25th

Yesterday my pre-sentencing report arrived: the probation office recommends to the judge that I be sentenced to between ten and 16 months in prison. Today, while Phil snores on his bunk, I do yoga. I sit peacefully, talking to Christ, asking for help, guidance, light. Christ transforms my spirit. I rarely feel this centered on the outside. This is the only clarity I know these days: Christ wants me to stay close to him. That is enough.

*

Jo Becker, director of the Fellowship of Reconciliation, visits this morning. This weekend, she attended FOR's "Women of Color" conference. Jo speaks of the energy and action plans emerging from the women. I share with her my new life behind bars, and tell her that if she ever wants to get away from it all, jail is the place to be. We both laugh.

Jesus speaks openly in the Temple, we read in our scripture. The bystanders ask, "Isn't this the one they're trying to kill? Haven't they killed him yet?" What a callous, hateful question! He cries out, "I know God because I am from God and God sent me" (Jn 7:29). Then, as they try to arrest him, he slips away. It amazes me that Jesus continues to share his true self with others, even though they refuse to believe him, dismiss him and plot to kill him.

Dear God, you suffer so much because of our hardened hearts. You reach out and invite us into your life even though we keep refusing your offer. I pray that I may not reject you, that I may love you and be your faithful friend all my days. Help us to accept your loving invitation.

May 26th

Good supportive letters arrive from Dan Berrigan, Henri Nouwen, Jim Douglass, Joan Chittister, and Fr. Bill O'Donnell in Berkeley, and Fr. Chris Ponnet in Los Angeles. When Chris entered the hospital earlier in the year for heart surgery, he asked his parishioners and friends to write us and he offered up his suffering on our behalf, for the struggle for peace. He is on the mend now. Lynn writes nearly every day, telling us about the other women she's with, the jailers, the greasy food, the stifling conditions at the Albermarle District jail, our shared struggles and her resilient hopes. "Close your eyes," she closes one letter, "and imagine that cool, salty ocean breeze; feel the sun on your face and be at peace."

We spend the morning discussing Jesus' prophetic act of nonviolent resistance at the climax of the Feast of Tabernacles (Jn 7:31-39). On the last day, as the urns of water are poured over the altar and thousands pray solemnly for rain, Jesus stands up and disrupts the entire religious high feast. He cries out, "Let anyone who thirsts come to me and drink. Whoever believes in me, as scripture says: 'Rivers of living water will flow from within.'" As Wes Howard Brook writes in his new book, *Becoming Children of God*, "Can we begin to imagine the effect of this shockingly 'inappropriate' action? In the history of bold acts of nonviolent resistance, is there any parallel to such an astounding action?" Jesus' quote from the scriptures combines the Torah, the Psalms, Wisdom literature and the prophets all in one verse. Which text is being cited? Does the river of living water flow from Christ or from the believer? John's genius leaves it ambiguously open: Jesus proclaims himself as a thirst-quenching source greater than the entire Hebrew scriptural tradition! On top of this, we are told of the coming of the Holy Spirit. John invokes *sophia*, the wisdom figure of the scriptures. In both Hebrew (*ruah*) and Greek (*pneuma*), "spirit" is feminine. Jesus incarnates *sophia*. Here we glimpse the feminine side of God, gathering her children together.

May 27th

The prosecutor, Bill Webb, has asked that we each receive another year in prison. My cousin Mary Anne Muller's ten-year-old son Joseph sends another hilarious letter in code (each letter of the alphabet represents a corresponding letter of the alphabet in reverse order): "GSV NXIGRZMH SZEV OZMWVW GZMGLI RH OLLHV. Don't let them know! It will mean destruction to the whole rebellion if they find out. . . . Sincerely, Red Squirrel."

At Phil's urging, Mike took us out to stand in the open garage this morning. For one hour, I stand by the chain-link garage fence, feeling the breeze of the fresh spring air. I talk at length with Miguel, who will plea bargain this week and expects perhaps ten years in prison. I speak with Mike about nonviolence. Later, Bruce and I visit with Gene McCreesh, S.J. and Tom Gaunt, S.J. and Shelley Douglass sends me Madeleine L'Engle's book *A Wrinkle in Time*. A full day.

May 28th

We keep busy though we are confined to this narrow dungeon: Bible study, Eucharist, check-in, long discussions about sentencing and supervised probation, writing, reading, letter writing, and praying. Mary Ryder and Patrick O'Neill are the parents of a beautiful baby girl, Maura, named after the Maryknoll sister and martyr, Maura Clarke. God is good.

May 29th

Jesus climbs the Mount of Olives to the Garden of Gethsemane to commune in agonizing prayer with God. The new Moses, he descends, enters the Temple, and teaches the crowds the new law of non-violence: love one another. Just then, the Scribes and Pharisees bring forward a woman they have captured in the act of adultery. (The man is nowhere to be found.) They make her stand in the middle of the crowd. They publicly humiliate her. They threaten to stone her to death. These so-called religious people have no sense of their cruelty. "Moses said we should kill her," they tell Jesus. "What do you say?" Like everyone else, they test Jesus' nonviolence. We always want to justify our killings, to make an excuse for one more murder.

Jesus remains calm, like Buddha, a center of nonviolence. Drawing in the sand, he issues a new law and literally disarms them. "Let the one without sin be the first to cast a stone" (Jn 8:1-11). Not only does he save the woman's life, he saves their lives, for the one who looks on a couple in the act has committed sin and is to be stoned according to their own law. They recognize their own sin and walk away. Then, Jesus says "Is there no one left to condemn? Then neither will I. Go and sin no more." The only sinless person, Jesus, refuses to kill or condemn anyone. Jesus shows mercy, forgiveness and compassion. This disarming Jesus speaks to us today: "Let the one without sin throw the switch on the electric chair or drop the bombs or push the button for nuclear war." Jesus disarms and transforms the murderous crowd. That is our job today.

Memorial Day, May 30th

Last evening, I reflected on the negative letters I received from friends and relatives in the past few weeks since I was found "guilty." They dismiss my action and my jail witness. This rejection is hard to bear. I value friendship; indeed, as a celibate, it's all I've got. People write the most critical things and I am stunned that they can be harsh while I sit locked up in jail. I think of Jesus who was rejected by everyone, thought crazy by his mother, betrayed and denied by friends. Rejection is to be expected if one follows Jesus.

I could not sleep last night. I am angry, hurt, upset. I spoke with Bruce. He tells me that people are challenged by my presence in jail in contrast to their materialistic lifestyle. I must accept this bitter cup. Someday, when I encounter my friends who have written me off, I hope to respond with love, compassion, understanding, forgiveness and truth—like Jesus.

May 31st

Someone sent Phil a copy of T.S. Eliot's *Four Quartets*, which I read throughout the day yesterday. This morning, I sit Buddha-like in quiet meditation, after yoga, at deep peace, seeking that "still point" of eternity that T.S. Eliot speaks of. The still point in jail is very still: a place of deep peace which the world cannot give.

"I am the light of the world," we read in John's Gospel. "Whoever follows me will not walk in darkness but walks in the light of life" (Jn 8:12). Jesus speaks to the Pharisees about testimony, judgment, and his origin. He is on trial. Though he is the judge of humanity, he judges no one. In the darkness of the domination system, Jesus offers the light of love, truth and peace.

In the cell with us sits a 34-year-old African-American who was sentenced to three years in prison for involuntary manslaughter. He killed his brother "in self-defense." The brother was threatening him, so he stabbed him in the leg and the brother bled to death. He speaks through a thick drawl. Though he's not a Christian, he spends his day reading a pocket New Testament. He's nervous about prison life and I find myself telling him not to worry. Another new inmate is in his early 50s. Though he is uneducated, poor and practically toothless, he speaks with great dignity. These broken poor are Christ in prison. We are here with them, keeping watch with Christ.

June 1st

My niece Jennifer Dear was born today at 6:17 a.m. She is a miracle. We thought she might not make it into the world, but here she is. Karen is well too.

Life abounds. God is at work. I take heart once more. Today I thank God for this child and pray for her and all the children of the world, that they may grow up in peace. We recommit ourselves to creating a more peaceful future for her generation. We pray that she may come to know the fullness of God's love and walk the way of nonviolence.

*

We discuss Jesus' conversation with the hostile Judeans. "You will die in your sin," Jesus tells them (Jn 8:21). "The one who sent me is with me." These words are lost on his hearers. But Jesus' insistence on God, on faith, on life, and on the cross, challenges us to a deeper faith. Rather than die in our sinful violence and cultural injustice, we hope to live in the fullness of life, resisting every variation of systemic and personal sin.

The problem that plagues the faithful in the first world is that we practice a private spirituality, sitting solemnly in luxurious retreat houses awaiting the spiritual breakthrough that will make us a "spiritual" people. Instead, we must act our way into a new spirituality. We need to take bold, public actions for justice and peace. Then, we shall receive a new social spirituality that will come, along with our sufferings and persecution, as a consequence of our action. We will be pruned, purified and taken into the life of the poor and oppressed. We will be blessed. The poor of the world eagerly await this new action-packed spirituality which the Gospels promise for all the faithful.

June 2nd

"If you remain in my word, "Jesus declares, "you will truly be my disciples and you will know the truth and the truth will set you free." The Judeans respond, "But we're already free. We're the chosen people." They are blind to reality and this invitation to new life. We North Americans are equally blind. Do we see how enslaved we are to possessions, money, prestige, power, weapons and despair? Do we recognize our need for liberation? We are as enslaved as they were. Because our hearts focus on false security, we are miserable and lifeless.

June 3rd

For the first time in six months, I slept alone in my own cell. Bruce moved into the cell with Phil. Now I have this little cell to myself. The peace and quiet of the night were extraordinary and I fell asleep quickly. This morning, our break day, I sit here silently and think and pray in solitude. I read my mail and my mind drifts to Jesus. I find myself reflecting on stages of my life as they have led me to this radical experiment in faith. I feel like a pioneer in the science of nonviolence. I sail on new waters, uncharted in our country. It is crucial that I am here. As of yet, I have not tapped into the spiritually explosive dimension of contemplative nonviolence, into the prayerful presence of God, yet that is where I'm headed. The political struggle we engage in is in reality an inner journey. The fruit of our inner struggle is born in the public struggle for justice and peace. Peacemaking, to quote the new Billy Joel song blasting on MTV, is "all about soul."

*

Last night, Horace joined us. This morning he was happily bailed out. After lunch, I read from Jonah's prayer of thanksgiving which he offers from the belly of the whale. We too offer thanks and praise to God from this whale's belly. There is much to be thankful for—for life, for food, for friends, for the Gospel, for God's reign of nonviolence, for Jesus, for the whole human family, and now for baby Jennifer. Though death circles the globe and hunts us down, life continually pushes us forward.

June 4th

It's 11:45 p.m.—a long, quiet day. As with every other day, we sit with the Gospels. Today we read Jesus' arguments with the Judeans. Instead of siding with God and truth, they prefer lying and murder. If Jesus says this to the liberal Pharisees, what does he say to us Americans?

I feel cooped up. I sit and pray and appeal to God.

June 5th

The national propaganda machine runs at full steam tonight as all the news celebrates tomorrow's 50th anniversary of D-Day. The Pentagon's officials, the president, the Congress and the veterans profess the glory of war. I want to hide. I want to flee from the culture like a desert father. So few oppose the mad military spending that eats us like cancer. These days reveal that we do not believe in the God of life, but worship the false gods of death.

Time stands still. We look for the next meal. We take long naps. We watch TV. We write a stream of letters. We talk for hours about the scriptures and our upcoming sentencing. We say our prayers. We hang by our fingertips.

June 6th

The nation's elite mark the 50th anniversary of D-Day. I sit in my cell, fasting, praying for peace, trying to cultivate a spirit of non-violence. We spend the morning discussing the climax of John's Gospel in chapter 8. "If you keep my words, you will never see death" Jesus proclaims to the brutal Judeans of the Temple. They denounce him, judge and condemn him. When he identifies himself with God, they pick up stones to carry out their death sentence. But he eludes them and leaves.

I confess my own complicity in this culture of death. In my fast and prayer today, I pray for all of us North Americans that we will repent of the sin of war and keep the word of peace. It is a somber day. We feel alone, yet we believe in God and trust that God hears our prayer for disarmament and that God's reign of nonviolence will be victorious. I beg God to purge me of violence and grant me a humble heart. This day, like all days, is in God's hands.

June 7th

Today marks six months since our action. Alone in my cell after a quiet day of fasting and discussing the scriptures with Bruce and Phil, I feel grateful to God for these difficult but grace-filled days. I marvel at the life and stamina of Nelson Mandela. How did he survive 27 years behind bars, including many years of solitary confinement? How did he break rocks day after day? How has he been able to transcend hatred and bitterness and reach out to his enemies in reconciliation? I have much to learn.

Yes, I have regrets. I have more questions about this action and my presence here than my harshest critics. Yet I know that the scriptures call us to disarm, that I too must take up the long journey of nonviolent resistance. I have been blessed, disciplined, and purified through the crucible of suffering. The deep immersion in the Gospel has been a daily confirmation of the imperative of Gospel nonviolence. Effectiveness? Success? I am way beyond the question of results. I am in a whole new territory. I swim in uncharted waters. I am trying to follow Jesus. I know I fail, but I long to try to be faithful, to be open to the mercy of God, to be a true channel of Christ's peace, a public peacemaker, a saint. I do not see where this experience is leading. Still

I am convinced that our action was marked by the Spirit's presence and guided by God. I walk the way of peace by faith alone. That is reason enough for gratitude.

June 8th

The healing of the blind beggar (John 9) is one of the great stories of the Bible. We are well into it now and I find it rich with wisdom and light. Standing in the center of the Temple, Jesus has just told a crowd of Pharisees that he is God and they pick up stones to kill him. As Jesus escapes, we are told in the original Greek, "he saw humanity blind from birth" (Jn 9:1)—not just "a man," but "humanity"! The story symbolizes the healing Christ offers to all humanity, and the way of discipleship we must all walk. Instead of inquiring after Jesus who has just barely escaped assassination and instead of seeking to help the poor blind beggar, the disciples start to philosophize about the meaning of suffering. "While I am in the world, I am the light of the world," Jesus asserts. With that, he spits on the ground, makes clay with the dirt, rubs it on the man's eyes and tells him to go wash in the Pool of the Sent. The image evokes Genesis and the God who creates humanity. It reminds us of baptism. We know the use of spit violates Jewish custom and law because it is unclean. Shortly, we learn that he has done this random act of kindness on the Sabbath. Finally, the man is sent. He symbolizes every human being and certainly every disciple. Humanity washes and sees.

Instantly, the once blind man is attacked by his neighbors, the Pharisees and his relatives. He fights them all off in the Temple, testifying to the truth, telling it like it is. They eventually kick him out. Hearing of this, Jesus seeks him out. "Do you believe in the Messiah?" Jesus asks. "Tell me who he is," the man replies. "You are seeing him and he is speaking to you," Jesus replies. "I do believe," the man says as he falls to the ground in worship.

What a story! This person is the model disciple. His story is our story. After our suffering, persecution, and excommunication from the Temple, Christ seeks us out and asks us about our belief. He reveals himself to us. We too can affirm him and worship him, but only after healing, confrontations and rejections. This story symbolizes my journey and helps me to understand the persecution and rejection I suffer. More and more, I hear Christ asking me now, as never before, "Do you believe in me?" With all my heart, I say, "I do believe," and fall on my knees in worship.

O God, I do believe. Help thou my unbelief. I worship you, Christ of peace. You are my Lord and my God. I love you. I thank you. I praise you. You Christ: you are our life, our sweetness and our hope. Amen. Amen.

June 9th

Yesterday, we shared a marvelous visit with Carol Brothers. She has convinced the local pastor to host a "Festival of Hope" at the church here in Edenton, the evening before our sentencing next month. Judge Boyle is one of the parish leaders. He teaches bible classes and runs the parish building committee. The plot thickens.

This morning, I spoke with Mev. She is now receiving radiation treatments. She gets outside daily for walks. Her new book, *The Struggle Is One*, is out to critical acclaim. She will speak in August at the Pax Christi National Assembly. She shares that she has many ups and downs and struggles with her fear of death. May God give her peace, strength, health, and many more years with us.

I did not sleep well last night. I went to bed early and woke up at 12:45 and lay awake until 5 a.m. The walls close in on me and I feel anxiety. But I did yoga and prayed for help. I visualize being outdoors at the North Carolina beaches or on Block Island or at Yosemite National Park, and soon feel some peace.

The story of the formerly blind disciple continues to energize me. It touches me at some deep level. I believe Christ is seeking me out and asking me, "Do you believe in the Anointed One? You are seeing him and he is speaking to you." With all my heart I believe, I tell Christ. In this spirit, I am at peace, focused on Christ, centered in faith, ready to endure anything.

June 10th

Jim and Shelley Douglass visit with us this morning for a glorious three hours. Jim returned Wednesday night from Bosnia after trying to help the religious leaders of Sarajevo get together for a pilgrimage of repentance for peace. They drove 12 hours yesterday from Birmingham, Alabama to be with us.

"We are in a time of greater danger of nuclear war," Jim said. "It is inevitable that nuclear weapons will be used somewhere, somehow, and many people will be killed in some catastrophic event. And we need to prepare now for that event. Suddenly people will become aware about the need for disarmament. At the same time, governments will split and become even more nationalistic and fascist. How do we prepare for such a time?" Jim asks. "That is the question I've been pondering. On that day, nonviolent actions such as Plowshares actions will offer great hope."

In the afternoon, Frank Moan, S.J., from my community on K Street in Washington, D.C., visits. He has just returned from Sarajevo and Palestine, where he investigated the treatment of refugees for his advocacy organization, *Refugee Voices*. He brings hundreds of pictures of war-torn Sarajevo: tall buildings bombed out and burned; the bombed out market-place; graves in public parks; also pictures of orphans in Gaza and militarized Israel. The striking photos vividly remind me why I continue to sit in silent witness here in jail: to call for disarmament and peace.

June 11th

A very quiet morning. For the second day in a row, we have given ourselves a rest from the intense bible study conversations so we can relax and pray and catch up on our mounds of correspondence. Here in my cell, I sit and look around at the ugly walls with the light brown paint falling off in sheets and I wonder where God is. "You are seeing him and it is he who is speaking to you," I hear the Gospel proclaim. Like the healed man, I fall in worship of Christ.

I pray that these days in jail may make me a person of faith and worship, that I may not be embittered, but rather more loving, compassionate, a kinder, gentler John Dear. So far it seems to be a losing battle. I can be self-righteous, arrogant and judgmental. I know that this is not my true self. I pray that I may be more loving, more inviting, and more affirming, so that others too may be willing to take new risks for disarmament. I pray for the gift of prayer.

June 12th

According to the Gospel, as we follow Jesus, are healed, stand up to resist the forces of darkness, and suffer the consequences, we are invited to a deeper faith. In the midst of suffering and persecution, we meet Christ. It is in this moment of ultimate crisis that we learn about faith and discover God. As we suffer expulsion from the Temple like the formerly blind beggar (in our case, expulsion from society into jail), we are sought out by Christ and invited into contemplation. Active resistance leads to a prayerful contemplation and a deepening faith in Christ. This morning, I am emboldened to watch for Christ who is seeking me out, finding me and asking me if I believe in him.

June 13th

Again, we delve into John's Gospel, the challenge of Jesus' healing touch, his sending forth, and his final inquiry into the formerly blind man's faith. Christ seeks us on the margins after we too have been kicked out of society. It is there—alone, rejected, on the periphery when we think our spiritual life is over—that Jesus approaches. We think we have been healed. We think we are disciples. We think we have been through it all—but like the formerly blind man, we still do not know Christ, who longs for us to know him. During these months in jail, Christ seeks us out, revealing himself to us and inviting us to faith.

June 14th

A heavy-set local named Billy, doing 30 days for drunk driving, joins us. He moves into the cell with me. He's nervous and unhappy but personable and polite. He is Christ and we welcome him.

"I came so that you might have life and have it more abundantly" (Jn 10:10). Jesus speaks to us of being the gate of the sheep, the voice the sheep listen to, the good shepherd. Some are thieves, robbers, hirelings, and, like Herod, foxes. They "steal and kill and destroy." Jesus is the nonviolent one. He promotes life. He brings people together in the sheepfold to rest in community. He also sends them out to speak and act and live in the pasture.

We struggle with this text but marvel at its beauty. Surely we know there are those who steal, kill and destroy. We trust in the shepherd who calls us, leads us, and cares for us. We are frail, lost, and helpless. We need a shepherd. The good news is that we have one, who is good, loving and devoted. Here in jail, he watches over us.

16

Life Beyond the Edge

Wednesday, June 15th, 1994

As I reflect on what it means to be a Christian, a priest, and a member of the Catholic church in these tumultuous times, I do not find myself preoccupied with the predominant questions of the mainstream, institutional church. On the one hand, the closing of churches, the scandals, the declining number of seminarians, the financial crises, and the lifestyle and politics of Church officials disappoint me. And I hope that someday the Catholic Church will allow priests to marry, will ordain women, will welcome all God's children, and give its land, property and wealth to the poor. But these issues are not my key concerns.

As I look at the church from the perspective of this dungeon, I wonder when North American Catholics as a people will take the Gospel seriously. When are we going to allow Jesus to disarm us and fashion us into people of disarming love? When will we put the demands of justice and peace at the center of church life?

The other morning, as we reflected on the meaning of discipleship, Phil described Christian faith as life on the edge which then moves beyond the edge into the unknown realm of faith.

This image captures not only our lives as disciples, but also what it means to be church today: we are a people on the cutting edge of society who take a step beyond the edge into unknown territory.

The church begins at the edge of society and goes beyond the edge. The church is Jesus' community. It is found among the poor, the homeless, the oppressed, the suffering and the marginalized. It thrives among those who take faith risks to announce God's reign of justice and peace and to denounce the world's systemic injustice. It promotes life by confronting the powers of death. The church is every community which practices Gospel nonviolence.

If anyone ever went beyond the edge, it is Jesus. His life does not stop with the formation of community, with his preaching of the good news of God's reign, or his liberating works among the poor; it begins there. From that locus, Jesus walks like a one-person crime wave into downtown Jerusalem, to the Temple, and turns over the tables in the greatest act of nonviolent resistance in history. His trouble-making life culminates with his swift arrest, jailing, trial, torture and execution.

The Gospels insist that the cross is the fullest revelation of Jesus' glory. As he goes to his death—resisting evil, loving his enemies, forgiving everyone, faithful to God—he shows us how to be human. In his resurrection, he stirs his community to resume where he left off. He sends his spirit upon his community to continue his mission of revolutionary nonviolence.

The church is nothing more and nothing less than this ever-present community of disciples who continue to practice active nonviolence. Church people today walk together the way of the cross, like Jesus, from the world of the poor to the world of power and take nonviolent direct action against the murderous, unjust status quo. Liberated from the shackles of power, the church today should take to the streets across the country in public demonstrations against the forces of death which kill us spiritually and physically. The church must denounce militarism, nuclear weapons, war preparations, homelessness, the death penalty and our demonic consumerism which leaves the third world to die like Lazarus on our doorstep.

Unfortunately, the institutional church rarely confronts the principalities and powers. The jails are not filled with Christ-centered, nonviolent resisters. The courts are not crowded with Catholics on trial for subverting the structures of injustice. The witness stands are not used to testify to Christ and his way of nonviolence. Few Catholics stand at the edge of anything.

Jesus faced exactly this problem in his day. When Jesus explains that his way of nonviolent love and resistance will not result in mass conversions but in his arrest, imprisonment, trial, torture and execution, Peter roundly rebukes him (Mk 8:33). The next time Jesus shares with them his way of nonviolence, the gang starts discussing which of them is the greatest (Mk 9:30-37). The third time Jesus risks the truth of nonviolence with his community, James and John demand a place at his right and left side in glory (Mk 10:32-41).

As the ruling authorities seek him out, Jesus offers himself completely, intimately, eternally in the Eucharist. Hours later, the disciples sleep as Jesus agonizes in prayer over the suffering that befalls him. As the soldiers arrest Jesus, the disciples ask him altogether, "Lord, shall we strike with a sword?" (Lk 22:50). Jesus is hauled away still trying to teach nonviolence to his disciples. "Stop, no more of this!" he cries (Lk 22:51). This plea for disarmament is the last thing they hear Jesus saying. The evangelists cannot stress the point enough: everyone had trouble following the nonviolent Jesus. "They all left him and fled," Mark writes (14:50). At the hour of his glory, as he dies on the cross, James and John do not die at his right and left side where they belong; rather, two violent revolutionaries hang with Jesus.

Though Jesus is abandoned and his way of nonviolence is misunderstood, he comes back risen, at peace, forgiving, loving and still insisting that his community embrace nonviolence. For nearly 2,000 years, his Holy Spirit has been trying to make us obey his way of life: "Love one another. Love your enemies. Forgive each other. Sell all that you possess and give to the poor. Seek first God and God's reign. Put down the sword. Take up the cross for nonviolent resistance to injustice. Do not be afraid. Have faith in God. Trust me. Take that leap off the edge."

Reading the Gospel in these confines confirms my conviction that the church today is summoned to spiritual maturity, to take up the cross. The cross is not a head cold or a hangnail or a cantankerous relative. The cross is the suffering, arrest, jailing, trial, imprisonment and possible execution that come as legal consequences of one's nonviolent confrontation with institutionalized violence. Every disciple is invited to this suffering love. "Those who wish to come after me must deny themselves, take up their crosses daily and follow me" (Lk 9:23).

Despite their fears and disbeliefs, the disciples do eventually adopt Jesus' way of active nonviolence. According to the Acts of the Apostles, they return to the scene of the crime. They commit divine obedience and civil disobedience—repeatedly. Filled with the Spirit, they are in and out of jail. One by one and by the thousands, they are martyred. Their last words are breathtaking in their simplicity and boldness. "We no longer take up 'sword against nation' nor do we 'wage war anymore,' having become children of peace for the sake of Jesus," Origen wrote. "We who once killed each other," Justin Martyr confessed, "not only do not make war on each other, but in order not to lie or deceive our inquisitors we gladly die for the confession of Christ." We need to recapture the faith of the saints.

As I reflect on the Word of God and share Eucharist each morning in our cell, I sense that we are being stretched into becoming a new church—right here in North America: the church of nonviolence, the church of resistance, the peacemaking church, the crucified church, the church beyond the edge.

Our journey over the edge begins at the margins of mainstream society, among the poor and disenfranchised. Life on the edge is the life of service to the poor, solidarity with the poor and action on behalf of the poor that leads to a sharing in their life. Defending the poor from systemic violence and accompanying Christ in the poor and in our enemies means going over the edge. It means becoming a prophetic community which denounces state-sanctioned violence and oppression. In the spirit of Jesus, we go on the nonviolent offensive, confronting the government centers of war which rob the poor and threaten to kill all humanity. In jail, this church keeps watch, listens for God, studies the scriptures, and prays: "Lord, I believe. Help my unbelief."

This church beyond the edge shares a living solidarity with the poor in prison. We become very much one with the poor. We minister in jail not only to fellow inmates but to those on the outside. Prison is the ultimate site for the church of nonviolence. It is the cross, and we accept it, fearfully, reluctantly, with sweat and tears, but willingly, obediently, joyfully. In these Calvaries, we suffer a living cross in witness against imperial violence and in obedience to the God of peace. In jail and prison, we let go of the culture, even the cultural church, and embark upon the water. In this violent world, the church of Christ can not do better than to stand prophetically present in every jail and prison, under sentence for loving disobedience and steadfast resistance.

The old church which blessed war and injustice is dying. A new church of nonviolence and resistance to evil is being born. As with every birth, there is pain and struggle. I take heart because though we stumble and fall, Jesus is with us. He fashions us into a community after his own heart.

June 16th

I am up to my ears in bombs bursting in air, bodies tossed about, bullets flying, men hiding in the trenches, killing rats while waiting to get killed. Erich Maria Remarque's *All Quiet on the Western Front* paints a ghastly and accurate portrait of war. It reminds me why I am here: to oppose killing, even at the price of my freedom. Though I am one of only a handful of war resisters currently imprisoned, I am grateful to be here for opposing war.

The highlight of the day: our jailer Glen let us borrow the electric razor and I cut Bruce's, Phil's and my own hair. I feel somewhat human again.

June 17th

All Quiet on the Western Front records the suffering that millions and millions of people have endured through the insanity of war. I finished it today and sit pondering the madness of the world. It puts my suffering in perspective and helps me accept suffering voluntarily for the noble cause of peace.

June 18th

We quietly reflect on Jesus' intimate relationship with his disciples (Jn 10:22-30). "My sheep hear my voice. I know them and they follow me. I give them eternal life and they shall never perish. No one can take them out of my hand." Jesus holds us in his hand. He protects us and cares for us. We are safe with him.

My brother Steve visited yesterday afternoon. I am so grateful for his abiding care and faithful love. He has shared every step of this journey with me.

June 19th

A downer of a day. I am depressed and unhappy. I try to pray, try some yoga, read some books, write some letters, but can't shake my ugly mood. I am mean to Bruce and Phil and generally grumpy toward everyone. I understand in my mind the significance of being here; the physical reality I find hard to endure. This small space is getting to me. I'm tired of the routine. I need some fresh air. I need space to move and breathe, to let my spirit soar. I don't want resentment and bitterness to eat away at me. God help me.

June 20th

There have been few visitors in the last two months (except for our new friends here in Edenton, and now Steve's visit). We feel very much alone and on our own. At least we have each other, Phil notes; Lynn is completely isolated.

I remain in a foul mood. I'm reading Ched Myers' great new book, *Who Will Roll Away the Stone?* My cellmate Billy compensates for the absence of cigarettes by eating like a pig. A new inmate, Roosevelt, a short, thin man in his 50s, has joined us. Today, we are all miserable.

June 21st

Lazarus has died and Jesus is on his way to be with him (Jn 11:1-16). We embark on that journey with Jesus to the tomb of Lazarus. Jesus loved Martha, Mary and Lazarus. Why did he not dash off at the first report of Lazarus' illness? His hesitancy perplexes us. But Jesus asserts that this illness will not end in death but in greater glory for God. The disciples, meanwhile, fear going back into that territory where Jesus was almost killed a few days before. They fear death. Jesus looks death in the face and insists on life. He heads off, regardless of trouble.

Meanwhile, I am as grouchy as ever. My mood swing has struck an all time low. Everyone annoys me, beginning with Phil and Bruce and my family and including the world and myself. And God. But where do you go in jail if you are miserable? What can you do? Nothing. I am sick of this cell and our confinement. I am tired of the stale air, the blasted television, the jail food, these orange fluorescent clothes and sandals, and the metal door. I have had enough of the whole experiment. I do not discuss this with Bruce and Phil. I sit alone on my top bunk all day long, with 300-pound Billy snoring away on the bottom bunk. Bruce and Phil know all too well about my foul mood and (wisely) leave me to myself, hoping I will cheer up.

How I wish I were outside, free, at the beach, at peace with myself and humanity.

In times of desolation, St. Ignatius advises, pray for consolation.

Lord, I'm ready: Send me consolation.

June 22nd

Suddenly, a full day that lifts me out of the depths. After breakfast and Eucharist, the "Faith and Ethics" reporter from the *Toronto Star*, spends the morning interviewing us. The conversation and her interest stimulate us and we finish exhausted but uplifted.

We take to our Gospel text like drowning men to air. The disciples try to talk Jesus out of returning to the Jerusalem vicinity, for fear of the murderous Judeans (Jn 11:11-20). "Our friend Lazarus is asleep and I am going to awaken him," Jesus tells them. Lazarus is their friend, too! We would expect them to show the same willingness to risk their lives. We speak about friendship and our attitudes toward our friends. We notice Jesus' attitude towards death: Lazarus is asleep. Death is a time of transition, a time of resting. Eventually, he explains: "Lazarus has died. I am rejoicing for you that I was not there that you may believe." Jesus does not talk here to Judeans and other unbelievers, but to the disciples who still do not believe. "Let us go to him," Jesus commands. He names and recognizes death. He does not fear death nor does he see it as the ultimate end. Thomas boldly proclaims, "Let us go and die with him." I am impressed with this great assertion of solidarity. And yet, it betrays their despair and misunderstanding. Christ is about life, not death; glory, not despair. Not only do they not die with Christ, they do not even go with him; the next verse describes Jesus arriving alone! We only read about the disciples again well after the saga is over when Jesus is again with them in the desert! Meanwhile, Martha, Mary and the Judeans, perhaps including the ones who want to kill Jesus, are well into the ritual 30 days of mourning. Martha hears that Jesus has arrived and runs off to greet him. She turns her back on the culture's attitude toward death. Mary eventually joins her. Phil, Bruce and I discuss the death of friends, funerals, mourning, and the Mass of the resurrection. The Gospel summons us once again to follow the God of life, to turn our backs on the culture of death, and greet the One who is the fullness of life.

June 23rd

Long ago, the Roman historian Tacitus described the martyrdom of early Christians under Nero:

> Nero looked around for a scapegoat and inflicted the most fiendish tortures on a group of persons already hated by the people for their crimes. This was the sect known as Christians. Their founder, one Christus, had been put to death by the procurator Pontius Pilate in the reign of Tiberius. This checked the abominable superstition for a while, but it broke out again and spread, not merely through Judea, where it originated, but even to Rome itself, the great reservoir and collecting ground for every kind of depravity and filth. Those who confessed to being Christians were at once arrested, but on their testimony, a great crowd of people were convicted. . . . of hatred of the entire human race. They were put to death amid every kind of mockery. Dressed in the skins of wild beasts, they were torn to pieces by dogs, or were crucified or burned to death: when night came, they served as human torches to provide lights. Nero threw open his gardens for their entertainment. . . . These Christians were guilty and well deserved their fate. (in Wes Howard Brook's, *Becoming Children of God*, Orbis, 1994, 258).

For the early Christians, discipleship entailed jail, brutal torture and death. How can I grumble? Although I have not been outdoors in seven months, how does my confinement compare to the persecution of the early Christians? I ponder the raising of Lazarus: First, Martha, in anger, disappointment and hope, complains to Jesus: "Lord, if you had been here, my brother would not have died." I too share disappointment and anger—at the injustice and wars which kill people, and the apparent absence of God. If Christ were here, I murmur, so many people would not have died. Such feelings betray my lack of faith. Jesus gets right to the heart of the matter: "I am the resurrection and the life. The one who believes in me, even though they should die, will live. Everyone living and believing in me will never die at all." Faith in Christ takes us well beyond death and its metaphors into the spiritual truth of reality. Death is separation from Christ. Be united in Christ and you will live, the early community shows us.

*

This morning, I begin to turn a corner. I am granted new strength, new hope, a new spirit. The presence of Jesus calms me, pacifies me, tames the violence within me. I imagine myself sitting with Christ below Mohegan cliffs at the edge of Block Island, looking on the ocean, soothing my restless spirit. The grace of God protects me. I will always be in recovery from violence and will have to continue begging God for the grace of nonviolence. Left on my own, I am dead. United to Jesus, I live, at peace, lovingly, truly myself, communing with others. I pray that Christ never leaves me alone.

June 24th

Daniel Berrigan has written a letter to Judge Boyle:

Sir: Permit me a reflection or two on the proceedings of the past seven months against the Plowshares group. My first reaction was a considerable puzzlement of spirit, as I watched you deny prior access to counsel, isolate the defendants from one another, and once the trial was underway, rule out of order reasonable arguments and topics. In ways that astounded, I saw day after day how you trashed the law you were hired to administer.

I was given to understand that you are a Catholic parishioner. The fact is astonishing. I strove to absorb apparent irreconcilables: that the same person could embrace the Catholic faith on the one hand, and act as a cover for the Air Force on the other. I was led back to scripture and the severe language of St. James with regard to judges. Stay away from the courts, settle your own affairs, is the advice of James (as well as of Jesus).

James goes on to reflect that judges invariably "favor the rich." And I thought of the Air Force, and of the hideous bombers of Seymour Johnson. I thought of the days and nights when, some 26 years ago, I cowered in bomb shelters in Hanoi, as I strove to evacuate three pilots the Vietnamese were releasing. I wondered if Judge Boyle realized that he was "favoring the rich," defending the enormous criminal entity that prowls the skies of the world, shadows the economy of North Carolina—and lords it in the courtroom of Terrence Boyle.

Yours was the worst judicial charade I have witnessed in some 30 years of resisting wars—ethically shabby, truculent and cruel.

None the less I am comforted, if spasmodically, by a reflection. Of course the Air Force, the most criminal arm of the American killer machine, requires legitimation of its crimes. You should tremble in your robes. For the judges will be judged.

Dan also writes to the prosecutors, William Webb and Christine Hamilton:

Sir and Madame: Now that the proceedings against the Plowshares defendants are ended, permit me to reflect on your conduct. Such unswerving malevolence as yours strikes me as unusual, even for American courts. You set yourself a task, and in my estimate, succeeded. You silenced and denigrated the noble defendants and turned a purported legal performance into a straightfaced theater of cruelty. Your behavior would have been applauded in an older, alas presently defunct, South Africa or Soviet Union.

In an otherwise riveting performance, I saw only one matter, perhaps a picayune one, that would have merited improvement. You would have offered a moment of truth beyond compare, had you entered court in the uniforms of the Air Force.

Permit me to recall a moment that to me summed up everything: it was a courtroom exchange between Mr. Webb and an entity of the FBI whose name escapes me. The latter said something to the effect that such defendants "made one ashamed to be a Catholic." And Mr. Webb, ever the witty and wise, responded that after all, they were "slime." This be it noted, within earshot of the families and friends of the defendants.

As to the first remark, kindly report to the Catholic eminence that he has matters slightly awry. He should in truth, declared Catholic as he would have it, be ashamed to sit in court at the side of those who "prosecute the saints of God, night and day."(Revelation)

(The text might possibly be a source of embarrassment to yourselves; it places in question your works and pomps. Are these to be thought properly demonic?)

And as to Mr. Webb's riposte as quoted above, one reflects that after all, "slime" is in the eye of the beholder.

June 25th

When the Judeans and Mary go out to greet Jesus, they are totally focused on death (Jn 11:28-37). They have no faith in Jesus. According to the Greek text, Jesus is enraged—much more than "perturbed" (as our translation describes him). Why? Not because Lazarus is dead, but because they have no faith in him or in the God of life. Confronted with their tears and lack of faith, he weeps—not for Lazarus, but for their lack of faith. They misunderstand and comment: "See how much he loved him. But couldn't he have done something?" Their question highlights their lack of faith. We all shake our heads with similar disbelief. If only you had done something! If only you would do something! If only . . . We are fixated with results and effectiveness. This desire for results and action has led us to develop weapons like the F15E. The Pentagon knows how to get results. Its weapons kill everyone in their paths and kill the souls of their creators and supporters. Meanwhile, we remains oblivious to all that God has already done for us, to all that God is doing, and to all that God is about to do for us. We do not trust God. Jesus weeps over our lack of faith.

In response to this faithlessness, Jesus is furious. He issues the first of three commands, "Take away the stone!" This great command resounds through the ages to the present day. "Roll back the stone that keeps us locked in the tomb, in the culture of death, in the empire of violence." How few hear this command. We not only disobey; we resist. We do not want resurrection. We do not want new life. Like the professional mourners, we live off despair and death.

And thus in the story: Of all people, Martha, the one who wanted Lazarus raised the most, speaks up in protest: "Lord, he is already smelling and he is dead four days now." Like the others, she has no faith and is overwhelmed by the despairing reality of death. And who can deny her claims? The body is rotting and stinking. According to tradition, after three days, the soul leaves the body. There is no hope. Nothing can be done. Lazarus is doomed. So are we.

And there stands Jesus, the God of life. "Take away the stone!"

*

We are six now. Along with Billy, Harold, a talkative, tall, thin man and Fred, a frail, bent over, gray-haired man have joined us. Both are here for failure to pay child support. They are friendly, but our tiny rooms are crowded. We eat our meals sitting on the floor. Two will sleep on the floor as well. We share our grace before dinner and ask God's blessing upon us all. Though we are in the tomb of the culture of death, the belly of the whale, we are still alive. God blesses us.

June 26th

They "lifted up the stone but Jesus lifted up his eyes to God and said, 'Thank you God for hearing me'" (Jn 11:41-44). The unbelieving crowds focus on earthly death, while Jesus is focused on his heavenly God. Rolling away the stone and confronting death require prayer. For the first time in John's Gospel, here at this climactic moment, Jesus speaks directly to God. Instead of the prayer that Martha hoped for—in which Jesus would ask God some great favor instead Jesus says simply, "Thank you." (Then, he explains himself to God, that he speaks simply "for humanity's sake," not for God's sake.)

He cries out in a loud voice, the second great command: "Lazarus, Come Out!" The Good Shepherd calls his sheep by name and they hear his voice. Lazarus represents humanity, all of us buried in the culture's tombs (from the Roman Empire to Seymour Johnson Air Force Base). Come out! Jesus cries. Live! Leave your tomb! Get up and walk away from death!

Lazarus appears! But he is bound in tight burial clothes—ears, eyes, mouth, hands, and feet. He cannot hear, see, speak, reach out, walk, or follow Jesus. He is still a victim of the culture of death.

Jesus issues his third and final command: Unbind him and let him go! Mark records the command to "bind the strong man" (the forces of death). Now comes the flip side, the command to unbind the weak, the poor and oppressed, and let them go free. The people standing by are ordered to do this. Life is not fully restored until we all pitch in and unbind one another and set each other free.

The story ends with this command. Do they obey? Does Lazarus go free? The command lingers. Our job today could not be more clear: to unbind humanity from the shroud of death which enslaves it and set it free to live in peace, justice and nonviolence.

The commands remain: Take away the stone! Lazarus, come out! Unbind him and let him go free!

June 27th

It rains all day today. Tornado warnings have been announced on the TV. We sit quietly, reading, writing, praying, talking with each other.

Mother Teresa writes from Calcutta: "I am sorry to hear that you have been arrested. Be glad that you are to proclaim the love of Jesus even to the poor in prison. Give Jesus your pain and limitation and trust in him. In your weakness, his power will be a protection and a strength. Be assured of my prayers for you. If I am in the U.S.A, I will get in touch with you. God bless you."

June 28th

Jesus' raising of Lazarus symbolizes all struggles of liberation from oppression and death. During the 60s, Dr. King and the civil rights movement called forth African-Americans from the tomb of racial injustice and unbound them. In South Africa, Mandela and the resisting masses ordered the stone of apartheid rolled back and the South African people to come forward. Whoever thought apartheid could be dismantled? At times, it appeared easier to raise someone from the dead than to end the systemic enslavement of 25 million black South Africans. Likewise, we are trying to take away the stone that keeps us entombed in our culture's militarism. Everyone tells us it is impossible. Despair has overwhelmed us. The voice of Jesus cries out: Take away the stone! Lazarus, come out! Unbind him and let him go free! In other words: "Disarm your weapons of mass destruction! Become a people of nonviolence! Put aside your love of death and live together in peace and justice!"

*

Lynn sends her "Joke of the Week" (which Larry loved):

Q: How many jailers does it take to screw in a light bulb?

A: Five. It's not a joke. She saw it happen.

*

This morning, Phil asked me about my funk. I shared with him my claustrophobia and anxiety; the lack of support I feel from many people on whom I had counted; my apprehension about our uncertain future; my loneliness; my fears; my worries for my parents; and my disappointment in myself and others. Like Bruce, he is encouraging and compassionate.

June 29th

Our overweight cellmate, Billy, left at midnight, after climbing the walls these last few days. Leo arrives this morning to take his place. He enters my cell this afternoon: "You guys are alright. I used to be in the Air Force at Seymour Johnson but now I hate all those preparations for war and killing people. It's just terrible. It doesn't solve anything. I support you for doing what you did to end war." I am dumbfounded by his clear grasp of our action and his total support, especially when I compare it with the educated churchfolk who write me stinging letters of opposition.

Bruce and Phil are eager to appear in court for our sentencing, not just for the opportunity to leave the cell but for the chance to speak out. I dread the whole affair. My stomach is in knots. I will stand before the judge and speak out because I must. I do not like confrontation: yet my whole life has become one confrontation after another.

The Gospel tells how Caiaphas declares that Jesus must die so that the nation might live. The chief priests argue that if Jesus is left alone, "all will believe in him and the Romans will come and take away both our land and our nation" (Jn 11:48). The state always punishes those who threaten its power. This dynamic plays out in our own lives: the authorities know that if everyone heard about Plowshares actions, supported them, and started enacting them at military bases around the country, the American establishment would be profoundly challenged. So, we are locked up "for the good of the nation."

June 30th

Patrick O'Neill visits this morning. Later, our friends Jeff and Carlotta from the Norfolk Catholic Worker visit. I tell Carlotta that we are discussing the story of Lazarus and she lights up. "The problem we have with resurrection," she observes, "is that we can't handle that much freedom. It's too much freedom! We can't control people if they're rising from the dead." She sums up the entire episode: Jesus offers freedom from death. The culture prefers death to the freedom of life, and so it kills him.

Afterwards, the jailer Mike Chinsolo takes us out to the jail's garage to show us his motorcycle, a huge, expensive two-seater that is almost as big as a car. We marvel at it, and are returned to our cell.

July 1st

"Things of fundamental importance to people," Gandhi wrote, "are not secured by reason alone, but have to be purchased with suffering. Suffering is the law of human beings; war is the law of the jungle. But suffering is infinitely more powerful than the law of the jungle for converting the opponent and opening their ears, which are otherwise shut, to the voice of reason. Nobody has probably drawn up more petitions or espoused more forlorn causes than I and I have come to this fundamental conclusion that if you want something really important to be done, you must not merely satisfy the reason, you must move the heart also. The appeal of reason is more to the head but the penetration of the heart comes from suffering. It opens up the inner understanding in people. Suffering is the badge of the human race, not the sword" (from *All Men Are Brothers*, p. 118).

The only way peace will come to our wartorn world is if people are willing to suffer nonviolently for it. Unearned suffering in the cause of disarmament, justice, and peace is redemptive. The reason we have no peace and so few peacemakers is because so few are willing to suffer for peace. But when we look at the lives of all noble people who struggled for peace, we see they did so through the power of voluntary suffering, and that makes all the difference.

July 2

Yesterday was a day of quiet rest. I spent most of the day reading Madeleine L'Engle's *A Wind in the Door*, a gift from Shelley Douglass. In the afternoon, Jack and Felice Cohen-Joppa visited. They had driven all the way from Tucson, Arizona. For over a decade, they have published *The Nuclear Resister*, a regular account of nonviolent direct actions and people in prison. They are a consistent voice of resistance to the war machine. We enjoyed their company tremendously.

This morning, we read John's account of Mary of Bethany's extravagant love for Jesus, how she pushes past the arrogant (male) disciples and pours out "a ton of expensive cologne" on Jesus' feet. (The ointment cost about $18,000 in today's dollars. It was only used to bury people). The disciples balk. "That money could have been used for the poor!" Judas Iscariot complains (Jn 12:1-11). "Leave her alone," Jesus says. "The poor you will always have with you, but you will not always have me. She has prepared me for burial." In other words, only Mary accepts Jesus' way of the cross, only she accepts him with love as the suffering servant. The men are caught up in ideology. The poor, Jesus says, will be with you in your communities. Support me as I give my life for them.

Jesus is constantly rejected. This is perhaps the only instance in John's Gospel where someone has done something kind to him. What is our attitude towards Jesus on the eve of his death? How do we approach Jesus in our prayer? How do we approach those who take up the cross in discipleship to Jesus? Do we support their walk to the cross?

This leads to a long reflection on how so many people, including family, friends and even community members, reject us and let us down. On more than one day, we have felt abandoned. Few people ask how we are doing. Most of those who visit do most of the talking. There's not much we can do, except try to be loving and try to listen to them and try not to complain and try to support one another here in jail and to pray for everyone.

July 3rd

It is Sunday evening and I sit on my bunk alone in this cell while my friends watch a film, *A River Runs Through It*, where two brothers explore the spirituality of fly-fishing in Montana. The outdoors come beautifully alive on the screen. Indoors, here, we dwell in a dungeon.

There are no words to describe the pain of jail. It is not romantic, as the writers of resistance literature might paint it. It is lonely. It is a dying. It is one long present moment. Time takes center stage. We wait all the day long. Each day resembles the day before. Day after day after day, life passes. Being in jail is like being sick. Our presence here, we hope, will be a balm for our culture.

I try to remain calm. Though the walls close in on me, I try not to panic. The sentencing approaches and I tell myself that my life is in God's hands. Whatever God wants, I accept.

My mother and father visit today, in good spirits, full of news and interest, cheering me up.

This morning, we ponder John's account of Jesus' entry into Jerusalem through the palm-branch-waving crowd. "Fear no more," we are told. "See your king comes riding on an ass's colt," the symbol of peace. Jesus incarnates humble nonviolence. We speak of putting aside our fears. It is a constant struggle: to look beyond fear to the nonviolent Jesus.

I am reading *Autobiography of a Yogi* by Paramahansa Yogananda and *A Swiftly Tilting Planet* by Madeleine L'Engle. Last night, I did yoga and sat in meditation, feeling close to God. I long to be close to God. Sitting in peace, trying to be aware of God's abiding love, helps.

July 4th

"The hour has come for the human one to be glorified," Jesus says. "Truly I say to you: unless the grain of wheat falls to the earth and dies, it remains alone; but if it dies, it bears much fruit." Jesus proclaims his hour as the Greeks come to see him (Jn 12:20-26). Using this image of wheat, John speaks of domesticated bread grain that must be broken up and sown to bear a good harvest. This work is done primarily by women. The scriptures invoke a feminine image for discipleship. What's more, the Greek word for "grain" is plural: not only does Jesus mean that he himself will fall to the ground, die and bear fruit, but all his followers will as well.

"Whoever serves me, follows me; where I am, there will my servant be." We seek to serve Jesus, to follow him and thus to be with him wherever he is. If Jesus goes to the Temple, gets arrested, jailed, tried and sentenced, so must his followers. If he gets executed, so must his followers. And so, we sit here on our journey toward Jesus.

Perhaps that journey, that personal transformation, is the most significant event of these days. It is not what we have done or what we are doing that is ultimately important, but rather, what God is doing in us. What God has been doing in me—leading me to disarm a nuclear fighter bomber, disarming my heart through this experience of suffering and confinement—is what is crucial and essential. God is at work. God is transforming us. What God is doing in us, God wants to do in everyone.

July 5th

We do not know what tomorrow holds. We might be released; we may be shipped off to prison; we do not know. After breakfast, I thank Phil and Bruce for these days—long, arduous, exacting, some painful, a rare few ecstatic; days of inner search, spiritual fortitude, conversations with other inmates and jailers; days of keeping watch, keeping the faith, keeping our spirits high; days of the cross and the resurrection. Both Phil and Bruce have stood by my side through all my ups and downs. They possess tremendous faith and wisdom. We read from the Psalms. We break the bread and pass the cup. We bow our heads in silent prayer. Blessing upon blessing.

Then, on cable TV, we watch the film *Hamlet*.

Tomorrow, I will stand in court in spiritual solidarity with Jesus who also stood in court. I will speak from my heart. I will try to speak for the victims of war, for all who long for peace, and indeed, for the God of peace. I pray to stand as Jesus' ambassador, his representative, appealing for conversion to nonviolence. May he give me the words, the heart, the spirit to offer that invitation. May he be there, in power and glory, to be glorified anew.

17

The Sentencing

At 4:30 a.m., the jailers awaken us. We are carted to Elizabeth City at 5:30 a.m., not 7:30 a.m., so that our supporters are unable to greet us at the courthouse. Phil appears before judge Boyle first. After Phil's remarks and Ramsey Clark's statement of support, the judge sentences him to one more month in jail, four months under "house arrest," and three years supervised probation. Lynn and Bruce appear separately in the afternoon and are sentenced to six and seven more months in jail, respectively, without any rationale given.

When the judge asks me if I have anything to say before he sentences me, I offer the following reflection:

> Judge Boyle, sisters and brothers: I would like to begin by thanking everyone who has helped me these past years, and especially during the last seven months of my imprisonment, to try and stand for peace, to try to stand with the nonviolent Christ, to try to stand publicly with the God of disarming love. Indeed, I would like to thank God this morning for bringing me to this day and for offering to us all the gifts of life and peace and nonviolence.
>
> Secondly, I would like you to know, Judge Boyle, that I have deep respect and love for you, as well as for Mr. Webb and Ms. Hamilton, and that it is in this Spirit of respect and love that I offer these reflections.
>
> I have often wondered what I would have done if I had lived in Nazi Germany. Would I have been a good, law-abiding, obedient German citizen? or, rather, would I have been a good, Gospel-

222

abiding Christian, obedient and faithful to the God of nonviolent love—and thus necessarily disobedient to the State's murderous policies? I hope I would have had the grace and the strength and the spiritual fortitude to walk into those German death camps and begin to take apart the gas chambers and cremation ovens, to literally and symbolically start dismantling those legal instruments of mass destruction. I suppose if I were not shot then and there, I would have been arrested, jailed and quickly tried in court for breaking the law, perhaps for "willfully, destroying government property."

I believe we're all faced with a similar situation today. As I look at the United States, the most violent nation not only in the world, but in the history of the world; the inventor of the atomic bomb and the hydrogen bomb and the F15E; the one nation so far to drop nuclear weapons on human beings; the nation that possesses a nuclear arsenal of unimaginable proportions; I conclude that what the Nazis tried to do to the Jews and others, our country threatens to do and is preparing to do to the whole of humanity. Despite all the recent changes, including the collapse of the Soviet Union, the us continues on its course of global destruction. And I conclude that all of us have a responsibility to do what we can to stop the killing, to dismantle our nuclear arsenal, to renounce war, as well as to promote peace and life for all people.

And so, coming from my work among the poor and the homeless, on December 7th, 1993, my friends and I walked unarmed and in the Spirit of nonviolence through the war games of Seymour Johnson Air Force Base and hammered briefly on one of the many F15E nuclear bombers to begin anew the process of disarmament.

I undertook this modest act of disarmament in order simply to be faithful to the God of peace and to call our country to stop preparing for war and to "Disarm and Live," as our banner read. I went because of my desire to follow the nonviolent Jesus and to obey God's commandments: "Thou shalt not kill. Put down the sword. Beat swords into plowshares. Love one another. Forgive 70 times seven times. Love your enemies." Like Gandhi, Martin Luther King, Jr., Dorothy Day and so many others, I simply want to obey God and God's law of nonviolence.

By our action, we say that the time has come to disarm every F15 nuclear fighter bomber, every nuclear weapon, and every weapon of death. The time has come, we say, to spend our resources on real human needs—to feed the starving masses, to house the homeless, to clean up the environment, and to provide healthcare, education and jobs for all. The time has come to disarm our hearts as a people and to live in peace together with all humanity as the sisters and brothers we are, children of a loving God. The time for disarmament has indeed come.

We are faced with the greatest spiritual crisis in history, a crisis of soul. Today, over two-thirds of humanity suffer under systemic poverty, misery and oppression. Forty thousand children die every day of starvation and hunger-related diseases. Our country's militarism and nuclear arsenal, as well as its consumeristic lifestyle cause this global suffering. Fifty years after Pearl Harbor, D-Day, Hiroshima and Nagasaki, our country has still not learned the way of peace. This is a spiritual crisis, a matter of life or death, a crisis of the soul.

We continue to promote and prepare for war, to thrive on the big business of death. This fiscal year, for example, the U.S. will spend $588 billion on nuclear weapons, war and preparations for war. Even after all the peace treaties are fully enacted, the U.S. will still have over 20,000 nuclear warheads. We are up to our ears in militarism and killing. We have not yet learned that war solves nothing; that violence only breeds further violence; that war is immoral and wrong. If we do not reverse our course, we shall continue down this spiral of violence to our doom. We cannot afford to waste another minute or another dime on war.

The time has come to disarm, because our warmaking is killing us spiritually. We are deep into mortal sin. We are in the process of losing our souls. We need to stop sinning and repent of our violence. Building, producing, paying for, maintaining, using and legally defending weapons of mass destruction like the F15E nuclear bomber is sinful. To the extent that we support war and these weapons of death, we oppose the God of life. We then stand in direct disobedience to the God of nonviolence. This spiritual crisis bears down on each and every one of us, whether we like it or not. We as a people have become servants of death. The choice before us is whether or not we will become servants of life.

It seems to me that either we support this culture of death, its wars, its F15Es, its nuclear weapons, its institutionalized injustice, its imperial oppression of the world's poor, its plans to destroy the planet, and the consequences of all this—the loss of our souls—Or, we support the God of life and God's Way of nonviolence and disarmament and God's reign of justice and peace and we obey God's command to love our enemies and we join God's struggle, God's movement against the forces of death and so share in the fullness of life.

This Kairos moment summons each and every one of us to take a new stand for disarmament and peace. Like so many others, I am trying to stand with the God of life, to walk God's way of peace, to practice God's command of nonviolence which requires our public opposition to war. This choice, this summons, brought me to Seymour Johnson Air Force Base.

This morning, I wish to share my hope and prayer that we as a people will hear the summons of God, the judgment of God, and choose to disarm and live in peace. I envision a day when thousands of people across the country will enter military bases and nuclear installations, as the scriptures instruct, and peacefully, prayerfully, dismantle our gas chambers, our legal instruments of mass destruction. I foresee a day when Plowshares actions will not only be legal, but be cause for nationwide repentance and conversion and celebration. I see a great day coming when the last nuclear weapon will be dismantled, when there are no more F15Es, when war is forever outlawed, and when we as a people embrace the wisdom of nonviolence.

And so, with all due respect and in hope for the coming of that day, I would like to invite you, Judge Boyle, to join us in this mission of disarmament and nonviolence.

I appeal to you and to everyone in our country: Let's not support or defend the F15E or other weapons of mass destruction. Let's not support mass murder any longer. Let's not be instruments or puppets of the warmaking, nuclear establishment. Let's not support the system which makes these idolatrous weapons possible and respectable. Let's not allow war to happen in our name. Let's not be like the good people of Nazi Germany, obedient citizens who allowed their nation to incinerate other human beings in a global holocaust. Let's not be servants of death.

We can do better than that. We can all do better than that.

Instead, let's be people of peace, people who love life, people dedicated to God's reign of life and love for all. Let's obey God's law of nonviolence. Let's be God's own people and thus reflect

God's own nonviolent love for everyone. Together, you and I and all of us, let's take a bold stand for peace, disarmament and life. Let's help make possible the coming of that day when war will be no more and everyone will walk the Way of nonviolence. Let's be servants of life. For this I pray, in the name of Jesus. Thank you for listening. God bless you.

*

The judge was livid and exploded with anger. "I'm proud to be an American," he railed. "I'm proud of all of the people who have gone before me and all the struggle and sacrifice and death that has gone on to make America what it is."

My lawyer friend, Joe Cosgrove, spoke up. "Although slavery is enshrined in the Constitution, slavery is no longer acceptable in our culture. We have changed our minds on things that we thought were solidly accepted institutions. It took a great deal to change that. What we have before U.S. is someone who has a vision for change." Bishop Thomas Gumbleton spoke as a character witness. When questioned about our Plowshares action, he told the prosecutor, "I would not see the destruction of an evil weapon as any different than what Jesus did in the Temple. To me, that's not a criminal act. . . . The use of nuclear weapons kills us physically and spiritually. . . . There will be times when you confront the civil authorities and act against them," he concluded. "John did it and we are called to do the same thing." Mr. Webb called me "a liar, a common criminal and a vandal." To put me in a category with Martin Luther King, Jr. and Gandhi, he concluded, was "just plain obscene." Then, Judge Boyle sentenced me to two more weeks in jail, four and half months under house arrest and three years of supervised probation.

I thank God for our witness and look forward to getting out and carrying on the struggle for peace.

Epilogue

Lessons from Jail

ONE YEAR TO THE DAY FROM OUR PLOWSHARES ACTION, I SIT HERE IN our Jesuit community row house home in Washington, D.C. under "house arrest." I was released just after midnight on the morning of July 22nd, 1994 to my parents and our friend, Patrick O'Neill. The jailers stood out in the parking lot talking with us for 45 minutes before we finally said good night. My liberation from jail was an experience of deep joy.

Phil was brought to the Alexandria, Virginia jail and eventually before another judge on a different charge for demonstrating at the Pentagon in August, 1993 on the Hiroshima anniversary. He was sentenced to several more months in jail and then further months under house arrest. He was released on October 5th, his birthday, to four months of house arrest. Bruce and Lynn were released for four weeks in August and turned themselves in to federal prisons in West Virginia on September 1st, where they remain until early 1995.

The probation officers assigned me to the wrong department and because of their mix-up, they have extended my house arrest several more months into 1995. I am allowed outside several hours a day. They monitor me closely, coming by the house for surprise visits and calling at odd hours to assure themselves that I am here. But I am reminded in the concluding lines of the Acts of the Apostles, how St. Paul underwent house arrest in Rome for two years. He spent his time receiving people and talking about Jesus and the reign of God. So I try to do likewise.

These days, as I walk outdoors, visit with family and friends, and resume my ministry in inner-city Washington, D.C., I ponder the meaning of my experience in jail—and where the grace of God lies in it. I will learn from and reflect upon my jail experience for the rest of my life. However, some primary lessons stand out.

1. Jail is awful. Nelson Mandela emerged from 27 years in a South African prison to offer his nation and the world the hope of reconciliation and healing. Gandhi, King, and Dorothy Day urged young people to "fill the jails" in opposition to war and injustice. Thoreau wrote that the only place for a just person in an unjust society is in jail. Nevertheless, there is nothing romantic about jail.

There are over one and a half million people currently in U.S. jails and prisons, and that figure promises to skyrocket. What I learned first hand is that the system does not work. It cannot heal people or rehabilitate people because it is set up to be cruel and inhuman. In the typically overcrowded Robeson County jail, where we were part of a handful of white inmates among nearly four hundred African-Americans, the jailers treated us coldly, as if we were not human beings. We ate poorly. Our cells were searched at random in the middle of the night by a squad of rubber-glove-wearing officers. We had to agitate to receive any books, including the Bible.

In the Chowan County Jail, Phil, Bruce and I shared two tiny cells with a small, connecting third room with three other inmates. We never left that fishbowl area in five months, and despite all the support we received from friends and family, the pressure and claustrophobia began to wear on us. How do people survive under such inhuman circumstances? Most do not. One thing I know is that barring a miracle from God, violent offenders can only emerge from jail and prison more violent. Our nation's commitment to building more jails and prisons instead of fighting crime at its roots by insuring justice for the poor will doom us to a future of violence. We should build new schools and not new jails, just as we should send food and medicine to our enemies and not bombs.

2. Personal nonviolence is crucial if you want to survive in jail. From the jailers to the federal marshals to the other inmates, violence is the name of the game. One is constantly provoked. Though fights and even murders happen in prisons all the time, it is more amazing that there is not more violence. I often wondered why the inmates did not go completely crazy and kill one another. Nonviolence is crucial for prisoners and needs to be taught. I discovered that showing respect to the other inmates and to the jailers can be very disarming. The practice of personal nonviolence can humanize relationships between prisoners and soften the attitude of even the cruelest guard.

3. The Bible and the Eucharist can sustain us through anything. Each morning, Phil, Bruce and I spent two to three hours studying the Gospel. I studied four years in theology school but I have never been so immersed in the scriptures. In the context of jail, the scriptures came alive. Each text spoke to our predicament and gave us new insight into our lives, our world, and the hope offered in Christ. Over and over, I heard the basic commandment to believe in God. Though my faith was tried through the fires of jail, the scriptures gave me daily, even hourly, encouragement to carry on in hope.

After each bible study session, we took a piece of Wonder Bread and a cup of grape juice and offered these humble gifts for our Eucharist. We presented our petitions, prayed the Lord's prayer, gave each other the sign of peace, and found strength to live through the dull monotony of jail. The scriptures and the Eucharist are our greatest gift. They sustain us through whatever persecution and trials we must endure.

4. Community is essential. During my first week and a half in jail, I was on my own in a cellblock with poor, young, brutalized men. I found the pressure and the loneliness overwhelming. When I was reunited with Phil and Bruce, I knew I would be able to survive. From then on, each morning after Eucharist, we had a "check-in" time. Even though we had not left the cellblock and knew everything about each other's lives, still we found it necessary to formalize a time each day to share with one another what was on our minds and in our hearts.

Community is not only essential to any dramatic act of civil disobedience or solidarity with the poor, it is crucial for those of us called to risk imprisonment for the sake of justice and peace. Without a supportive community, we might not survive. But through communal sharing and love, we can talk out our day to day concerns, share our joys and sorrows, and find in one another the strength to endure.

5. *Christ is present among the imprisoned poor.* Matthew 25 insists that Christ is present among those in prison. Our jails and prisons are packed with the poor and the marginalized, especially with African-Americans and Latinos. Since scripture maintains that God takes the side of the oppressed and is determined to liberate them, I knew that God was in our midst.

I liked to compare ourselves with Shadrach, Meshach and Abednego, in the fiery furnace for refusing to worship the emperor's idols. While the flames burned around us, we remained unburned, and a fourth person like a Son of God stood in our midst. We realized that Christ presented himself to us in the suffering prisoners around us.

Some inmates were violent and broken, others were friendly and jovial. During our last few months, we shared our space with Harold, Fred, and Leo, rural Carolinians in jail for not paying child support. Fred simply had no money and had been homeless and hungry. Leo took him in and they both eventually landed in jail when Leo too ran out of funds. Harold had worked as a construction worker every day for over a year and was relieved to have time off in jail. He saw it as vacation and enjoyed his naps and television. Fred had not eaten a square meal in a long time. Their attitude—and gratitude—toward their six week imprisonment challenged me and made me more aware of the plight of the poor.

Going to jail on behalf of disarmament and peace offers a living solidarity with the poor that is not available in any other way. I found myself without any possessions and without the freedom to do as I please. I tasted for a few months the bitter poverty, powerlessness and helplessness which is the daily lot for most of humanity. For someone with a vow of poverty, it was nothing less than a revelation. Christ among the poor is teaching me a new lesson.

6. *Go and visit the imprisoned.* I cherished my visits with family members, other Jesuits, supporters and friends. They broke the monotony and drudgery of day to day confinement. Those who took the time to listen to my story healed the pain I felt and gave me new strength to carry on for a few more days. Visiting the imprisoned is a great ministry. The smallest act of compassion toward a prisoner can go a long way. Listening to their tales of woe, doing small favors for them, and being present to their suffering are tremendous acts of charity that do more than lift the human spirit. They help people survive an inhuman situation.

7. *Jailers are human, too.* One of Nelson Mandela's closest friends is the jailer who had charge over him during his last 15 years in prison. They still visit several times a week. Political conversion has a very human dimension in the day to day world. The jailers we encountered in the Robeson County Jail, by and large, were brutal and mean. Even the friendliest of them could turn on you. They hold the keys. Some of them are armed. They have dominating power over you. How do we respond in the Spirit of nonviolent love to jailers and guards? We tried to be as respectful as we could, to resist injustice as much as we could, and to concentrate our energies on our own survival and hanging out with our cellmates. Then we met Mike Chinsolo.

As the chief jailer of the Chowan County Jail, Mike came in to visit with us every morning at 7 a.m. from the first day we arrived in his jail. For weeks, he would sit down and tell us the difficulties of running a jail, the lack of state funding, the "security" problems, the troubles of the other inmates and the crises in his personal life. Over time, he began to ask about us. He wanted to know our life stories. He argued with us about our action. Quickly, he grew to respect us and we him. He befriended our families and friends and lobbied to keep us together in his jail. He ordered our books and asked us to sign them. As our sentencing approached, he even arranged press interviews for us with the local media.

As we got to know Mike and other friendly jailers, we encouraged them to improve life for the imprisoned and change their own employment so that they would not have to spend their lives locking people up. Through it all, I began to understand St. Paul's excitement in his letter to the Philippians as he told of converting members of the Praetorium guard. We kept inviting Mike to let us go just as the early Christians in the "Acts of the Apostles" were set miraculously free. When I was eventually released in the wee hours of the morning, he told me, with a smile, that he was sorry to see me go.

8. *Contemplative prayer is a basic requirement.* The solitude and silence which I have so richly treasured in my 12 previous years as a Jesuit ended the minute I entered the jail. The TV blares all day long. People yell at one another. The prison doors slam shut with a loud thud and you have no privacy whatsoever. How does one pray in such an environment? How can one listen to the still, small voice of God coming through the breeze in a noisy, crowded jail cell? Where is God in jail?

Over the years, I have come to experience God as a God of peace and unconditional love. God is gentle and nonviolent. In my Ignatian prayer, God reveals God's self to me as Jesus my brother. I like to sit in solitude and spend time being in relationship to Jesus Christ. Jail disrupted this quiet rhythm. Perhaps my faith is very weak. Perhaps I was too worried and anxious. Eventually, I found a new way to center myself in meditation despite the surrounding din. Prayer became a matter of breathing, of being present, of dwelling in God's abiding love in an inhuman environment. Now out of jail, I appreciate not only the glories of creation, but the silence of solitude. Yet I now know that one can pray anywhere, even in jail.

9. *Hope is granted in daily doses to those who hope for it.* I had many hard days in jail. But oddly enough, my friends and I found ourselves more hopeful than ever. Phil used to joke that we had more hope than we could stand. If we can rise above the institutionalized despair of jail and prison, we can be people of living hope. We found great hope in our action, modest though it was, as a symbol of disarmament. We found hope in the faces of our fellow inmates and in the strength and support of friends and relatives. We found hope in the thousands of people who wrote to us and shared their desire for peace and renewed commitment to nonviolence.

Most of all, I found hope in the life, teachings, suffering, death and resurrection of Jesus. Through our bible study, Eucharist, and prayer, we were immersed in the story of Jesus and were given strength to carry on the witness of nonviolent love. Though nuclear weapons, war and violence continue to inflict pain and destruction on the human family, God is greater than human violence. Though we were in jail, we believed anew in the power of nonviolence. We are all convinced: one day war will be abolished. Nuclear weapons will be outlawed. The church will teach nonviolence as a matter of course. We learned to trust in God and God's nonviolent transformation of humanity.

*10. **Disarmament is still a priority.*** As we mark the 50th anniversary of the atomic bombings of Hiroshima and Nagasaki, we reflect that disarmament is needed as much now as ever before. We saw with our own eyes in the early morning hours of December 7th, 1993, that the war machine rolls on. Despite the end of the Cold War, the United States still possesses over 20,000 nuclear weapons. The Clinton administration has bowed to the Pentagon's wish to maintain the nuclear arsenal. With the proliferation of nuclear weapons and other weapons of mass destruction, humanity is not safe by any measure. As we discovered during our trials, the courts work actively to defend such weapons legally, despite international law, the Nuremberg principles, and God's law of nonviolence. During our time in jail, we reflected at length on the world's militarism and how our nation's addiction to violence is destroying our cities and our souls. As long as one nuclear weapon exists, as long as injustice continues to plague humanity, as long as the earth is threatened, some Christians will still have to go to jail in protest.

*11. **We can live the Gospel in our daily lives: the choice is ours.*** The choice before us is simple: we can spend our lives making a positive contribution to the nonviolent transformation of the world, or we can selfishly pursue career and money at the expense of suffering humanity and allow the world to disintegrate before our eyes. As one of the Salvadoran Jesuit martyrs wrote, the only way to be truly human in the world today is to dedicate ourselves to the abolition of poverty, oppression and militarism. We can choose to make a difference in the world. We can take a stand for the vision of God's reign. Every day of our lives, we can choose justice, disarmament, peace. We can act in the faith that our lives will sow seeds of peace and bear fruit someday for future generation. The choice is ours.

*12. **Social change comes about through our sharing in the Paschal Mystery of Jesus.*** "Unearned suffering is redemptive," Martin Luther King, Jr. taught. More and more, I am learning that social change does not come about through lobbying, letter writing, speaking or preaching; it comes about through our willingness to suffer for it. For years, my friends and I have debated the tactics and strategies of social change. We have tried every legal avenue until we felt compelled to take nonviolent direct action to challenge the existence of weapons of mass destruction. Though the 75 F15E fighter bombers continue to await bombing missions, and though the Clinton Administration has not decided to disband the military because of our action, nevertheless I am convinced that our willingness to suffer imprisonment for the sake of disarmament and peace is the greatest contribution we could make for our country and humanity.

This is an old lesson. From the abolitionist movement to the civil rights, anti-war, and women's movements, history demonstrates that social change comes through sacrifice. As the scriptures teach, social change comes about through our sharing in the cross and resurrection of Jesus. As we undergo what he underwent in service to God's reign, we are transformed and the love of God is spread, more and more, in anticipation of that day when justice shall roll down like waters and righteousness like a mighty stream.

In jail, such lessons come hard, but over time their wisdom is understood as a great grace.

Sheed & Ward

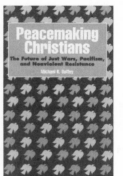